IRAN: A REVOLUTION IN TURMOIL

IRAN
A Revolution in Turmoil

Edited by

Haleh Afshar

State University of New York Press

First published
in U.S.A. by
State University of New York Press
Albany

Printed in Hong Kong

Library of Congress Cataloging in Publication Data
Main entry under title:
Iran, a revolution in turmoil
Includes index.
1. Iran—History—Mohammed Reza Pahlavi, 1941–1979—
Addresses, essays, lectures.   2. Iran—Politics and
government—1979-   —Addresses, essays, lectures.
I. Afshar, Haleh, 1944–
DS318.I686   1985   955′.053   85–2824
ISBN 0–88706–125–7
ISBN 0–88706–126–5 (pbk.)

10 9 8 7 6 5 4 3 2 1

Contents

List of Tables

Acknowledgements

My thanks to each of the contributors for making this book possible. They and many others have helped and encouraged me with this project. In particular I would like to thank Maurice Dodson without whose constant help, support and encouragement this book would never have been completed, and Marlyn Ellison for typing so many of the chapters to such a tight schedule.

H.A.

Notes on the Contributors

Ervand Abrahamian teaches modern history at Baruch College in the City University of New York and is the author of *Iran between Two Revolutions*.

Haleh Afshar is a lecturer in Developmental Studies at the University of Bradford. Before the revolution she worked as a civil servant at the Ministry of Cooperative and Rural Development and was an economic correspondent for the daily paper *Kayhan International*.

Kamran Afshar graduated from Shiraz University, Iran, and continued his education at Oxford and at Florida State University. He is currently Assistant Professor of Economics and Business at Moravian College, USA.

Reza Fazel received his Ph.D. degree from the University of California at Berkeley in 1971. Currently he is an Associate Professor of Anthropology at the University of Massachusetts in Boston. Dr Fazel has done extensive research on tribal populations inhabiting the Zagros mountains and the Persian Gulf regions of Iran.

Fereidun Fesharaki is Co-ordinator of the OPEC Downstream Project at the East–West Center. He was born in Iran in 1947 and received his M.A. and Ph.D. in Economics from Sussex and Surrey Universities respectively. Formerly, he was a Visiting Fellow at the Center for Middle Eastern Studies at Harvard University, a Professor at the National University of Iran, and a Senior Fellow at the Institute for the International Political and Economic Studies in Tehran. During 1977–8, Dr Fesharaki served as the Energy Adviser to the Prime Minister of Iran. Currently, he is consultant to a number of Middle East governments, Asian governments and major oil companies.

Mohamad Hashem Pesaran was a Director of the Department of Economic Research of the Central Bank of Iran before the revolution, and is currently a Fellow of Trinity College, Cambridge.

Ayatollah Morteza Motahari was a well-known teacher first in Qum and from 1954 at the Faculty of Theology at Tehran University. He was involved with such societies as the *anjumanhayeh Eslami*, 'Islamic Associations' which included students, engineers, doctors, merchants, and formed the nucleus of the movement which was to become, eventually, the revolution. He was also a founder-member of the Hoseinieh Ershad, which played a central role in the religious life of the capital over the four years until its closure by the authorities in 1973 (it has now reopened). At the same time he maintained his contact with more traditional religious activities, teaching first in the Madraseyeh Marvi in Tehran and later in Qum, and preaching in mosques and other religious centres in Tehran and elsewhere in the country. Through his lectures and writings – both books and articles – he became a well-known and much-respected figure throughout Iran, but it was mainly among the students and teachers of the schools and universities that he was most influential, setting an example and inspiring them as a committed and socially-aware Muslim with a traditional education who could make an intelligent, appropriate and exciting response to modern secularising tendencies. His wide knowledge and scholarship, which combined a profound understanding of Islam with certain elements of the Western tradition, is reflected in the range of his works, which cover law, philosophy, theology, history and literature. (For a complete list of published and unpublished works, by Ayatollah Motahari, see Abd Al Karim Surush (ed.) *Yadnamehyeh Ostadeh Shid Morteza Motahari,* Tehran, 1981, pp. 436–556.) He was also one of the few high-ranking *ulama* who maintained links with Ayatollah Khomeini during the sixteen or so years in which the movement which led to the revolution was in progress, and he was actively engaged in all the stages through which this movement went. His life came to an abrupt and untimely end when he was fatally shot in the head coming out of a meeting of the Revolutionary Council, of which he had been appointed the first head by Ayatollah Khomeini, on the evening of 1 May 1979.

In a sense, Morteza Motahari can be regarded as the Islamic revolution's first ideologist, for not only had practically all the leading figures in the revolution, from both a traditional and a university background, been his pupils, but also his lectures and writings came second only to those of Ayatollah Khomeini himself in forming the foundation for post-revolutionary ideological trends.

Glossary

Ahl al-Bayt	Household of the Prophet
al amreh beh maruf va nahi al monker	'bidding to good and forbidding evil'
Aleyeh Salam	May peace be upon him (usually in reference to a saint)
Amir al-Muminin	Commander of the Faithful
Anjumanhayeh Eslami	Islamic Associations
Ayandegan	futures
Ayatollah	Leading religious figure, selected by other Ayatollahs
Azadi	freedom
bantu	South African system of segregation of black and whites
bast	sanctuary
bazaar	market-place and general trading or financial forum
boneh	small share cropping co-operative units
chaqou-keshan	Down town muscle men, usually armed with knives (*chaquo*)
dasteh-yeh azadi	ritual funeral procession
Donya	the world
etelaat	information
faqih/foqaha	wise divine/s, learned in religious matters/ leading religious figures
Fedayan	Marxist guerrilla group
gavbandan	share-cropping oxen-owners
Hadith	body of traditions relating to Mohamad
Hambastegi	Unity
haram	Islamically impure
Hazrat	saint
hejab	women's Islamic veil
Hejri	Islamic calendar
Hezb Allah	God's party
Hosseinieh	religious centre

Ithn'ashairi	'Twelver' Shiism branch of Islam
jahadeh danishgahi	committee of cultural revolution in universities
jahadi sazandegi	village reconstruction force
jahad	holy war
jezyeh	small per capita religious tax paid by non-muslims to a religious leader
joft	pair of oxen
Jonbesh	the movement
kadkhoda	village headman
Kayhan	the world
Kar	labour
Khavarej	followers of Ali who deserted him during the battle of Karbala
Khannameh	an account of activities of chieftains
khoms	a 20 per cent religious tax on surplus money paid by Shiia believers to the religious leader of their choice
khoshneshin(an)	landless labourer(s)
khounasham	bloodsucker
komiteh	revolutionary committee
jangal	forest
lutis	Downtown muscle men with a chauvinistic code of honour
maddrassah/maddaress	Islamic teaching institution
Majlis	Parliament
maktabi	orthodox
maktabi	clergy-controlled schools
Mardome	people
marja	Source
Marjayeh taqlid	a religious leader chosen by believers as 'a source of imitation' wisest and ultimate authority for interpreting Koranic laws
mohandesin	engineers
Mojahedin	one of the major guerrilla groups
mostahed	religious leader
mulla	muslim clergyman
Nabardeh Khalq	People's Struggle
nassaq	customary form of allocating land among share croppers
paksazi	cleaning-up process

pasdaran	revolutionary guards
Paykar	battle
pishmargan	Kurdish guerrilla fighters
qanat	underground aqueduct
Qiyameh Kargar	workers' uprising
resaleyeh amaliyeh	manuals on religious obligations
rial	unit of currency in Iran
rozeh khani	religious shiia morning sessions, reciting the heroic deeds of Ali and his disciples
Sadat	Descendants of the Prophet
Sepah Pasdaran	the revolutionary guards
Setareh Sorkh	Red Star
shahanshahi	royal (from shah)
Shahid	martyr
shahrak	small town
Sharia	Islamic laws
shora	administrative consultative unit
Shorahayeh Chariki	Freedom Fighters' Rural Councils
shorayeh fatwa	committee of *foqaha*
sofreh hazrat-eh abbas	female religious thanksgiving ceremony for fulfilment of a vow
takieha	mystery play theatres
taziyeh	passion play
tohid	divine unity
tohidi	unitary
ulama (plural of *alem*)	men of religion
zakat	a property tax

Abbreviations Used

bn	billion 100 000 000 (American)
m	million
AIOC	Anglo Iranian Oil Company
ARMISH	American Military Mission to the Iranian Imperial Army
CENTO	Central Treaty Organisation
CCUTU	Central Council of United Trade Unions
CFP	*Compagnie Française de Pétroles*
CORC	Central Organisation of Rural Co-operatives
Cfd	cubic feet per day
EGOCO	European Group of Oil Companies
ERAR	*Entreprise de Recherches et d'Activités Petrolières*
GENMISH	American Military Mission to the Iranian Imperial Gendarmeri
HM	His Majesty
HOPECO	Hormuz Petroleum Company
IMINICO	Iran Marine International Oil Company
INPECO	Iran Nippon Petroleum Company
IPAC	Iran Pan American Oil Company
IRP	Islamic Republican Party
IROS	Iran Oil Services Company (now renamed Kala)
LAPCO	Lavan Petroleum Company
LAREX	Lar Exploration Company
LDC	less-developed country
MAAG	Military Assistance Advisory Group
NGL	natural gas liquid
NIGC	National Iranian Gas Company
NIOC	National Iranian Oil Company
OPEC	Organisation of Petroleum Exporting Companies
OSCO	Oil Services Company of Iran
PLO	Palestinian Liberation Army

SAVAK	Sazemaneh Etalaat va Amniateh Keshvar
SAVAMA	Sazemaneh Etelaat va Amniateh Mihan
SIRIP	*Société Irano-Iraliène des Pétroles*

Introduction

The Iranian revolution came as an unwe ume surprise to the West and has seriously undermined many theories wedded to the belief that modernisation measures would naturally lead to long-term political stability in Third World countries. It is, however, in the domain of military alliance and the cold war that the failure of the Shah's regime has had the most serious repercussions. By depriving the West of one of its most reliable allies in the Gulf region, the Iranian revolution has opened a wide political schism in one of the most important oil regions in the world; a situation rendered all the more critical by the long-running Iran–Iraq war which continues to threaten the delicate political balance of the Gulf states.

Despite the appearance of authority and control, the internal instabilities in Iran are well-known to its people and the revolution was not expected for those living and working in that country. The dynamics of revolution were set in motion through the very process of modernisation that was expected to avert it. A major concern of this book is the practical reality of the development process in Iran. In particular we offer a critical assessment of the assumptions made by the orthodox theories which base growth on accumulation of wealth and the availability of foreign exchange. It will be shown that the oil revenue undermined agriculture and intensified the problems of the dual economy and seriously aggravated inequalities in the society.

The contributors to this book are specifically concerned with Iran, but their conclusions are of importance to all Third World countries as well as to those institutions concerned with economic growth and political stability. The needs of capital-intensive agriculture and industry place enormous strains not only on a country's economic resources but also on its socio-political fabric. Although able to obtain foreign exchange Iran was unable to contain the tensions emerging from the disruption of its traditional institutions. The threat presented to the indigenous merchant capital and to the clergy's Islamic ideology, by the penetration of foreign capital and Western culture, played a central part in reviving the old alliance between the merchant and the clergy

1

and precipitated the revolution. This book sets out to isolate the inherent contradictions in the attempts to modernise the Iranian economy and to evaluate the extent to which the clergy have appreciated these problems in their bid to gain political supremacy and economic control. The political ideology of the Muslim fundamentalists and their Islamic policies are also discussed to provide some insight into current events in Iran.

The authors reveal that the problems of dualistic development which contributed in large measure to the downfall of the Shah are recurring in Iran and that the revolutionary government, although at times aware of the problems, is unable to deal with them. In some cases the very nature of Islamic government makes any solution impossible. Thus, once the war with Iraq is over, it should not be altogether surprising if the Khomeini regime collapses as suddenly as did that of the Shah.

This collection of essays is written by Iranians, mainly academics who have been involved in the 1960s modernisation programmes. The concentration of these programmes on urban development and the failure of the government to improve the deteriorating terms of trade for agriculture, resulted in a rapidly increasing migration away from the agricultural sector. Grandiose plans for the creation of large agro-industrial complexes and brutally repressive measures against nomad tribes intensified the tide of migration without producing any increase in agricultural production. So long as the government was able to obtain sufficiently high prices for oil, these social and cultural imbalances and the failures in the nation economy could be sustained. However, the combination of the Shah's gross extravagance, the ensuing high inflation and grave social discontent, made the revolution inevitable.

The first part of this book analyses the problem of dualistic development policies. The second part discusses the social forces and institutions that supported or threatened the Shah's regime. The crowd and the power of street politics have been instrumental in deciding crucial political issues in Iran, and the massive rural urban migration led to an enormous increase in the numbers of effective potential opponents to the regime. Led by a charismatic and venerable figure, and benefiting from the climate of resistance created by the urban guerrillas, the crowd in a series of massive demonstrations, toppled the Shah.

But the revolution has not solved the country's economic problems. The spiralling inflation continues; it has been attributed to the profiteering trades, but harsh exemplary punishment handed out to them has alienated the regime's traditional allies among the merchant and

the guilds. Criticism and opposition are ruthlessly and brutally suppressed by the fanatical revolutionary guards which were created to
replace the army. To prevent a military *coup d'état*, Khomeini had
begun dismantling the army and replacing it by his new militia, a
process which came to a sudden halt with the Iraq invasion in 1981. The
revolutionary guards, who are fanatically devoted to Khomeini and
committed to die a martyr's death for the cause, are perhaps more
effective agents of oppression than the Shah's armed forces which, to a
large extent, consisted of conscripts who were unwilling to shoot
civilians and fellow-Muslim protestors. Thus, despite the national unity
brought about by the war, there are a number of parallels with the pre-
revolutionary Iran. This book suggests that the Iranian theocracy may
be more vulnerable than it appears, and that when the war ends the
government might find itself faced with a new counter-revolutionary
threat expressed by crowds as powerful and decisive as those which
overthrew the Shah.

This book begins with an introductory chapter by Mohamad Hashem Pesaran highlighting the roots of the 1978 revolution, and
providing an overview of the chapters that follow. Pesaran analyses the
inherent instability created by the modernisation policies of the Shah
and outlines the emergence of the dual economy and the dependent
nature of the oil's enclave development in Iran. This chapter provides
an authoritative critique of oil-based development policies; the oil
income was invested by the government in a few grandiose capital-
intensive industrial and agro-industrial schemes, which merely widened
the large inequality gap between the rich and the mass of the Iranian
people.

Pesaran argues that the modernisation policies alienated all but a
small part of the society. The penetration of western capital and culture
benefited the rich and served to raise the expectations of the poor.
Meanwhile, although the propaganda machine was projecting an image
of wealth and prosperity, the reality of everyday living was becoming
more difficult. The merchant classes, displaced by modern capital and
an inadvertent policy of import-substitution, were losing their central
role as traders and local financiers. At the same time, much of their
investment in agricultural land was lost through the land reform
measures, intended to return the land to the peasants. Pesaran points
out that by the time the land reforms had been modified by the *Majlis*
(parliament) and the landed interest, the policy merely served to
intensify the flow of the landless labourers to towns, and encourage
mechanisation and modernisation of agriculture. The mass of urban

slum-dwellers, and discontented merchants excluded from the development process, furnished the clergy with a receptive basis of support. The intelligentsia, many of whom had been arrested, tortured and killed by the secret police, provided a radical and revolutionary rhetoric that was soon taken up by the clergy. The historical tripartite alliance of the merchants, the clergy and the intelligentsia, gained massive popularity after the oil-price rises of 1973. The Shah's extravagance exacerbated the rising inflation, widened the poverty gap, without meeting the rising expectation of the Iranians, and hastened the inevitable revolution. The present revolutionary government, however, has not dealt with any of the fundamental social and economic problems, has failed to placate much of the intelligentsia and has lost the support of the merchant classes. But for the war with Iraq, a counter-revolution would have been almost inevitable. Pesaran's arguments are extended in succeeding chapters.

Kamran Afshar's brief chapter highlights the erroneous theoretical basis for the Shah's development policies. Using the Iranian government's own figures, Kamran Afshar demonstrates that the planners made the common mistake of classifying the agricultural sector as being simultaneously at a subsistence level and suffering from disguised unemployment. He shows that both assumptions were unfounded; unemployment was seasonal and agriculture was highly responsive to rising demand for food. Haleh Afshar's chapter on the rural sector extends the discussion by looking at the mistaken policies resulting from the false assumptions made by planners, and brings us up to date with the current government's rural policies.

Agriculture, the largest employer and the largest single contributor to the GNP, was erroneously considered to be backward and at a subsistence level. This assumption was consistent with modernisation theories, but in the case of Iran, the agricultural sector had for decades produced a surplus which had kept up with the population growth. But in the late 1960s, the policies of consolidation of holdings and concentration of resources on the modern, capital-intensive rural concerns, deprived small peasant proprietors of much needed credit and displaced many without providing them with alternative employment. The resulting widespread rural proverty led to large-scale rural–urban migration. The availability of a pool of cheap labour in rural areas did not, as developmentalists would have argued, result in a lowering of wage rates and a cheaper industrial workforce. For, despite the absence of powerful trade unions, the sophisticated technological demands of Iran's industrial sector excluded all but a small, relatively skilled élite industrial labour force. The migrants – poor, illiterate, frequently unemployed and discontented – were a serious political threat to the regime which sought to placate them, primarily through a cheap food policy. This policy, which subsidised imported foodstuffs, sold at controlled prices, further depressed Iranian agriculture.

Despite its stated policy of rural development, the Khomeini regime has failed to make any radical changes in the agricultural sector. Indeed, the clergy have always opposed land reforms on religious grounds, and so not surprisingly have been unable to formulate a satisfactory policy for the redistribution of holdings. Although many land-owners have left Iran and the foreign capital invested in agri-business units has been withdrawn, the peasants are yet to obtain the legal right to cultivate these lands. The legal processes initiated by some landlords against *ad hoc* take-overs of their holdings by the cultivators have resulted in an overall fall in food production and a new wave of rural–urban migration. The current regime's cheap food policies, and the large imports of foreign wheat and grain, are repetitions of the mistakes of the Shah. Haleh Afshar's chapter illustrates the point made both by Pesaran and Kamran Afshar, that erroneous policies merely exacerbate the critical economic conditions. Unless it concentrates seriously on the development of the rural economy, the Islamic government will be faced with a major crisis.

Future development policies must include help for the pastoral tribes who, for the past fifty years, have been persecuted and isolated from national politics and institutions. Reza Fazel's chapter on the tribes describes the plight of this important group and discusses the historic roots of the opposition of the tribes and minorities to the central government. Although a Muslim country, Iran is linguistically, cultur-ally and ethnically diverse, and less than half the population (mainly those living in the central areas) speak the official language, *Farsi*, as a first language. Nevertheless, the Shah represented Iran as a *Farsi*-speaking, homogeneous society and the modernist policies worked mainly to the advantage of the central province at the expense of the outer regions and minorities. But before the Pahlavis, Iran's numerous minorities, particularly the tribes, had enjoyed a considerable degree of autonomy while maintaining a loose allegiance to the monarchy. Many, such as the Kurds, Turkmans, and the Arab tribes in Khouzes-tan, maintained close ties with their tribal relatives across national borders, and had at one time or another waged war on the central government.

The Pahlavis sought to destroy the power of the tribes by turning them into settled farming communities. Communally-owned tribal lands were distributed, and much of their pasture was nationalised. These measures effectively disbarred large numbers of tribesmen from their traditional rights and access to their means of livelihood. The result was a fall in production of livestock and a rise in the number of landless and destitute rural inhabitants.

Fazel argues that potentially the Islamic government could have bridged the wide gap between the tribal people and the central government. The institutions of Shiia tribes in particular have important similarities with those of the current government. Using the Boyr Ahmad and Kuhgilu tribes as examples, Fazel shows that tribal religious leaders play a central role in the day-to-day lives of tribes people and as final arbitrators in major disputes. The conservative policies of government, with regard to the exclusion of women from the public sphere and endorsement of traditional values, find ready acceptance amongst Shiia tribes who had lost much by the Pahlavi's modernisation policies but held to Islamic values. Although there are less structural contradictions between Shiia tribes and the Islamic government, the latter has no clear policies for assistance and economic aid to the tribes. On the other hand, the 5 m. Suni nomads have found the present regime as autocratic as its predecessor and have taken up arms to obtain tribal autonomy.

These articles on the rural sector clearly demonstrate that decades of mistaken policies had undermined this resilient sector and had finally resulted in a mass exodus towards the more prosperous towns. The booming building industry, financed largely by oil money, was able to provide temporary employment for many of the migrants. But, as the chapter on oil by Feregdun Fesharaki demonstrates, the oil industry played an ambivalent part in maintaining the Shah's regime. The Shah's grandiose plans were matched by the West's apparently unlimited thirst for Iranian oil. However, the dominance of foreign interest in this sector on the one hand secured a large income, while on the other it provided ample evidence of the Shah's dependence on the West and, in the eyes of his people, deprived him of legitimacy to his crown. The Shah was seen, with some justification, as an agent of imperialism.

The oil industry which had funded much of the royal extravagance was in the end instrumental in his downfall. The long oil strike was a lethal blow to the Pahlavis' rule. The post-revolutionary government sought a separatist position from the major foreign oil interests and began its rule by sacking most of the expatriates working in this sector. The strong infrastructure of the oil industry and predominance of

Iranians in its workforce and management ranks has enabled the industry to continue operating although at a lower level of production. Nevertheless, as Fesharaki points out, the less sophisticated methods of extraction currently used might lead to rapid depletion and considerable production losses in the future.

In the international arena of oil negotiation, the Islamic government of Iran began by adopting an uncompromising position in OPEC and demanding very high prices. However, faced with the falling demand from the West and the rising costs of the war, the Iranians have been obliged to change their policies. As Fesharaki points out, the structural intermesh of Iranian oil with the capitalist realities of the free market, made it impossible for the current regime to maintain an independent and radical political position. The logic of the market-place and the needs of the industry have obliged the Iranian government to settle for lower oil prices and to re-employ considerable numbers of expatriates in the oil sector. Fesharaki maintains that the need to collaborate with international oil firms has not only replenished the nearly bankrupt treasury, but has also had a modernising effect on the policies of the revolutionary government.

Part II places the Iranian revolution in an historical perspective and discusses the character and formation of the revolutionary forces before and after the 1978 revolution. This sector begins with Errand Abrahamian's classic article on 'The Crowd in Iranian Politics' which gives a historical perspective to the alliance of merchant classes and the clergy and the ability of the former to mobilise the trade- and craft-workers and of the latter to command the support of the mass of poor and disillusioned slum-dwellers. His chapter provides an incisive analysis of revolutionary forces which can be, and have been, mobilised in Iran and elsewhere. The politics of the street, dictated by the crowd, have been instrumental in generating radical changes in Iran. The crowd secured a constitutional government for Iran and maintained it through years of civil war; it has staved off imperialism and first maintained and then rejected the monarchy as a system of government. It has been used as a decisive political lever, both by the left and the right, and was decisive in toppling the Pahlavi regime.

Abrahamian analyses the composition of the crowd and the traditional alliance of clergy, merchants and intelligentsia. He extends Pesaran's discussion on the role of the bazaar, pointing out that it has been the traditional granary, bank and workshop as well as the religious centre of Iranian society. Abrahamian demonstrates that far from being an amorphous mass of merchants, the *bazaar* is a tightly knit and hierarchical society, held together by a complex web of guilds and trade networks.

The close alliance of the *bazaar* with the clergy, who have been the traditional defenders of the merchants, has enabled the religious establishment to summon and obtain mass support. The crowd, drawn from the rank and file of the guilds, and financed by the merchants, has gained its religious authority from the clergy and its demands were placed in a theoretical framework by the intelligentsia. By 1950 political leaders such as Mossadeq had learned the importance of the crowd in Iranian politics, and were astute enough to use it to legitimise their authority. Khomeini is very much in the same mould of venerable, charismatic Iranians who have come to power and retained their position by direct appeal to the politics of the street. However, the crowd has not always been a decisive part in Iranian politics. In 1962 the Shah used his army to disperse mass demonstrations; the army fired indiscriminately into unarmed crowds and many were killed. This brutal reaction made the streets appear as an unsuitable arena for radical politics. Deprived of their most effective platform, groups of young intellectuals resorted to guerrilla activities to create what they called 'an atmosphere of resistance'. In Chapter 7, Abrahamian enlarges on Pesaran's view that moral indignation played an important part in the development of revolutionary force in Iran. Abrahamian shows that the urban guerrillas in Iran appeared during a period of economic prosperity and came largely from the affluent middle classes and formulated their strategy largely in accordance with the traditional political positions of their class.

One of the major guerrilla groups, the *Mojahedin*, was formed by the sons of the traditional middle classes, devout merchants, traders and the clergy. Almost all of the *Mojahedin* were Shiia Muslims, and in their literature the revolutionary Marxist ideology was tempered by Islamic language; they advocated a revolutionary Islam. By contrast, the other major guerrilla grouping, the *Fedayan*, advocated a classic Marxist armed struggle. The *Fedayan*, who included women among their leaders, were formed by the children of the modern middle classes, the professionals, teachers, and civil servants, and included Sunis and non-Muslims among their members.

After more than a decade of guerrilla warfare, however, neither group gained popular support. Nevertheless, they were a well-trained, independent armed force which provided invaluable support for the crowd in 1979 and indeed, defeated the Shah's famous imperial guards.

The failure of the post-revolutionary government to meet the expectations of the idealists and its rigorous suppression of freedom and human rights, has led to renewed urban guerrilla activity. To counteract both urban guerrillas and tribal freedom fighters, the revolutionary government calls on its fanatical revolutionary guards who have proved even more brutal than the Shah's army.

The strong centralised state buttressed by a large well-equipped army, was a recent phenomenon closely linked with the Pahlavis' ideals of modern Iran. The army was created by Reza Shah as a means of producing a new national élite, drawn from all classes and all regions in the country and controlled entirely by the Shah. It was made an effective vehicle of social mobility, offering education, wealth and prestige as well as permanent employment, and in time was to paper over national disunity and allow the Shah to act as the policeman of the Gulf. Haleh Afshar's chapter on the army will discuss its role as the linchpin of the Pahlavis' power and authority, both nationally and internationally. The presence of the extremely well-equipped Iranian armed forces secured a degree of national stability and an uneasy peace with neighbouring countries. But in this case, as in other aspects of the modernisation programme, appearances hid fundamental contradictions. The army, although a means of social mobility for the officers, relied on reluctant conscripts drawn from all areas and subjected to harsh military discipline. For illiterate peasants, accustomed to the easy tempo of the seasons, the military service represented a hateful and undeserved ordeal. Far from kindling love and loyalty, conscription served as a further means of alienating a discontented peasantry and at the same time greatly reduced the army's coercive powers; conscripts were reluctant to kill and repeatedly refused to fire on demonstrators.

The post-revolutionary government continued to view the armed forces as a potential threat. Despite the loyal support given to Khomeini by the air-force cadets and the eventual final decision by the high-ranking officers not to oppose him, Khomeini continued to fear a military coup, and began dismantling the army. Dismissal or imprisonment of high-ranking officers, and desertions by the conscripts, had seriously debilitated the army when the Iraquis invaded. The need for an army capable of resisting the invaders was clear and urgent. The derogatory slogans were forgotten and the armed services were built up again, there was a national mobilisation and the depleted ranks of officers were filled by releasing some of those in prison and by promotions from the ranks. To prevent a military coup the government installed members of the clergy as alternative 'moral' commanders, in the armed forces; and for the moment, the clergy and the armed forces coexist uneasily.

It is the devout revolutionary guards who are now engaged in warfare against urban guerrillas and in the numerous battles against tribal uprisings. Manned by fanatical followers of Khomeini, and engaged in what they see as a holy war against his enemies, the revolutionary guards have, in practice, proved a far more deadly agent of oppression than the Shah's army had been. Ironically the army in Iran is beginning to be seen as a liberating force, and may, in the end, prove popular enough to launch a military coup.

Part III concentrates on the post-revolutionary situation in Iran. Extracts from Ayatollah Morteza Motahari's speeches on the revolution provides an illuminating example of the theoretical arguments presented by the clergy to formulate the ideology and political development of the revolution. Motahari exalts the militant nature of Islam and argues that it is Islamic ideology, rather than class-based struggle, which generated ardour in Iran. In an attempt to meet the criticism of the guerrillas, Motahari makes a distinction between the Islamic revolution and revolutionary Islam. The latter he denounces as the ill-conceived propaganda of the *Mojahedin* and their followers who, according to Motahari, wish to use Islam as a mere tool for achieving a socialist revolution. By contrast, Motahari says that the Islamic revolution was supported by all classes and serves the interest of all, the rich as well as the poor. He concludes that the revolution in Iran was not fuelled by social or economic forces, but by revulsion against the un-Islamic behaviour of the Shah. It follows that once an Islamic government had come to power, there was no longer any need for another class-based revolution. Although categorical about the total success of the revolution in Iran, Motahari does end with a note of caution, remarking that should the government prove brutal and oppressive, then the forces who advocate a revolutionary Islam might find popular support for their counter-revolutionary activities. Sadly, Motahari's calls fell on deaf ears, and the theocracy in Iran has proved far more ruthless than expected by its well-known ideologue.

The final chapter on the theocracy provides a critical analysis of Khomeini's writing about the financing and management of an Islamic government. Funded by religious taxes, such a government need not be either representative nor democratic. Khomeini argues that since its members merely serve to implement the will of God, such government should exact the obedience all Muslims owe to God.

The Islamic government's demands for a double taxation of the merchants might prove counter-productive. The merchants, who have traditionally provided both finance and political support for the clergy, are now finding themselves bereft of political impact. Their economic activities have been curtailed by policies to restrict and regulate trade, foreign exchange, travel, usury as well as the rationing and control of food distribution. The traditional financial heart and granary of the economy is once more under threat and the traditional alliance of merchants and clergy is at a breaking-point.

For the moment, the war has created a climate of unity which secures the survival of the regime. Severe economies and the monetarist policies of the government have seriously eroded their support among the unemployed urban slum-dwellers. The government can ill afford to face large-scale bread riots and once the war is over, it may well find itself faced with an insoluble crisis.

The book is concluded by an epilogue discussing some of the questions that have not been analysed in detail – the problems faced by women, by the educational institutions in the throes of Islamification, and by persecuted minorities, such as the Bahais. The debilitating cultural and social effects of the imposition of Shiia fundamentalism on the country are noted in this final chapter.

Part I
Dualistic Economic Development

1 Economic Development and Revolutionary Upheavals in Iran

M. H. PESARAN*

The tradition of all the dead generations weighs like a nightmare on the brain of the living. And just when they seem engaged in revolutionising themselves and things, in creating something entirely new, precisely in such epochs of revolutionary crisis they anxiously conjure up the spirits of the past to their service and borrow from them names, battle slogans and costumes in order to present the new scene of world history in this time-honoured disguise and this borrowed language. (Marx, 1851, p. 595)

INTRODUCTION

This chapter attempts to trace the economic and social forces which led to the Iranian Revolution of February 1979 that took the world by surprise, not only because it occurred in a country with a remarkable recent history of apparent political stability, but also because it involved demonstrations by masses on a scale, if not unprecedented, at least comparable with the great revolutions of this century.

As yet we are not far enough removed from the February Revolution for an objective account of it and the lasting impact that it might have

*This is a substantially revised and updated version of the paper that appeared in the September 1980 issue of the *Cambridge Journal of Economics*, under the pseudonym of Thomas Walton. The author wishes to thank Massoud Karshenas, Nikki Keddie, Suzy Paine, Hadi Shams and John Wells for their helpful and constructive comments on earlier drafts of this paper.

upon Iranian society to be given.[1] Furthermore, a detailed and exhaustive investigation of its causes is a formidable undertaking which is clearly beyond the scope of one single chapter.[2] Our purpose here is first to look at the Iranian development experience over the past thirty years and suggest the major socio-economic factors that were, in our view, responsible for turning a seemingly 'flourishing and prosperous economy' into a 'development disaster' and for creating conditions where a successful challenge to the regime could develop, and second, to speculate on the likely outcome of the revolution. We shall argue that, contrary to what might appear at first, the February Revolution came about not because of a sudden and dramatic Islamic resurgence, but mainly as a result of deteriorating socio-economic conditions, ever rising inequities and political suppression by the old regime that became intolerable as soon as the masses realised that it was possible to avoid them. In the process of challenging the old regime, the political influence of the *ulama* (the men of religion)[3] and their role of giving religious sanction to the already existing popular resentments and enabling the masses to realise their real strength in their struggle against the old regime is undeniable. Indeed it is difficult to believe that the wide-ranging mass demonstrations of 1978–9 could have taken place if it were not for the passive approval and support of the *ulama* to begin with and their active involvement later on. It would, nevertheless, be a mistake to regard this as a genuine manifestation of a new Islamic resurgence which would have taken place even in the absence of the hostile economic and political conditions that prevailed at the time. The abortive attempt of the clergy to oppose the Shah during the early 1960s culminating in Ayatollah Khomeini's exile in 1964 is a telling recent reminder of the limits to the clergy's power and influence in Iranian political life.[4,5]

The privileged position enjoyed by the clergy in Iran dates back to the establishment of the Safavid dynasty (1500–1722) which adopted 'Twelver Shiism' as the country's official religion.[6] A prominent role was given to the Shiite *ulama* whose position apart from being legitimised was later on institutionalised through the state's insistence upon rigid adherence to Islam's economic as well as social and legal codes. The Safavids stressed the obligatory nature of large alms to be administered by the *ulama* and endorsed the *ulama*'s control over the collection of religious taxes such as *khoms* and *zakat*.[7] The consolidation of the *ulama*'s economic and ideological power in turn meant their financial and political independence from the state. As they relied more heavily upon *khoms* and *zakat* and the voluntary contributions of rich merchants and traders they became more receptive to the *bazaar* (the place of the merchants, the shopkeepers and small traders) and public opinion rather than remaining subservient to the state. In Keddie's words 'what had been a pillar of state policy in early Safavid times later turned into a financial base for anti-government action' (see Keddie, 1969, p. 48). Therefore the alliance of state and religion was gradually replaced by that of the *bazaar* and the clergy in opposition to the state's intervention in the affairs of the *bazaar* and the mosque.[8]

The secular reformists and revolutionaries, that is, the intelligentsia,[9] who were fully aware of the potential power and influence that the *ulama* and *bazaar* had over the masses, have frequently formed apparently paradoxical alliances with them in the pursuit of their ideals of reform and social and political change. Indeed, it has been this tripartite and somewhat strange alliance that has been instrumental in ensuring the success of all three major anti-government protests and upheavals that have taken place in Iran over the past two centuries.[10] These alliances, especially that of the intelligentsia and the clergy, as to be expected, have generally undergone considerable strains or have even broken off as soon as the initial aim of the struggle, that is, the resistance to or the overthrow of the ruling regime, has been achieved. Perhaps it is worth mentioning that the 1951–3 Nationalist Movement led by Dr Mohamad Mossadeq and the clergy's 1961–3 opposition already mentioned failed even in the first stages because neither of them had the full sympathy and the support of the other members of the tripartite alliance. It is true that the overthrow of the legally-elected government of Dr Mossadeq was achieved by a *coup d'état* organised and financed by the United States' Central Intelligence Agency.[11] But the deterioration of the clergy's relation with Dr Mossadeq's government and the *bazaar*'s unease with the worsening of the economic conditions in 1952–3 made a crucial contribution to ensuring the success of the coup.[12]

In analysing revolutionary upheavals, we should, however, be careful not to mistake tactical alliances and political manoeuvrings of the sort discussed above for the fundamental underlying causes of revolutions. In the case of Iran the formation of new political alliances or the break-down of old ones have often been more the symptom than the cause of political unrest and social discontent. Now, without having any pretensions to be exhaustive in our treatment of the relevant political, social and economic factors that may have been responsible for bringing about the Iranian Revolution, we shall turn to Iran's development experience which we believe to be at the heart of the revolution.

EARLY ATTEMPTS AT INDUSTRIALISATION

Iran's economic development experience is yet another example of the by now almost bankrupt development strategy of the 1950s and 1960s with its undue emphasis upon maximal growth, industrialisation and foreign technical assistance at the expense of better income distribution, more balanced growth and greater economic self-reliance.

Although attempts at industrialisation and modernisation in Iran go back to the early 1920s, the idea of economic development within a planning framework did not materialise until the Allied military occupation of Iran in 1941–5 had come to an end. Iran's experience of industrialisation from 1921 to 1941, the period of Reza Shah's rise to power and his reign, was marked with symbolic and nationalistic construction programmes. Reza Shah established a state monopoly over foreign trade and imposed exchange controls; and was singularly successful in financing the construction of the Trans-Iranian Railway (1394 km of line) through forced savings obtained by the imposition of a tax on tea and sugar.[13]

Another important aspect of Reza Shah's modernisation which emerged quite clearly after his abdication (forced upon him by the British) has been emphasised by Lambton (1944) who writes:

> In spite of the apparent progress achieved during the reign of Reza Shah, and although Persia became more conscious of her new role as a national state belonging to Western Society, she had not yet found a sound basis for her new life, nor had she achieved a synthesis between the bases of Western Society and Persian tradition. The house had been swept of much of the past that remained but nothing solid has been put in its place. (p. 14)

There seems to be a general consensus that Reza Shah's reforms were 'carried out at too rapid a pace' and 'much that was old was removed and not enough that was new was put in its place',[14] a view to which we shall return with respect to Iran's more recent development experience.

The First Seven-Year Development Plan which was finally approved by the Iranian Parliament in 1949 having taken almost three years to prepare was deficient both in basic planning methodology and objectives. It was a partial plan and did not take account of investment by the private sector. In effect the Plan was a collection of 'high prestige' projects drawn up by an American consultant company to be executed by the newly established Plan Organisation.[15] However, because of the 1951-3 crisis over oil nationalisation and the subsequent loss of oil revenues which resulted from the British embargo on the purchase of Iranian oil, the implementation of the Plan had to be abandoned.

INCREASING AMERICAN PRESENCE IN IRAN

The rapid deterioration of the Iranian economy over the post-oil-nationalisation period caused the government of Dr Mossadeq to rely heavily, although reluctantly, upon US technical assistance, better known as the Point IV Programme.[16] In fact by June 1954, no fewer than thirty-eight projects approved by Point IV Mission were among the First Plan projects which had previously had to be postponed. This increased American involvement in Iran covered a variety of areas such as agriculture, industry, public health, education and public administration, and was later reinforced and augmented by their covert operations in the overthrow of Dr Mossadeq in August 1953,[17] thus paving the way for Iran's subsequent economic and military domination by the United States. The Mutual Security Act of 1954 and its amendments provided a general umbrella for this purpose.[18] The 1955 Law for the Attraction and Protection of Foreign Investment in Iran, by effectively safeguarding foreign companies against expropriation and nationalisation and guaranteeing them 'prompt, adequate and effective' compensation in such events, opened the way for private foreign investment and influence.

According to Baldwin (1967) pp. 200-4, the combination of American economic and military aid to Iran during the period 1950-64 amounted to well over a billion dollars, which was larger than that received by any country in the Western hemisphere, Africa and Middle East, with the exception of Turkey. A more up-to-date figure of $2.3 bn is given by Ramazani (1976) p. 327, for the period 1950-70.

The increasing US presence in Iran during the post-1953 period, the American pro-British posture in the Anglo-Iranian conflict over the oil-nationalisation crises, not to mention the CIA's involvement in the overthrow of Dr Mossadeq's government, planted the seeds of suspicion of US intentions in Iran and revived the resentment of foreign power rivalries and interventions in Iranian Society.[19]

PERIOD OF CYCLICAL GROWTH: 1954–63

After the overthrow of Mossadeq's government, with the resumption of oil production and export in 1954 and the acceleration in the technical and financial assistance from the United States, the Second Seven Year Development Plan (1955–62) was launched.[20] This Plan again emphasised a handful of large prestigious projects and did not have a comprehensive or coherent development strategy.[21] Almost all the Plan's allocation to the agricultural sector was devoted to the completion of three large dams, namely Karaj, Sefid Rud and Dez. The Plan's achievements in the industrial sector were confined to the construction and modernisation of large textile, sugar and cement factories.[22] In the area of transportation and communication, the construction of inter-city highways and the extension of the railway network were emphasised and no serious attempts at improving transportation facilities in the countryside were made.

Like its predecessor, the Second Plan was a medium-term government financial programme and, apart from some minor exceptions, it did not play an important role in stimulating private sector investment. Nevertheless the 1957 devaluation of the rial provided a convenient excuse for the authorities to increase the money supply by the amount equivalent to the rise in rial value of the country's stock of gold and foreign exchange.[23] Furthermore, the devaluation of the rial also meant a considerable once-for-all rise in rial revenues of the government and a subsequent rise in government expenditures.[24]

The amount of high-powered money that was thus created as a result of rial devaluation amounted to 7.1 bn rials which was directly lent to the private sector for investment in agriculture and industry over the three-year period 1956–8.[25] In consequence the credit extended to the private sector rose by 46.1 per cent in 1957, 60.5 per cent in 1958, and 32.4 per cent in 1959.[26] The rising government expenditure together with the unprecedented expansion in the private sector credit produced Iran's first major economic boom. The expansion was most pronounced in urban housing and industry in the post-1945 period. The private sector investment in construction in the city of Tehran rose by 85 and 130 per cent in 1958 and 1959 respectively.[27] Unfortunately, no reliable overall measures of economic activity for the pre-1959 period are available. But indicators such as domestic oil consumption and cigarette sales show a considerable rise over the 1957–9 period.[28]

This monetary-induced boom inevitably had to come to an end when the country faced both excessively rising prices and large current account deficits, and towards the end of 1960 the government was forced to embark upon an 'Economic Stabilisation Programme' prescribed by the International Monetary Fund.[29] The stabilisation programme consisted of a set of standard IMF 'medicines' such as direct control of private sector credits, raising of interest rates, restriction of imports and cuts in government expenditures.[30]

As a result of these measures the boom of 1957–60 was soon turned into a deep recession. Real gross domestic fixed capital formation by the private sector declined by 7.7 and 9.5 per cent in 1961 and 1962 respectively.[31] Public sector investment also dropped by 11.6 per cent in 1962. Among the various economic sectors, the traditional sectors, namely agriculture, construction and domestic trade, were most seriously affected by the recession (see Table 1.1). Domestic Trade, which covers the economic activities of the *bazaar*, was the hardest hit by the import and credit restrictions of the 'Stabilisation Programme'. The value added of this sector declined by 2.3 per cent in 1961 and showed only a marginal rise in 1962 at constant prices. The recession, however, had relatively little adverse impact upon the modern sectors of the economy. The value added of manufacturing and mining (excluding oil) at constant prices rose by 8.4 and 13.6 per cent in the 'depressed' years of 1961 and 1962 respectively.

TABLE 1.1 *Annual percentage changes in value added of key sectors of Iranian economy at constant 1959 prices*

Sectors	1960	1961	1962	1963	1964
Agriculture	2.0	0.9	1.0	1.7	2.1
Oil	12.5	9.5	15.9	9.8	13.0
Manufacturing and mines	9.0	8.4	13.6	8.8	4.6
Construction	0.7	6.1	− 0.8	15.6	5.2
Domestic Trade	7.5	− 2.3	1.7	3.6	12.8
Others	5.1	1.2	5.7	7.5	11.7
Gross Domestic Product (at factor costs)	5.9	3.5	6.7	6.6	8.4
Non-oil GDP	4.5	2.2	4.6	5.9	9.2

SOURCE *National Income of Iran: 1959–1972,* Central Bank of Iran, Mordad 1353 (1974) Table 16.

The asymmetrical impact of the 'Stabilisation Programme' upon the traditional and the modern sectors of the economy came about on the top of the boom which had produced its own type of social and economic dislocation and inequities, largely fuelled by the excessive emphasis of the Point IV Programme upon the modern and westernised sectors of the economy during the 1950s.[32] In the words of Senator Hubert Humphrey who was speaking before the US Senate Committee on Foreign Relations:

In Iran the rich in the country are getting richer, and the poor are not getting much better off. This is not the observation of any one person. This is the usual observation.[33]

These mounting social and economic problems resulted in mass discontentment among low-income urban-dwellers, a large proportion of whom were unemployed migrant construction workers, and the *bazaar* which had lost most from the government Stabilisation Programme. The Shah's response, apparently under pressure from the newly-elected Kennedy Administration,[34] to the deteriorating conditions was his six-point reform programme of land redistribution, profit-sharing in industry, female suffrage, nationalisation of forests, return of state industries to private enterprise and the formation of a literacy corps. These proposed reforms presented a real threat to the interests of the landed upper and the propertied middle classes and were regarded by the opposition groups as fraudulent and an American conspiracy for further political and economic domination of Iran. Thus, instead of relieving the social tensions, they in fact aggravated the economic and political uncertainties that existed at the time and caused a revival of old alliances, particularly that of the *ulama* and the *bazaar* in opposition to the regime.[35] The political unrest throughout 1962–3 and the mass demonstrations of June 1963 however, failed to overthrow the regime, not only because the regime exercised brute force to quash the wide-spread uprisings, but also because the Economic Stabilisation Programme that was so much detested by the *bazaar* was brought to an end in 1961 and signs of economic recovery could clearly be seen during the first half of 1963 (see Table 1.1).

A sociological explanation of revolutionary upheavals advanced by Davies (1962) – the so-called J-curve hypothesis – might be relevant here. He argues that 'Revolutions are most likely to occur when a prolonged period of objective economic and social development is followed by a short period of sharp reversal'.[36] Although the 1957–9 boom was not sufficiently prolonged in Davies' sense, there is no doubt that the sharp 'reversal' of 1960–2 was crucial in fermenting revolutionary fervour and opposition to the regime. The recession of 1960–2 clearly could not have brought about the events of 1962–3 by itself, and as we have pointed out earlier, the role of the *ulama* in the organisation of political opposition and the mobilisation of the masses in Iran is indisputable. Invariably, it has been the development of socio-economic forces hostile to the ruling regime (often a direct result of 'internal autocracy and/or foreign hegomony') that have provided the appropriate environment for the *ulama*'s particular brand of opposition to flourish and even succeed. The events of 1963 undoubtedly enhanced and gave fresh impetus to the *ulama*'s opposition (both at home and in exile) to the Shah's regime which was to be so crucial in the February 1979 Revolution and its aftermath.

We shall now concentrate on the major socio-economic forces that made the 1978–9 re-emergence of the defeated opposition of 1963 possible.

PERIOD OF SUSTAINED GROWTH AND INDUSTRIALISATION: 1963–72

Ironically, the Economic Stabilisation Programme that was responsible for the sharp 'reversal' of 1960–2, embodied an important ingredient of Iran's industrialisation strategy throughout the 1960s and early 1970s. The restriction of imports of non-essential items which was intended to solve the country's balance-of-payment problems laid down, perhaps inadvertently, the foundation of an import-substitution industrialisation strategy. The policy of import controls was later complemented with generous fiscal incentives, exclusive industrial licensing, low or non-existent profit taxes and easily accessible low-interest loans for investment in the manufacturing sector. The rather haphazard planning methods inherent in the first two plans were also modified in favour of more comprehensive five-year plans so that public and private sector investments could be better co-ordinated. In short, Iran joined the ranks of many other developing countries which had embarked upon the first stage of an import-substitution industrialisation strategy,[37] but with one major difference: while most other developing countries, apart from relying on primary exports and foreign loans, also promoted their manufacturing exports to pay for a proportion of their imports of capital and intermediate goods, Iran continued instead to rely heavily and almost exclusively upon oil exports. During 1963–72 foreign exchange receipts from oil and gas accounted for 76 per cent of the country's total export earnings (see Table 1.2) and the average annual rate of growth of oil and gas revenues during the Third and Fourth Plans amounted to 14.5 and 25 per cent respectively. The growth of oil revenues during this period was, however, achieved by a fast rate of reserve depletion rather than higher oil prices. The rise in 'per barrel' oil revenues during 1960–70 was meagre indeed: increasing from $0.80 in 1960 to $0.86 in 1970. Nevertheless, as a result of OPEC's successful strategy of 'cash and control', Iran's per barrel revenues increased to $1.25 in 1971 and to $1.36 in 1972.[38]

TABLE 1.2   *Percentage share of the oil and gas sector in government revenues, foreign exchange receipts and gross domestic product during five-year plans*

	In government revenues	In current foreign exchange receipts	In gross domestic product
Third Plan (1963–7)	48.1	75.8	18.7
Fourth Plan (1968–72)	55.2	76.2	24.0
Fifth Plan (1973–7)	77.7	84.7	37.4

SOURCE   *Annual Reports,* 1346 (1967), 1351 (1972) and 1356 (1977) Central Bank of Iran.

The adoption of an import-substitution strategy, together with the rising oil revenues and the country's political stability produced high profit expectation and thus ensured a high and sustained growth of the industrial sector. Manufacturing value added grew on average by 12.3 per cent per annum over the period 1963–72 (see Table 1.3) and its share in total domestic value added increased from 12.6 per cent to 14.5 per cent. Iran's manufacturing sector grew about twice as fast as the average growth of this sector in other developing countries, see UNIDO (1979, p. 38). This high degree of industrialisation was achieved by a considerable amount of investment in construction and imported machinery and equipment. The average annual growth of gross domestic fixed capital formation reached 16 per cent and that of fixed investment in machinery and equipment amounted to over 20 per

TABLE 1.3 *Average annual real rate of growth of major sectors of Iranian economy during the five-year plans[1] (shown as percentage)*

Sectors	Third Plan (1963–7)	Fourth Plan (1968–72)	Fifth Plan (1973–7)	1963–77
Agriculture	4.6	3.9	4.6	4.4
Domestic oil	13.6	15.2	−0.7	9.4
Industries and mines	13.7	13.0	15.5	14.1
Manufacturing and mines	(11.8)	(12.8)	(15.8)	(13.5)
Construction	(12.0)	(8.6)	(14.4)	(11.7)
Services	8.0	14.2	15.3	12.5
Gross domestic product (GDP)	9.7	11.4	6.9	10.8
Non-oil GDP	8.7	10.4	13.3	9.4

Note:

[1] Because of deficiencies in the compilation of statistics and particularly because of possible underestimation of price increases, the published growth figures (except for the oil sector) might very well be overestimated. The overestimation of the growth of the agricultural sector, however, seems to be more serious than that of the industrial sector. The evidence on imports of industrial machinery and equipment supports the published high figure for the growth of the manufacturing sector, but as suggested by Amuzegar and Fekrat (1971, p. 48), a realised real rate of growth of 2.8 per cent per annum for agriculture during the Third Plan seems more plausible.

SOURCE *Annual Reports*, Central Bank of Iran.

cent during the Third and Fourth Plans (see Table 1.4). The rise in imports of intermediate and capital goods as to be expected, from an import-substitution industrialisation strategy, was accompanied by a shift away from consumer goods in total imports. The share of this category of imports in the total non-military merchandise imports declined uniformly from 30 per cent in 1959 to less than 11 per cent in 1969. (See Table 1.5.)

Another important feature of Iran's industrialisation during the period 1963–72 was the remarkable degree of price stability that accompanied the fast growth of output. The implicit price deflator of non-oil GDP during the Third and Fourth Plans, grew on average by only 0.9 and 3.8 per cents respectively (see Table 1.6).

TABLE 1.4 *Average annual rate of growth of real gross domestic fixed capital formation, by types of capital goods (shown as percentage)*

	Third Plan (1963–7)	Fourth Plan (1968–72)	Fifth Plan (1973–7)	1963–77
Gross domestic fixed capital formation	18.5	13.7	22.9	18.4
Construction	16.0	13.1	19.5	16.2
Machinery and equipment	25.9	14.8	28.7	23.1

SOURCE *National Income of Iran: 1959–72*, and *Annual Reports*, Central Bank of Iran.

TABLE 1.5   *Commodity composition of Iran's imports classified by their use[1]*
(shown as percentage)

Type of use	1959	1962	1967	1969	1972	1977
Consumer goods	30.2	21.8	12.6	10.9	12.9	18.6
Intermediate goods	49.2	57.2	59.7	64.0	62.1	54.2
Capital goods	20.6	21.0	27.7	25.1	25.0	27.2
Total	100.0	100.0	100.0	100.0	100.0	100.0

Note:
[1] Excludes military imports.

SOURCE   *Annual Reports,* 1349 (1970) and 1356 (1977) Central Bank of Iran.

TABLE 1.6   *Some indicators of price inflation in the Iranian economy during the five-year plans*

	Third Plan (1963-7)	Fourth Plan (1968-72)	Fifth Plan (1973-7)
Implicit price deflator of non-oil GDP	0.9	3.8	15.5
Index of wholesale prices	1.3	4.2	12.7
Index of retail prices	1.5	3.7	15.7

SOURCES   *National Income of Iran: 1959-72,* and *Annual Reports,* Central Bank of Iran.

Iran, however, was not immune to the unfavourable economic and social consequences of a hasty industrialisation promoted largely by import controls and easy private sector credits, and sustained exclusively by means of excessive exploitation of the country's exhaustible oil reserves.

In this process certain members of the Shah's family and their close business associates played a detrimental role. In the pursuit of quick and easy profit, the Pahlavi family used their unrestrained political leverage to ensure first, that they became business partners of most major manufacturing enterprises, hotels, banks and insurance companies; and second, by resort to bribery, arm-twisting and enforcement of changes in the country's trade and banking regulations, they created an appropriate environment for their purposes which often proved contrary to the objective of achieving balanced growth and a more equitable distribution of income. The establishment of new banks by close business associates of the Pahlavi family paved the way for their easy access to private sector deposits as well as to public sector funds (loans and credits from the Central Bank of Iran) and were instrumental in their capital transfers abroad. These banks were also used to grant loans to companies, often in excess of their worth, which belonged to the Pahlavi family or their associates. The Pahlavi Foundation (now renamed as 'The Foundation for the Oppressed') which was established in 1958 as a charity organisation, was another key institution used by the Pahlavi family to extend their influence over the economy.[39]

This hasty industrialisation in quest of quick and easy profits inevitably created acute geographical and sectoral imbalances. The agricultural sector, which in 1966 accounted for over 47 per cent of the country's employed labour force, grew on average by less than a third of the growth of the industrial sector. Consequently, the share of agricultural value added in the total GDP (at factor cost) declined from 26.5 per cent in 1963 to 16.1 per cent in 1972. Since it is quite likely that the official figures for the growth of the agricultural sector are exaggerated, the fall in the share of this sector has probably been much more pronounced.[40]

High tariffs on consumer goods, overvaluation of the rial and control of food prices in the politically sensitive urban areas through government food imports and generous subsidies, made possible only because of rising oil revenues,[41] were among important factors which caused the deterioration of the terms of trade of the agricultural sector and worked against a balanced development of the rural areas. As a result, real investment in agricultural machinery and equipment during 1963–71 grew by only 6.7 per cent per annum as compared with an average annual rate of 20 per cent for the total investment and its share declined from 16.6 per cent in 1963 to 5.1 per cent in 1971.[42]

The implementation of the first two stages of the Land Reform Law of 1962 and its amendments also brought about a number of important unanticipated social changes in village life that reinforced even further the undesirable social consequences of the neglect of the agricultural and rural sector of the economy. Like many other 'bourgeois-capitalist' reforms, Iranian land reform was a political response to mounting internal and external pressures. It was not very well thought out and as it moved from its first phase, it became less and less effective as an instrument of land redistribution.

The implementation of the first stage of the land reform programme started in 1962 and covered all estates in excess of one village, or parts of different villages that together could be regarded as equivalent to one whole village. Tea and fruit orchards and mechanised farms using modern agricultural machinery were exempted. The second stage of the land reform commenced in 1965 and set limits of 20–150 hectares to landowners' holdings according to the type of land and its proximity to the market, but furnished the landlords with the following five options:

1. letting the land to the occupying peasants on a 30-year lease;
2. selling the land to the peasants;
3. dividing the land between themselves and the peasants in the same proportion as under the crop-sharing agreement;
4. forming a farm co-operative with the peasants;
5. purchasing the peasants' rights of the use of land, assuming that they are willing.

As a result of the implementation of this phase many peasants could not become landowners. The third and final stage of the reform that started in 1969 was an attempt to eliminate the tenancy relations in farming which the second stage had failed to deal with effectively. This stage, however, coincided with the government's policy of creating farm corporations in order to facilitate mechanisations of farming and to increase agricultural productivity. The scheme meant that the peasants were forced to transfer the use of their land permanently to the farm corporations in exchange for shares equivalent to the value of their land and other farm assets. This was seen by many peasants as a reversal of the land-distribution programme and, as far as they were concerned, they had again ceased to be landowners and had reverted to their previous social status of being mere agricultural labourers.[43]

Thus the subsequent amendments to the Land Reform Law enabled many landlords to keep a sizeable proportion of the most fertile lands in a village and those unlucky farmers who happened to be cultivating the land retained by the landlord became landless. As a result, in many villages relatively homogenous communities of 'landless' peasants, became stratified overnight into the 'landed' and the 'landless' (*khoshneshin*) classes.[44] The pre-land-reform predominance of 'landlords' in village life was therefore replaced by a new class of peasant proprietors and government officials. The *khoshneshin*, who by the end of the 1960s had lost all hope of becoming landholders and found themselves forced to work with other peasants, became quite bitter and resentful of both the landed peasants and the government in

Tehran. Craig (1978) in his case study of a village before and after land reform in the Fars province concluded that:

> The White Revolution undeniably changed the *status quo* between 1965 and 1973: land titles changed hands, the *kadkhoda* (the village headman) and the landlord were excised from village affairs, and new institutions were established. However, in many ways the changes came full circle and several of the pre-reform problems remained unsolved ten years after the reform. While at the outset there had been optimism and co-operation on the villagers' part, there was now factionalism, stratification and disenchantment with the government. What the political import of these frustrated expectations will be remains to be gauged. (p. 153)

The regime's failure to fill effectively the organisational and physical vacuum created by the half-hearted removal of landlords, and its neglect of agricultural investment left many disenchanted and disappointed *khoshneshin* with little option but to look for work in the fast-growing industrial centres. Unfortunately, reliable figures for the rate of rural–urban migration are not available.[45] However, if we assume that in the absence of rural–urban migration the population of urban areas would have increased at the country's rate of population growth, it immediately follows that the annual number of rural–urban migrants increased by 78 per cent during 1966–76 as compared with the period 1956–66. In other words, while rural migrants comprised 44 per cent of the increase in population of urban areas between 1956 and 1966, these migrants accounted for as much as 50 per cent of the increase in the urban population during the period 1966–76. As a result the degree of urbanisation rose very sharply from 31.4 per cent in 1956 to 46.9 per cent in 1976 (see Table 1.7).[46] Furthermore, most of the discontented migrants under the pull of the high and rising demand for labour, particularly for unskilled construction workers in urban centres eventually found their way into large overcrowded cities such as Tehran, Isfahan and Tabriz, thereby intensifying the already acute problems of traffic, housing, water shortage and air pollution in these politically important centres of population.[47]

Finally contrary to the regime's highly publicised objective of greater social and economic equity embodied in the Shah's social reforms of the early 1960s, it gradually became clear that the benefits of industrialisation and land reform were not 'trickling down' at a satisfactory rate, and income distribution both in urban and rural areas became

TABLE 1.7   *Iran's population by urban and rural areas*

	Total (000s)	Urban (000s)	Rural (000s)	Degree of urbanisation[1] (%)
1956[a]	18955	5954	13001	31.4
1966[a]	25789	9794	15995	38.0
1976[a]	33662	15797	17865	46.9
1978[b]	35509	17342	18167	58.8

Notes: [a] Census data; [b] Estimated
[1] The percentage of total population residing in urban areas.

SOURCE   *Annual Reports*, 1351 (1977) and 1357 (1978) Central Bank of Iran.

increasingly unequal over the whole of the post-1963 period. In an early study of income distribution in Iran, the International Labour Office concluded that the Gini coefficient for Iran's income distribution in 1969–70 was 'higher than any country in East and South-east Asia, considerably higher than in Western countries and probably as high or higher than in Latin American countries for which data are available'.[48] Over the whole period from 1959 to 1974, the expenditure share of the top 20 per cent of households in urban areas increased uniformly from 52 per cent to 56 per cent and the share of the bottom 40 per cent of households declined from 14 per cent to 11 per cent. Similar trends can also be observed for rural areas.[49] The rapid expansion of consumer goods industries in the vicinity of fast-growing urban centres such as Tehran, Isfahan and Tabriz, together with neglect of the rural-agricultural sector, also aggravated the significant regional disparities that existed among the various regions with respect to income, provisions of health care, educational facilities, etc. According to urban–rural Household Budget Surveys carried out by the Statistical Centre of Iran, the average household expenditure in the central province was 2.7 times that in Kerman, twice that in Sistan and Baluchestan and 1.4 times that in Kordestan provinces in 1971–2 (see Pesaran, 1976a, p. 285). In the area of health care, about half the country's doctors in 1973 were located in Tehran where there was one doctor for every 878 inhabitants, while for the rest of the country this figure was only one for every 5011, and in some remote provinces such as Elam it was only one for every 12 570. The regional disparity in the degree of literacy was also extremely marked. The rate of literacy in Tehran was estimated in 1973 to be 76 per cent, while the figure for the rest of the country was 38 per cent.

Provinces such as Elam with 21.5 per cent and Kordestan with 22.8 per cent, had the lowest rates of literacy in the country.[50]

Therefore, only a decade after the political unrests of 1963 and promises of social and economic reforms for a more equitable society, the discontented and disillusioned rural migrants were arriving in towns in large numbers and the masses were realising that the rich were still getting richer while the gap separating them from the poor continued to widen even further. Indeed in the early 1970s James Bill in his study of informal politics in Iran concluded that: 'Mohammed Reza Shah's White Revolution which is in many ways designed to buttress traditional relations carries serious unintended consequences as aspirations are heightened and expectations sharpened'.[51]

A MISSED OPPORTUNITY: 1973–8

Apart from having unfavourable social consequences, the rapid growth and industrialisation during the Third and Fourth Plans also produced a series of balance-of-payments problems. In all but the first year of these two five-year plans, the current account of the balance-of-payments was in the red. Over the period 1963–72, the accumulated deficit of the current account amounted to $2617m, all of which was financed by long-term loans.[52] By 1970 the situation appeared alarming.[53] Indeed if it were not for the dramatic rise in oil prices during the early 1970s, the adoption of some kind of Economic Stabilisation Programme would have become inevitable.[54] The Tehran Agreement of February 1971 and the subsequent quadrupling of oil prices in 1973–4 which increased Iran's 'per barrel' oil revenue from $0.98 in January 1971 to $9.49 in January 1974,[55] not only solved Iran's foreign exchange problems overnight, but presented the regime with another golden opportunity to redress the economic and social inequities that its ill-considered social reforms and the rapid industrialisation of the 1960s had created. The increase in oil prices also meant that for the first time the government was in a position to reduce the rate of extraction of Iran's fast-dwindling oil reserves without undermining the country's growth potential or causing a deep economic recession. However, the regime, and particularly the Shah himself, opted for an acceleration of the social and economic trends of the 1960s.

In the summer of 1974, contrary to the advice given by economists and planners in the Central Bank of Iran and the Plan and Budget Organisation, the total expenditure of the Fifth Five Year Plan whose implementation had started in March 1973, was doubled.[56] The planners' objections that the revised Plan would create shortages of skilled manpower and acute infrastructural bottlenecks and would worsen the economy's already precarious balance were discounted with contempt by the regime. The Shah's answer to shortages of skilled and experienced manpower was 'computers', 'foreign experts' and 'imported advisers'. Being in great haste to reach his ideal of a 'Great Civilisation', the Shah once again underestimated the impact that rapid industrialisation, urbanisation, and rising dependence on Western technology and culture might have upon Iran's social and political structure.

As early as March 1975 a Hudson special report on the Shah's ambition of making Iran the world's 'fifth greatest power' concluded:

> However, this wealth will be highly unevenly distributed, apart from maldistribution by class, there will be a great concentration of wealth in the cities in glaring contrast to the underdeveloped countryside. Social tensions, and political trouble would seem inevitable.[57]

The doubling of the Fifth Plan's expenditure seemed also to have had the blessing of the United States for two reasons. First, the envisaged high level of government expenditure would not only have expanded the export markets of the Western industrialised countries in Iran, but would also have drained Iran's foreign exchange reserves, thus forcing the regime to increase or at least not to curtail the country's oil exports. In this way the threat of supply shortages and higher oil prices would have been averted.[58] Second, the higher expenditure would have enabled Iran to fill the military and political vacuums created by the withdrawal of the British forces from the Persian Gulf in 1971, without any new costs to the Western Alliance; thus ensuring the success of the so-called 'Nixon Doctrine' in the region.[59]

As was expected, the implementation of the revised Plan produced the worst that the planners had feared. The bottlenecks created in the ports and the transportation networks meant that up to 200 ships at a time had to queue to unload their cargoes with an average waiting time of 160 days.[60] The shortages of electricity meant frequent blackouts in urban areas and costly disruption of industrial production. The manpower shortages resulted in considerable wage increases in almost all sectors and a considerable inflow of foreign workers both from the industrialised and the developing countries. The lack of preparation of the government's bureaucratic machinery to handle such a large expenditure invariably resulted in wastage and amplified the inherent weaknesses of Iranian public administration. Corruption took new dimensions and the public's discontent with government officials reached new heights.[61]

With increasing government expenditure out of oil revenues, the country's dependence upon oil increased even further. The share of the oil and gas sectors in total government revenues rose from 55 per cent in the Fourth Plan to about 78 per cent in the Fifth Plan (see Table 1.2). The urgency in reforming the archaic and unjust tax system once again disappeared. The situation was even worse in the case of foreign trade. The share of oil and gas revenues in total current foreign exchange receipts rose from 76 per cent in the Fourth Plan to 85 per cent in the Fifth Plan (see Table 1.2).[62] By 1977, it became quite clear that the policy of expanding non-oil exports had failed. The share of non-oil merchandise exports in the total foreign exchange revenues was a mere 1.8 per cent. More strikingly perhaps, the ratio of exports of manufacturing to the manufacturing valued added had declined from 3.4 per cent in 1972 to only 2 per cent in 1977.[63]

The expansion of domestic demand far beyond the country's output potential and the capacity to import goods and services, inevitably resulted in a marked acceleration of the domestic rate of price inflation.[64] The rate of increase of retail prices rose from 3.7 per cent per annum during the Fourth Plan to 15.5 per cent in 1974 (see Table 1.6). In order to curb the price rises, instead of reducing public sector expenditure and restricting the expansion of private sector credits, the regime embarked upon an anti-profiteering campaign which sowed the seeds of distrust and resentment of the government by the *bazaar* and at the same time revived and harboured the historical alliance of the *ulama* and the *bazaar*.[65] Later on as the ineffectiveness and the disruptive nature of this type of control was increasingly recognised, the government started adopting a tighter monetary and fiscal policy in mid-1975. However, because of the suppressed inflationary pressures that still existed in the system and the government's failure effectively to remove the bottlenecks, consumer prices started accelerating from 9.9 per cent in 1975 to 16.6 per cent in 1976 and finally to 25.1 per cent in 1977, while at the same time the growth of domestic value added started declining. The growth of real investment in construction which had amounted to 53.2 per cent in 1975 and 22.9 per cent in 1976, declined to 2.7 per cent in 1977. The total gross domestic fixed capital formation at constant prices which had grown by 64 per cent in 1975 and 21 per cent in 1976, grew by only 3.4 per cent.[66] In fact for the first time since 1969 real investment of the private sector in machinery and equipment decreased by 6.8 per cent in this year and largely as a result of a dry year, value added of the agricultural sector also declined by 0.8 per cent in 1977.

The complete lifting of restrictions on foreign exchange transactions in December 1974, coupled with the implementation of the 1975 Share Participation scheme requiring owners of manufacturing companies to sell 49 per cent of their shares to their employees and the public, also had an adverse effect upon private sector manufacturing investment and brought about an unprecedented flight of capital out of the country. This massive capital outflow not only represented a loss of faith by the industrialist community in the Shah's regime, but also provided the opposition groups with a very powerful instrument to incite the masses against the regime.

In short, expectations of ever-rising material wealth were becoming increasingly frustrated and the people's tolerance for the continually rising social and economic inequities which had been in process ever since the abortive protests of 1963, was becoming rapidly exhausted. People may be prepared to tolerate what they perceive as inequities as long as they expect the existing disparities and injustices to diminish eventually. But if this does not happen, the inevitable result under autocratic regimes will be social tension, political protests and potentially revolutionary upheavals.[67]

The mood of discontent in 1977 was further reinforced by a prolonged period of political suppression and the torture of political prisoners of which people were becoming increasingly aware,[68] and the relatively large presence of US military personnel in Iran that revived the anti-American sentiments of the 1950s.[69] These two additional factors together with the corruption of the government officials already referred to, provided the opposition groups with excellent legitimate weapons for the mobilisation of the already discontented and disillusioned masses against the regime.

The stage was set. The repressed intelligentsia who were waiting for an opportune moment to strike at the old regime encouraged by the Shah's liberalisation policy, presumably implemented within the framework of Carter's administration policy of Human Rights,[70] stepped up their activities against the regime and demanded prompt and effective observance of the articles of the 1906 Constitution and the Universal Declaration of Human Rights.[71] The *bazaar*, economically alienated and badly humiliated in the aftermath of the anti-profiteering campaign, and the clergy, with its deep-rooted resentment of the Shah's pro-Western anti-Islamic policies, were ready for a decisive revival of the old traditional alliances. As before, the *bazaar* with its financial strength and its network of information, the clergy with their strong religious power over the masses, and the intelligentsia with their influence *vis-à-vis* the élite and the university students, together had little difficulty in mobilising the discontented and disillusioned masses. The centuries-old network and organisation that existed in the *bazaars* and the mosques for religious gatherings and processions to comme-morate the martyrdom of the Imams, particularly that of the Third Imam, Hosein the Lord of Martyrs, was at the disposal of the *bazaar*–clergy alliance. It was through organising *rozeh khani* (religious sermons), *ta'ziyeh* (passion plays), *dastehyeh azadari* (ritual funeral processions), *sofreh hazrat-eh abbas* (female religious gatherings to fulfil a vow) and other forms of religious rituals that they succeeded in mobilising the discontented masses against the regime.[72] By the end of Ramadam (the month of fasting) in September 1978, the opposition groups headed by the clergy managed to incite over a million inhabi-tants of Tehran to participate in public prayers and processions. This also marked the start of a series of street mass demonstrations, strikes by private and public sector employees, notably the strike by the oil workers in Khuzestan province that crippled industries and disrupted life in the urban centres all of which were eventually instrumental in bringing about the Shah's departure and ensuring the fall of his regime in February 1979.[73]

The reliance of the tripartite alliance upon religious demonstrations and mass prayers as the most expedient method of opposing the regime, soon resulted in a *de facto* approval of the clergy's leadership and looked as if a marked tendency towards Islamic fundamentalism was taking place. The religious colouring of the demonstrations was much the same as that of the earlier uprisings as witnessed in the Tobacco Protests of 1891–2, the Constitutional Revolution of 1905–11 and the 1962–3 violent demonstrations.[74] As with the other successful uprisings, although the mosque, the bazaar and the universities were united in their determination to overthrow the regime, each was hoping that as soon as its aim was achieved it would influence the outcome of the revolution in accordance with its own ideologies and vested interests.

REVOLUTION AND ITS AFTERMATH

The February Revolution was primarily a political revolution in the sense that an established political order was overthrown suddenly and violently with overwhelming popular support. It was neither a Socialist nor – in spite of its outcome – an Islamic revolution in essence. The potentially revolutionary situation was the direct and inevitable consequence of the people's expectations rising at a much faster rate than the actual satisfaction of their needs and the non-responsive nature of the Shah's autocratic regime. The people simply wanted a change of regime. They did not seem to care much what replaced it. Islam as a unifying force and Shiism as a doctrine denying the Shah's rule its legitimacy served to raise the uprising's chances of success. Islamic resurgence was not the *cause* of the February Revolution, it was its *effect*. It is not the first time that the immediate outcome of a revolution is determined more by the instruments and the personalities of those who help to achieve it than by the fundamental social and economic forces that were truly responsible for its occurrence. However, without a prompt resolution of the basic and socio-economic dislocations and inequities of pre-revolutionary Iran, it seems rather doubtful that such a fundamentalist Islamic outcome can be sustained for long. The fact that the ruling clergy have invoked the opinion prevalent among Shiia *ulama* which alleges that only Shiia *mujtahed* (religious leaders who are capable of exercising individual judgement or endeavour) can be deputies of the Hidden Imam and that they are the only legitimate authority during his absence, has undoubtedly been a significant factor in consolidating their political leadership in post-revolutionary Iran.[75] But the clergy's long-term claim to legitimacy can be sustained only if they prove capable of solving the country's pressing socio-economic problems and establish a more responsive system of government. As is aptly pointed out by Dunn (1972, p. 15) 'The legitimacy of revolutionary élites in the process of struggle comes from their claim to be able to solve (or go some distance towards solving) some of the problems of their societies. It is a legitimacy which can only survive their success intact if they do contrive to solve some of these.'

Every revolution has its romantic phase which coincides with the victory over the old regime and embodies the heroic and romantic deeds of the revolutionaries and depicts man to be the master of his own destiny. This phase is usually rather brief and in most great revolutions has not lasted more than a few months.[76] The Iranian experience does not seem to have been an exception and, if it had not been for the seizure of the United States Embassy in Tehran in November 1979, it would have come to an end even sooner. The revival of the revolutionary fervour in the wake of the hostage crisis was instrumental in helping the clergy to achieve their prime objectives of legalising their authorities before the termination of the romantic phase. During this phase (just over one year after the fall of the Shah) they succeeded, by resort to repeated referendums, in establishing an Islamic Republic and in consolidating their political power in judicial, legislative and executive matters.

Initially, the clergy exercised their authority through a secret Revolutionary Council, a large number of revolutionary committees (*komiteh*) that mushroomed all over the country immediately after the revolution, and Islamic revolutionary courts. The running of the bureaucratic machinery, however, was left to moderate secular politicians mainly of Iran's Liberation Movement which had close links with the clergy. Members of the militant left-wing guerrilla organisations which had played a crucial role in the overthrow of the old regime were conspicuously excluded from the government. The Muslim fundamentalists not being themselves completely ready to take over the government machinery which they distrusted, started creating parallel military and civilian organisations. The Revolutionary Guards were formed to operate alongside the armed forces. The 'Organisation for Construction Crusade', 'Foundation for the Powerless Ones' and the 'Housing Foundation' were set up as counterparts to a number of key ministries responsible for infrastructure, agriculture, rural development and housing.

It was, however, the secular provisional government headed by Bazargan which found itself faced with the formidable dual task of regenerating the economy and restoring normal conditions while at the same time proceeding with the social and institutional transformation of the Iranian society at a rate fast enough to be acceptable to the Muslim fundamentalists as well as to the militant left-wing groups who were excluded from the government. As was to be expected, the duality of authority implicit in the creation of the revolutionary organs, the extremists' demand for a rate of social change incompatible with the objective of normalising economic conditions, and the uprisings in the provinces involving Kurdish, Arab and Turkoman Sunni minorities demanding some degree of autonomy, increasingly weakened the Bazargan government and eventually forced its downfall in the wake of the occupation of the United States Embassy by the militant students.

Rule by the moderates in the immediate post-revolutionary period and a relatively swift termination of their government is by no means confined to the Iranian experience and has been quite prevalent amongst the revolutions that Friedrich (1966) categorises as being 'unlimited'. Brinton (1953) in his account of 'The Anatomy of

Revolution' has argued in some detail why the rule by the moderates in the English, French and Russian revolutions had to, and in fact did, come to an end shortly after their victory over the old regimes. He summarises his findings as:

> We may say then that in all our revolutions there is a tendency for power to go from Right to Centre to Left, from the conservatives of the old regime to the moderates to the radicals or extremists. As power moves along this line, it gets more and more concentrated, more and more narrows its base in the country and among the people, since at each important crisis the defeated group has to drop out of politics. (p. 136)

The fall of the Bazargan government and the taking of the US hostages brought about a definite move towards a less moderate and a more clergy-dominated administration. A complete transfer of power to the hard line clergy was however, *temporarily* halted by Khomeini forbidding religious leaders to stand as candidates for the presidency of the newly formed Republic. Khomeini's personal intervention was instrumental in paving the way for the election of Abolhassan Bani Sadre, a secular French educated economist, as Iran's first president in January 1980 and in keeping the hard-line clergy out of the presidential race. However, it was not long before the political balance in favour of the hard-line clergy was restored. The religious alliance led by Ayatollah Beheshti within the framework of the Islamic Republican Party (IRP) scored a decisive victory in the new *Majlis* (national assembly) elections and won around 130 seats out of the 247 seats contested at the time.[77] This sweeping victory of the IRP in the *Majlis* election not only legitimised the clergy's involvement in running the government machinery, but more importantly, it proved crucial in neutralising Bani Sadre's political activities and eventually in ousting him from office in June 1981. Bani Sadre's failure to unify the opposition to the hard-line clergy and his ineffectiveness in creating a viable political organisation capable of counteracting the IRP was also instrumental in speeding his downfall. However, one should not overlook the fact that without Khomeini's support Bani Sadre would have stood little chance of succeeding in the post-revolutionary political turmoils, and since it was unlikely that Khomeini would back Bani Sadre *against* the fundamentalists, it was therefore not surprising that it was Bani Sadre and not the IRP which had to go when Khomeini repeatedly failed to reconcile them.

The dismissal of Bani Sadre as Commander-in-Chief of the armed forces and his subsequent impeachment by the IRP dominated *Majlis* completed the *total* take-over of power by the hard-line clergy and started a new phase in Iran's revolutionary upheavals. This pattern also fits well with Brinton's phenomenology of the revolutionary process. The rule of the moderates ended with the accession of the hard-line clergy who were finding themselves increasingly isolated as the secular politicians, left-wing groups, the intelligentsia and even the *bazaari* were joining the ranks of opposition to their rule.

The 1978–9 tactical alliance of the intelligentsia and the clergy was the first of the links in the tripartite alliance to break down in the aftermath of the revolution. The universities soon became the focal point of the 'Cultural Revolution' and until very recently were closed down. The bureaucracy was made subject to widespread purges. Although the alliance of the clergy and the *bazaar* remained intact at first, it soon started to show some signs of cracking. A rigorous implementation of the regulations for the total nationalisation of foreign trade and the government's anti-profiteering campaign is likely to exert more pressure on the *bazaari* and push them further away from the ruling clergy. The political isolation of the ruling clergy has already manifested itself in waves of repression, arrests and the execution of their political opponents on a massive scale, notably the *Mojahedin*. The executions became particularly intensified in the wake of the bombing of the IRP headquarters which killed Ayatollah Beheshti and more than seventy-one other leading figures of the IRP (including four ministers, six deputy ministers and eighteen members of the *Majlis*) and the subsequent explosion at the prime minister's office on 30 August 1981 which killed both the newly-elected president, Mr Mohammad Ali Reja'i and his prime minister, Dr Mohammad Javad Bahonar. The government's response to these political assassinations was further arrests, imprisonments and executions. The revolution began a new phase. The hard-line clergy having secured the total control of the government were determined to maintain their rule in the face of opposition by terror and repression. Iran in effect entered a revolutionary phase often described as the 'Reign of Terror'.

Meanwhile, the political and economic uncertainties, the continuation of war with Iraq, the lack of a clear economic policy, international isolation (partly self-inflicted) and acute shortages of raw materials and managerial skills have all prevented the economy from returning to acceptable levels of capacity utilisation. In the nine months immediately after the revolution, the economy did show some signs of returning to normality. The index of manufacturing output of large establishments started to rise steadily and by the third quarter of 1979–80 reached 88 per cent of its pre-revolution level (in the third quarter of 1977–8) and was 10 per cent higher than its level in the third quarter of 1978–9. This normalisation process, however, came to an abrupt halt with the fall of the Bazargan government and was subsequently reversed in the aftermath of the seizure of the US Embassy in November 1979. The output of large manufacturing establishments fell by 19.2 per cent over the year from the third quarter of 1979–80 to the third quarter of 1980–1. It was only after the complete take over of the state apparatus by the hard-line clergy that the manufacturing output began to rise again (see Table 1.8). Nevertheless, in the third quarter of 1982–3 (four years after the triumph of the Revolution) the output of large manufacturing establishments was still 3.9 per cent below its pre-revolution peak value. The collapse of the industrial sector as a whole was even more pronounced. According to the provisional national income statistics recently released by the Central Bank of Iran, the value added of the Industries and Mines (excluding oil) at constant prices declined by an average annual rate of 8.7 per cent over the period from 1977–8 to 1981–2 compared with an average annual real rate of growth of 16.0 per cent over the period from 1970–1 to 1977–8. Despite these unfavourable output trends, manufacturing employment not only did not fall, but because of political pressure from Workers' Councils continued to rise at an average annual rate of 4.2 per cent over the period from 1977–8 to 1981–2 (see Table 1.8).[78]

Not surprisingly, the agricultural sector was hardly affected by the urban-based revolutionary upheavals. The average annual real rate of growth of this sector is estimated to have been around 4.7 per cent over the period from 1977–8 to 1981–2, which is high even by historical standards. But given the persistence of the old agrarian relations, the continued expansion of the agriculture sector at such a high rate may not be sustainable. In fact very little has been done by the ruling clergy to alter the country's dependence on food imports and oil revenues in a fundamental way.[79]

Furthermore, the government policy of artificially maintaining the high level of industrial employment by subsidising industries that are working well below the normal levels of capacity utilisations has also led to high levels of effective demand without a corresponding rise in domestic production. This has been particularly true of the large establishments that were nationalised immediately after the revolu-

TABLE 1.8 *Quarterly movements in output and employment of large manufacturing establishments* (1974–5 = 100)

Year	Output				Employment			
	Q1	Q2	Q3	Q4	Q1	Q2	Q3	Q4
1975–6	103.3	106.1	121.9	127.4	108.1	110.4	111.2	111.8
1976–7	123.5	124.5	145.0	145.5	116.0	117.1	117.6	118.5
1977–8	133.9	136.7	159.9	169.7	118.0	119.6	119.5	121.4
1978–9	158.9	162.3	128.1	66.3	126.4	127.9	125.5	121.6
1979–80	125.1	121.7	140.8	133.8	128.2	131.6	133.0	133.2
1980–1	126.4	127.7	113.7	118.1	136.9	138.7	137.2	137.1
1981–2	118.3	125.5	155.8	150.2	139.8	142.5	142.5	141.6
1982–3	138.8	143.0	163.0	*n.a.*	145.0	147.5	148.8	*n.a.*

SOURCE *Bank Markazi Iran Bulletin*, various issues.

tion.[80] The result has been a widening inflationary gap which together with uncertainties surrounding imports have caused prices to soar. Official figures have put the average annual rate of inflation (measured in terms of consumer prices) over the period from 1980–1 to 1982–3 at 22 per cent, but other sources have estimated inflation to be running at rates as high as 50 per cent per annum.[81]

It is difficult to predict where we may go from here. One thing however is certain. A country ruled by terror and an economy in a state of disarray was not exactly what most of those who took part in the mass demonstrations of 1978–9 had hoped for. Nevertheless, Ayatollah Khomeini's charismatic leadership, continued repression and the crushing of all types of opposition in the name of Islam, the prolongation and possible intensification of the war of attrition with Iraq and, finally, the highly fragmented nature of opposition to Khomeini's regime are likely to persuade the majority of Iranians that, so long as Khomeini is alive, the best course open to them is to wait and see. It looks as if, unlike Engels' proclamation that revolutions are authoritarian in manner and liberating in effect, the Iranian Revolution has been liberating in manner and is becoming extremely authoritarian in effect.

NOTES

1. A brief account of the particular events that, in just over a year, led to the fall of the old regime can be found in Forbis (1980) pp. 3–9; Graham (1979)

pp. 208–41; Halliday (1979a) pp. 310–22; Zabih (1979); Katouzian (1981) pp. 332–53, and Keddie (1981) pp. 231–58. Among these published accounts, Zabih's is the most detailed and comprehensive.

2. However, see Halliday (1979b) who attempts a general discussion of the genesis of the February Revolution and lists the autocratic character of the old regime and its institutionalised repression, its make-believe development programme and its international alignment as the roots of its downfall. Halliday's paper is in effect a useful résumé of his book cited above but does not contain any additional insights. Keddie's recent book (Keddie, 1981) despite its eye-catching title, *Roots of Revolution*, is primarily a useful descriptive text on Iran's modern political and religious history and falls rather short of providing a comprehensive analysis of Iran's revolutionary upheavals.

3. It should be emphasised that the *ulama* are not a priesthood but in the words of Algar (1969) p. vi 'The *ulama* are essentially those who have acquired prominence in religious learning transmitted by former generations, and who can lay no claim to ultimate authority'.

4. For a description of the events that led to the June 1963 uprising and the historical background to the *ulama*'s power in twentieth-century Iran, see Algar (1972) who also argues convincingly that, contrary to the assertions made by the old regime, the reason for Khomeini's call to overthrow the regime was not his objection to the Shah's Land Reform and the enfranchisement of women, but rather seems to have been his uncompromising and resolute opposition to the Shah's violation of the 1906 Constitution; the granting of capitulatory rights to American personnel and their dependents in Iran; the purchase of military equipment from the United States; and Iran's expanding trade and diplomatic relations with Israel. Khomeini and his supporters regarded the Shah's six-point reform programme, the so-called 'White Revolution', as an American conspiracy aimed at Iran's cultural as well as political and economic domination.

5. An accurate account of Khomeini's exile first to Turkey in November 1964 and later on to Iraq in October 1965 can be found in Zonis (1971) pp. 44–7. The June 1963 cited by Algar (1972) p. 249, as the date of Khomeini's exile is incorrect.

6. The 'Ithnashari' or 'Twelver' Shiism branch of Islam is founded on a belief in the cycle of Twelve Imams which started with the Imam Ali, the cousin and the son-in-law of the prophet Mohammad, and culminated in the occultation of the last in the series, the Hidden Imam, *Mahdi*, who is to reappear before the day of judgement to restore justice and equity throughout the World. The dominant features of 'Twelver Shiism' are summarised, for example, by Algar (1969, Ch. 1) who also provides a scholarly documentation of the basis of the *ulama*'s power and influence in the Qajar period. The foundation of 'Twelver' Shiism has been discussed recently by Sachedina (1978). A critical discussion of the sources of the Shiite *ulama*'s effective political power can be found in Eliash (1979).

7. *Zakat* is a kind of property tax and *khoms* is a 20 per cent tax levied on one's 'surplus', measured as the excess of income over the 'necessary' expenses of maintaining one's household. Income is defined quite broadly and includes both earned and unearned categories. *Khoms* should also be

paid by the new owner on the value of land transferred, extracted minerals, precious or semi-precious stones and a few other less significant items. This is a Shiite interpretation of the Koranic ruling given in Sura 8:42. See Dawood's translation (Penguin Classics, 1974) p. 317.

8. It is estimated that the *bazaar* provided the clergy with 80 per cent of their financial needs in the pre-February Revolution. See Zabith (1979) p. 27.

9. Admittedly, our treatment of the intelligentsia is not altogether satisfactory as it is not a monolithic entity, but its use seems less objectionable during the pre- as compared with the post-revolutionary period.

10. These were, the successful 1891–2 protests against the granting of the Tobacco Concession to an English company in 1890, the Constitutional Revolution of 1905–11, and the recent revolutionary upheavals of 1978–9. A comprehensive account of the Tobacco Protest is given by Keddie (1966) who also stresses the role played by Sayyid Jamalud-Din al-Afghani, the prominent pan-Islamist in fostering the alliance of the clergy and the nationalists. The events leading to the Constitutional Revolution are discussed for example in Browne (1910) and Kasravi (1961).

11. The nature of the CIA's intervention in Iran, although neither admitted nor denied officially by the US government, is abundantly clear from the accounts given, for example, by Wise and Ross (1962) pp. 110–14; Tully (1962) ch. 7; and Roosevelt (1979).

12. The relationships between the clergy headed by Ayatollah Kashani and the government of Dr Mossadeq during the nationalisation crisis up to the royalist *coup d'état* are discussed by Cottam (1964) pp. 152–6, and more recently by Algar (1972) pp. 241–2. Although Kashani was instrumental in the organisation of mass support for Mossadeq's National Front movement in the early days of the campaign for the nationalisation of the oil industry, by 1953 Kashani's relations with Mossadeq had deteriorated beyond repair and, at the time of the *coup d'état*, Kashani not only did not oppose the overthrow of Mossadeq's government but, as pointed out by Algar, he even lent it his support.

13. A detailed discussion of Iran's economic development over the period 1921–41 can be found in Banani (1961), especially ch. 7; also see Katouzian (1981) Part II.

14. See Banani (1961) p. 151.

15. The origins and the institutional aspects of economic planning in Iran can be found in Baldwin (1967) pp. 22–52.

16. A detailed and relatively exhaustive account of the Point IV programme is given by Amuzegar (1966). The dilemma that the US government faced in Iran at the time of oil nationalisation is also fully discussed by Amuzegar (p. 78).

17. It is worth noting that the American presence in Iran during the pre-1950 period was mainly confined to private US citizens who acted either as missionaries or advisers to the Iranian government in the field of public finance. See Ramazani (1976).

18. See Public Law 535, 81st US Congress, 2nd Session.

19. Some of the reasons for the Iranian attitudes and reactions to US technical assistance are discussed in Amuzegar (1966) pp. 133–42. The general failure and shortcomings of the Point IV Programme in Iran are also

acknowledged by Baldwin (1967) p. 203. However, with a typical misinterpretation of the underlying social, institutional and spiritual foundations of Iranian society, Baldwin argues that the 'foreign presence' associated with the US technical assistance in Iran constituted one of the greatest indirect benefits of the programme!

20. The US financial aid over the period 1954–6 amounted to $148m as compared with $30m over the period 1950–3. See Greaves (1977) p. 79, and Ramazani (1976) p. 327.

21. Initially the Second Plan's total expenditure was set at 70bn rials but was later on revised upward to 87.2bn rials. A comparison of the expenditures of the First and the Second Plans can be found in the *Annual Report*, 1341 (1962), Central Bank of Iran.

22. For further details see Baldwin (1967) ch. VI, and Amuzegar and Fekrat (1971).

23. The official exchange rate of the rial was changed from 32.50 to 75.75 rials to a US dollar; a rate which prevailed until February 1973.

24. Because government revenues from oil are paid in dollars and oil revenues form a significant part of the total government revenues (see Table 1.2) any change in the rial/dollar exchange rate will directly influence the monetary consequences of the government fiscal operations.

25. See *Annual Report*, 1339 (1960) Central Bank of Iran (p. 9).

26. See *Annual Report*, 1340 (1961) Central Bank of Iran (p. 9).

27. Ibid, p. 18.

28. Ibid, pp. 16–19.

29. The total current account deficits for the years 1958 to 1961 amounted to $236.7m, which was equivalent to 66 per cent of the country's foreign exchange receipts from oil exports in 1960. See *Annual Reports*, 1339 (1960) and 1342 (1963) Central Bank of Iran. The deterioration of the balance of payments was further accentuated by the fall in the export price of oil over the period 1957–60. Iran's oil revenues per barrel declined from 84 cents in 1955 to 80 cents in 1960. On the oil price cuts of 1957 and the subsequent years see Adelman (1972) pp. 160–91.

30. See '*Annual Reports*' 1339 (1960) and 1340 (1961) Central Bank of Iran.

31. See '*National Income of Iran: 1959–1972*', Table 83, Central Bank of Iran.

32. Even Amuzegar (1966) who seems otherwise quite sympathetic towards the US assistance programme in Iran sounds very disenchanted with the impact of the Point IV Programme on economic conditions when he writes:

> The balance-of-payments problems of the mid-1950s which necessitated an austerity-oriented economic stabilisation programme in 1960 were also traceable, partly at least, to the 'demonstration effects' of Point IV activities. The major residential housing recession in the city of Tehran, starting in 1959 and continuing well into the 1960s was also partly caused by excessive and miscalculated local investments in modern quarters, presumably, to take care of the Mission technicians' increasing demand for American-type housing. (pp. 22–3)

33. See Hearings before the Senate Committee on Foreign Relations, May 13, 1959, 86th Congress, 1st Session.

34. See for example Halliday (1979a) p. 252.
35. See Algar (1972) pp. 245–9.
36. See Davies (1962) p. 5.
37. A critical analysis of import substitution strategy is given by Power (1966) and Hirschman (1966).
38. An interesting account of OPEC's strategy can be found in Rustow and Mugno (1976).
39. For the extent of the Foundation's assets and its operations during the old regime see Graham (1979) ch. 9.
40. See Footnote to Table 1.3. (*Editor's note*: For a detailed discussion of this sector see Chapters 2 and 3 on agriculture in this volume.)
41. Iran's imports of agricultural products rose from 6.8bn *rials* in 1963 to 8.7bn *rials* in 1970 and then jumped to 20.9bn *rials* in 1972; thus turning Iran from a net exporter to a net importer of agricultural products. (See IBRD, 1974, Table 10.5)
42. See *National Income of Iran: 1959–72*, Tables 91 and 92, Central Bank of Iran.
43. A survey and appraisal of Iranian land reform can be found, for example, in Lambton (1969); Keddie (1972) and Ajami (1976). (*Editor's* note: for further discussions of these policies see Chapters 2 and 3 on agriculture.)
44. Accurate statistics on the proportion of 'landless' in Iranian villages after the land reform are not available. But according to a number of case studies, it is estimated that *khoshneshin* probably comprise about 40 per cent of a village. See Miller (1964) and Craig (1978).
45. Information on lifetime migration in Iran is obtained in the Census years. We have not tried to use these statistics as they do not provide us with net rates of rural–urban migration.
46. The calculations are based on the statistics reported in Table 1.7.
47. For an analysis of why people migrate to Tehran and its likely consequences see Hemmassi (1976).
48. See ILO (1973) Appendix C, p. 6.
49. For further details see Pesaran (1976a) and Pesaran and Gahvary (1978).
50. For a more detailed account of these and other disparities and relevant statistical sources, see Pesaran (1976b).
51. See Bill (1973) p. 151.
52. See *Annual Reports*, 1349 (1970) and 1351 (1972) Central Bank of Iran.
53. The accumulated deficits of the current account over the period 1963–70 amounted to $2170 m which was 70 per cent higher than the country's total oil revenues in 1970.
54. As a matter of fact, in 1970 the Central Bank did embark upon a tight monetary policy and apart from imposing ceilings on the expansion of private sector credit, it also increased the legal reserve requirements of the commercial banks and required them to keep 16 per cent of the increase in their deposits in the form of government bonds. See *Annual Report*, 1349 (1970) pp. 24–6, Central Bank of Iran.
55. For the details of the events that led to the oil price rises of 1971–4, see Rustow and Mugno (1976) ch. 1.
56. A vivid and accurate account of this is given by Graham (1979) ch. 5.
57. See Langer (1975) p. 30.

58. In spite of the substantially higher oil prices, Iran's oil exports grew by 12.3 per cent in 1973 and her share of output in OPEC rose from 18.5 per cent in 1972 to 19.6 per cent in 1975. See *Annual Report*, 1356 (1977) pp. 180–1, Central Bank of Iran.

59. Military sales to Iran by the United States alone amounted to $15.2 bn during 1973–7 which was eight and a half times the figure for the whole of the period 1950–72 and accounted for as much as 18 per cent of Iran's total oil and gas revenues over the period 1973–7. See Halliday (1979a) p. 95. For the meaning and the application of 'Nixon's Doctrine' in the Persian Gulf see Martin (1977). (*Editor's* note: for a further discussion of arms expenditure see Chapter 8 on the army in this volume.)

60. During 1974–5, Iran paid well over $1.0bn in demurrage charges for delays in the unloading of ships. See Graham (1979) pp. 87–8.

61. See Halliday (1979a) p. 99, and references therein for some idea of the extent of the corruption in Iran's military purchases from the US.

62. The figures of 85 per cent should, however, be regarded as an underestimation of the overall contribution of the oil sector to Iran's foreign exchange earnings. In 1977, the interest received on Iran's foreign exchange reserves deposited abroad amounted to $769m. (about 3 per cent of total foreign exchange receipts) which was a by-product of rising oil revenues over the period 1973–6. See *Annual Report*, 1956 (1977) Central Bank of Iran, Tables 45 and 46.

63. For developing countries as a whole the ratio of manufacturing exports to gross value of manufacturing was 11.5 per cent in 1970. See UNIDO (1979) p. 152.

64. In order to expand the supply of consumer goods, a more liberal foreign trade policy was adopted, which resulted in a considerable increase in the share of consumer goods in Iran's merchandise imports, see Table 1.5.

65. According to official statistics, during the first ten months of the campaign more than 250,000 business units were fined or closed down in the city of Tehran alone. Some 8,000 merchants were sent to jail for two months to five years. See Zabih (1979) p. 31.

66. See *Annual Report*, 1356 (1977) Central Bank of Iran, pp. 168–9.

67. On this line of argument, see Hirschman (1973) for an excellent exposition.

68. The extent of the regime's political suppression and the use of torture and terror by the Shah's secret police SAVAK can be judged, for example, from Baraheni's (1976) article which is based on his testimony before the sub-committee on International Organisation of the US House Committee on International Relations. For more details see Halliday (1979a) ch. 4.

69. It is estimated that by 1977 around 26,000 US military personnel and their dependents were stationed in Iran, all of whom had diplomatic privileges under a 1964 Law. See Martin (1977). It is worth mentioning that one of Khomeini's reasons for fighting the regime in 1963 was his objection to granting capitulatory rights to the American personnel. See note 2. On the legal status of US personnel in pre-revolutionary Iran, see Pfau (1974), where he shows how diplomatic privileges were granted by the Shah to the American Military Community at the price of 2 hundred million dollars!

70. It is, however, quite plausible that the Shah's liberalisation policy was motivated by his own desire to smooth the transition of power, in due time,

to his son along the 'King Carlos' model in Spain. But the American advocacy of human rights was undoubtedly instrumental in giving added important stimuli to the intelligentsia to press for their demands.

71. For an example of open defiance of the regime by the intelligentsia see the text of the open letter sent to the Shah in June 1977 by leaders of the National Front. A translation of the letter can be found in Graham (1979) pp. 259–60.

72. An explicit account of the structure and organisation of religious gatherings and the martyrdom of Imam Hosein can be found in Thaiss (1972) where he also shows how these religious festivities were used by the clergy in 1963 to incite the people against the regime.

73. For further details see references cited in note 1.

74. Relevant references are cited in note 10.

75. This doctrinaire approach to the legitimacy of the *ulama*'s rule is by no means accepted by all the Shiia *ulama*. Recently, Eliash (1979) by resort to primary Shiia sources has argued that during the Greater Occultation of the Twelfth Imam no government whether headed by members of the clergy or not, can be regarded as legitimate or infallible. He rejects the notion of delegating the Imam's authority to a 'deputy' or 'agent'. The problem of the relation between state and religion, the function and the choice of *marja al-taqlid* (a *mojtahed* who is chosen by the believers as a 'source of imitation') in Shiism has also been considered by Lambton (1964) who provides a useful summary of the views held in 1962 by a number of prominent revolutionary figures such as Ayatollah Taleqani, Ayatollah Motahari, Ayatollah Beheshti, Engineer Bazargan and Tabataba'i on the political position of the *ulama* in a Shiia society.

76. For an interesting study of the stages through which revolutions are most likely to go, see Brinton (1953).

77. Voting for the election of the remaining twenty-three seats was postponed as a result of political unrest in some districts of Kurdistan, Baluchestan and other tribal regions.

78. Notice, however, that the employment figures given in Table 1.8 refer to large manufacturing establishments, and may very well exaggerate the growth of employment in the manufacturing sector as a whole. Unfortunately, employment data for the total manufacturing sector are not yet available.

79. On this see Pesaran (1982).

80. All banks, insurance companies and almost all the large manufacturing industries were nationalised during the Bazargan's provisional government.

81. See *Quarterly Economic Review of Iran*, 3rd Quarter 1981, the Economist Intelligence Unit, London, p. 11.

BIBLIOGRAPHY

Adelman, M. A. (1972) *The World Petroleum Market* (Baltimore: Johns Hopkins Press).

Ajami, J. (1976) 'Land reform and modernization of the farming structure in

Iran', in Farmanfarmaian (ed.) *The Social Sciences and Problems of Development*, pp. 189–207 (Princeton: Princeton University Program in Near Eastern Studies).

Algar, H. (1969) *Religion and State in Iran 1785–1906 – The Role of Ulama in the Qajar Period* (University of California Press).

Algar, H. (1972) 'The Oppositional Role of the Ulama in Twentieth-Century Iran', in N. R. Keddie (ed.) *Scholars, Saints and Sufis* (University of California Press).

Amuzegar, J. (1966) *Technical Assistance in Theory and Practice: The Case of Iran* (New York:) Praeger Special Studies in International Economics and Development.

Amuzegar, J. and M. A. Fekrat (1971) *Iran: Economic Development Under Dualistic Conditions* (The University of Chicago Press).

Baldwin, G. B. (1967) *Planning and Development in Iran* (Baltimore: The John Hopkins Press).

Banani, A. (1961) *The Modernization of Iran: 1921–41* (Stanford University Press).

Baraheni, R. (1976) 'Terror in Iran', *New York Review of Books*, October 28, pp. 21–5.

Bill, J. A. (1973) 'The Plasticity of Informal Politics: The Case of Iran', *The Middle East Journal*, pp. 131–51.

Brinton, C. C. (1953) *The Anatomy of Revolution* (London: Jonathan Cape).

Browne, E. G. (1910) *The Persian Revolution of 1905–1909* (London: Cass) (New impression, 1966).

Cottam, R. W. (1964) *Nationalism in Iran* (University of Pittsburgh Press: 1979 revised edition).

Craig, D. (1978) 'The Impact of Land Reform on an Iranian Village', *The Middle East Journal*, pp. 141–54.

Davies, J. C. (1962) 'Toward a Theory of Revolution', *American Sociological Review*, 27, pp. 5–19.

Dunn, J. (1972) *Modern Revolutions: An Introduction to the Analysis of a Political Phenomenon* (Cambridge: Cambridge University Press).

Eliash, J. (1979) 'Misconceptions Regarding the Juridical Status of the Iranian *ulama*', *International Journal of Middle East Studies*, 10, pp. 9–25.

Forbis, W. H. (1980) *Fall of the Peacock Throne: The Story of Iran* (New York: Harper & Row).

Friedrich, C. J. (1966) 'An Introductory Note on Revolution', in Friedrich, C. J. (ed.) *Revolution* (New York: Atherton Press) pp. 3–9.

Graham, R. (1979) *Iran, the Illusion of Power* (London: Croom Helm) revised edn.

Greaves, R. (1977) '1942–1976: The Reign of Muhammad Riza Shah', in Amirsadeghi, H. (ed.) *Twentieth Century Iran* (London: Heinemann).

Halliday, F. (1979a) *Iran: Dictatorship and Development* (Penguin Books) 2nd edn.

Halliday, F. (1979b) 'The Genesis of the Iranian Revolution', *Third World Quarterly*, October issue, pp. 1–16; published in London by Third World Foundation.

Hemmassi, M. (1976) 'Migration and Problems of Development: the Case of Iran', in Farmanfarmaian K. (ed.) *The Social Sciences and Problems of*

Development, pp. 208–25 (Princeton: Princeton University Programme in Near Eastern Studies).

Hirschman, A. O. (1968) 'The Political Economy of Import-substituting Industrialization in Latin America', *Journal of Political Economy*, 82, pp. 2–32.

Hirschman, A. O. (1973) 'The Changing Tolerance for Income Inequality in the Course of Economic Development', *Quarterly Journal of Economics*, 87, pp. 544–66, with a mathematical appendix by M. Rothschild.

IBRD International Bank of Reconstruction and Development. (1974) 'The Economic Development of Iran', Vol. III; Statistical Appendix, Report No. 378 *Iran*.

ILO (1973) *Employment and Income Policies for Iran* (Geneva: International Labour Office).

Kasravi, A. (1961) *History of Iranian Constitution* (Tehran in Persian).

Katouzian, H. (1981) *The Political Economy of Modern Iran: Despotism and Pseudo-modernism, 1926–1979* (London: Macmillan).

Keddie, N. R. (1966) *Religion and Rebellion in Iran: The Tobacco Protest of 1891–1892* (London: Cass).

Keddie, N. R. (1969) 'The Roots of *ulama*'s Power in Modern Iran', *Studia Islamica*, 29, pp. 31–53.

Keddie, N. R. (1972) 'Stratification, Social Control and Capitalism in Iranian Villages: Before and After Land Reform' in R. Antoun and I. Harik (eds) *Rural Politics and Social Change in the Middle East*, pp. 364–402 (Indiana University Press).

Keddie, N. R. (1981) *Roots of Revolution: An Interpretive History of Modern Iran* (New Haven: Yale University Press).

Lambton, A. K. S. (1944) 'Persia', *Journal of the Royal Central Asian Society*, January, pp. 8–22.

Lambton, A. K. S. (1964) 'A Reconsideration of the Position of the *Marja al-taglid* and the Religious Institution', *Studia Islamica*, 20, pp. 115–35.

Lambton, A. K. S. (1969) *The Persian Land Reform, 1962–1966* (Oxford: Oxford University Press).

Langer, F. (1975) 'Iran: Oil Money and the Ambitions of a Nation', *The Hudson Letter* (Hudson Research Europe, March).

Martin, L. W. (1977) 'The Future Strategic Role of Iran', in Amirsadeghi, H. (ed.) *Twentieth Century Iran*, pp. 223–52 (London: Heinemann).

Marx, K. (1851) 'The Eighteenth Brumaire of Louis Bonaparte', published in Tucker, R. C. (ed.) *The Marx – Engels Reader* (New York: Norton) 2nd edn.

Miller, W. G. (1964) 'Hasseinabad: a Persian Village', *Middle East Journal*, 18, pp. 483–98.

Pesaran, M. H. (1976a) 'Income Distribution and its Major Determinants in Iran', in J. W. Jacqz, (ed.) *Iran: Past, Present and Future* (Aspen Institute for Humanistic Studies) pp. 267–86.

Pesaran, M. H. (1976b) 'Social Welfare and Planning', published in the proceedings of the Second National Seminar on Social Welfare, Tehran, April 1976 (in Persian).

Pesaran, M. H. (1982) 'The System of Dependent Capitalism in Pre- and Post-Revolutionary Iran', *International Journal of Middle East Studies*, 14, pp. 501–22.

Pesaran, M. H. and F. Gahvary (1978) 'Growth and Income Distribution in

Iran', in R. Stone and W. Peterson (eds) *Econometric Contributions to Public Policy* (London: Macmillan) pp. 231–48.

Pfau, R. (1974) 'The Legal Status of American Forces in Iran', *The Middle East Journal*, 28, pp. 141–53.

Power, J. H. (1966) 'Import Substitution as an Industrialization Strategy', *Philippine Economic Journal*, 5, pp. 167–204.

Ramazani, R. K. (1976) 'Iran and the United States: An Experiment in Enduring Friendship', *The Middle East Journal* 30, pp. 322–34.

Roosevelt, K. (1979) *Counter-Coup: the Struggle for the Control of Iran* (New York: McGraw-Hill).

Rustow, D. A. and J. F. Mugno (1976) *OPEC: Success and Prospects* (London: Martin Robertson).

Sachedina, A. (1978) 'A Treatise on the Occultation of the Twelfth Imamite Imam', *Studia Islamica*, 48, pp. 109–24.

Thaiss, G. (1972) 'Religious Symbolism and Social Change: the Drama of Husain', in Keddie, N. R. (ed.) *Scholars, Saints and Sufis* (University of California Press) pp. 349–66.

Tully, A. (1962) *CIA: The Inside Story* (London: Arthur Barker).

UNIDO (1979) *World Industry Since 1960: Progress and Prospects* (New York: United Nations Industrial Development Organization).

Wise, D. and T. B. Ross (1962) *The Invisible Government* (London: Jonathan Cape).

Zabih, S. (1979) *Iran's Revolutionary Upheaval: An Interpretive Essay* (San Francisco: Alchemy Books).

2 The Impact of the Urban Income per capita on the Agricultural Output: A Case Study of pre-1975 Iran

KAMRAN AFSHAR

The purpose of this paper is to test the impact of urban demand on agricultural output. The first part of the paper is a review of some of the theories of unlimited supply of labour and their applicability to the Iranian agricultural sector. The second part is devoted to building a model and testing it.

REVIEW OF THEORIES OF UNLIMITED SUPPLY OF LABOUR

The agricultural sector is usually considered backward in the less developed countries (LDC). Highly traditional, they are said to be over-conservative and rather stagnant. Agricultural sectors in most LDCs have passed the discovery of new frontiers. They have usually employed as much usable land as possible, and are now adding labour to a relatively fixed supply of land which is more or less of the same quality. As population grows the agrarian societies deploy more labour-intensive techniques until the 'marginal product of labour falls below zero.'[1] This results in disguised unemployment. W. Arthur Lewis argued that this unemployment in the agricultural sector can be considered as a blessing for the industrial sector,[2] which it provides with an unlimited supply of labour'. Ranis and Fei took this idea one step further arguing that not only a relatively unlimited supply of labour be available to the industrial sector, but this transfer of labour would release some hidden saving equal to the transferee's consumption.[3] Of course, the idea of an unlimited supply of labour of a particular quality is not undisputed. For example, I. M. D. Little argues that because of the nature of subsistence agriculture a reduction in the number of people on the farms will result in less need for production, thus reducing the output.[4] Another opponent of the theory of unlimited supply of labour is Dr Yong Sam Cho[5] who argues that observers dealing with average yearly unemployment do not fully appreciate the nature of seasonal changes in labour requirements in rural areas.

Dale W. Jorgenson also disagrees with the Fei–Ranis model. He argues that: 'transfer of labour from agriculture will result in a decline in agricultural production, thereby creating a problem of feeding the increasing urban population. As a result, the transformation may be delayed not only by a shortage of capital in non-farm jobs, but also by a shortage of food to support the non-farm workforce.'[6] Nakajima and Mellor in an attempt to develop a behaviour pattern for agricultural workers constructed a model including utility and production possibility surfaces of an average farmer. Mellor explains that 'farmers' decisions about labour allocation can be usefully portrayed by means of a utility surface ... depicting the transformation of leisure into material goods and services'.[7] Mellor explains that zero or near-zero marginal productivity is possible, but only for farmers who are pressed to put up more and more labour to make up, as much as is possible, for poor endowment, merely to produce enough to survive. The other group who can provide extra labour without reduction in output are the farmers whose production-possibilities function is not only above subsistence level but also above cultural subsistence level. At this level leisure gains more desirability and thus creates disguised unemployment. Accordingly, we can have idle labour in the agricultural sector at two technically different areas of marginal productivity, one at zero marginal productivity and another at a point with positive marginal productivity. W. Arthur Lewis' labour surplus theory requires high population densities in rural area, that push the marginal product of labour down to near zero. But Mellor's model can be applied to less populated areas.

Labour Force in Iran's Agricultural Sector

The 1960 data regarding the age distribution and work participation in Iran's rural areas suggest that 48.1 per cent of the population are between 14 and 60 years of age.[8,9] Of course, it should be added that females traditionally are assumed not to participate in work outside the home in all but two of the provinces. The work-participation ratio of the members of the farmer's family varies from 1.5 per cent in the provinces of Sistan and Baluchestan up to 42.2 per cent in the Central province. The Ministry of Agriculture estimated that in 1960 3 863 800 thousand hours of work were done in Iran's rural areas.[10] Accounting for the significant female participation in agricultural work in the Central and Northern provinces, a labour force of 4 475 000 can be estimated to exist in rural areas of Iran out of 7.4m people between the ages of 14 and 60 in 1960. This will round up to about 860 hours of work per year per person in the rural labour force – in other words, about 2.36 hours per day per person. Assuming a six-day working week of eight hours a day, mathematically, a labour force of 1 543 000 would prove sufficient to carry out the year's workload. Out of an available existing labour force of 4 475 000, a labour surplus of 2 952 000 or 66 per cent will be available for transfer, without considerably affecting the output. There is, of course, one great shortcoming. As Yong Sam Cho points out, agricultural labour requirements vary in accordance with the seasons. Figure 2.1 shows the percentage of the total work which is done by the farmer and hired workers in accordance with the seasons.

Thus, a smooth labour average requirement proves too much for off-seasons and too small for the peak of the harvest season. In some provinces like Kordestan and the territory of Chahar Mahal Va Bakhtiari, the work done by an average farmer was zero hours during the winter of 1962–3.[11] For example, in Kordestan province, 26 per cent of the total man-hours spent by the average farmer and his hired workers is in autumn, zero per cent in winter, 6 per cent in spring and 68 per cent in summer. But this 68 per cent translates to a labour force of 435.5 thousand, working seven days a week and for slightly more than eight hours a day, thus requiring the entire labour force of the province for the summer season, while the same province will have a surplus of close to 100 per cent of its labour force for the winter season. This constitutes a clear case of seasonal unemployment. On the other hand, in the Northern province the workload is more evenly distributed with 22 per cent of the work done in the autumn, 7

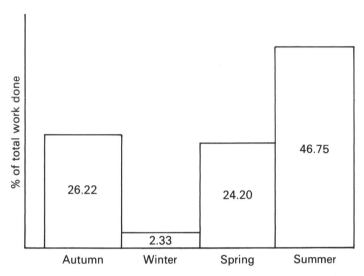

FIGURE 2.1   *Seasonal distribution of work in Iran's agricultural sector*
SOURCE   Ministry of Agriculture's Statistics, 1341 (1962).

per cent in winter, 40 per cent in spring and 31 per cent in summer. But even in the busiest season – spring – only 37.6 per cent of the labour force is required to do the job. This is a 62.4 per cent surplus of labour in the peak season. This clearly constitutes a case for the 'unlimited supply of labour' theory.

This seems to support the proposition that there is a surplus labour force of 66 per cent. But then we explored the technical application of this labour withdrawal and found that in peak seasons there are hardly enough people to do the job in some provinces. Thus, what this really means is a seasonal surplus of labour. This is not what industrialists are looking for, because, in the first place, high transportation costs will prevent most of these people from leaving home just for a possibility of a temporary job during the off-season. Second, and probably more important, this seasonal variation will make a high rate of labour turnover which will result in high training costs and low efficiency, which translates into a drop in the value of the marginal product of labour and an increase in the implicit wage-bill that the industrialist has to pay, which is higher than the wage that the labourer is receiving. Taking into account the transportation costs and the risk of not being able to find a job, the relatively high urban wages may translate into an implicit wage which is nearer to rural than urban wages. This obviously reduces the attraction of the urban job.

MAKING AND TESTING A MODEL

Using the theoretical background explained earlier and drawing upon the indications of the statistical data in reference to the unlimited supply of labour a set of assumptions are made upon which the model is based:

1. Agricultural consumption is on a subsistence basis, but its production is affected by the industrial sector's demand. Income per capita in the urban areas is used as a proxy for industrial sector's demand.
2. Agricultural exports to foreign countries are not considered to be part of the traditional sector that is being tested.
3. The level of investment is constant in the agricultural sector.

The Model

$$Ca/P = f_1(POPR) \tag{1.1}$$

$$Ia/P = bo \tag{1.2}$$

$$Ta/P = f_2(RUY) \tag{1.3}$$

$$Ya = Ca/P + Ia/P + Ta/P \tag{1.4}$$

$$Ya = g_1(POPR, RUY) \tag{1.5}$$

where

bo = constant
$POPR$ = agricultural sector's population
Ca = agricultural sector's consumption
Ia = agricultural sector's investment
Ta = agricultural sector's income from transfer of food to the industrial sector
RUY = real urban income per capita[12]
Ya = agricultural sector's real output
P = price index
$Yind$ = industrial sector's income
$POPU$ = industrial sector's population

If the agricultural sector is basically at subsistence level then the coefficient for RUY will not be significant. Even if the coefficient of RUY is significant, a very low elasticity only indicates the presence of the inevitable contact between the sectors at the margin but nothing substantial. Accordingly assumption (1) can be statistically accepted if both the above conditions are met.

Empirical Tests

Using seventeen observations[13] regression estimates of equation (1.5) are as follows.

(A)

$$Ya/P = -72.77 + 9.01 *POPR + 0.952 *RUY$$
$$T \qquad 2.9 \quad 4.5 \qquad\qquad 3.1$$

$$R^2 = 0.932$$

$$DW = 1.78$$

The above equation clearly indicates that the model is statistically acceptable and the industrial sector has a signficiant spread effect on the agricultural sector. But this meets only one of the conditions of assumption (1). To test the elasticity of RUY, assuming constant elasticity, a double log regression of equation (1.5) is estimated. The results are as follows:

(B)

$$\log(Ya/P) = -0.007 + 1.26 *\log(POPR) + 0.327 *\log(RUY)$$
$$T \qquad 0.02 \quad 3.7 \qquad\qquad\qquad 3.0$$

$$R^2 = 0.952$$

$$DW = 1.74$$

Although elasticity of RUY is relatively low considering that it deals with food and other primary products, an elasticity of 0.327 is not considered insignificant, thus providing the second requirement for accepting assumption (1) as statistically viable.

CONCLUSION

The results of the empirical tests provide statistical grounds to accept the model and thus its assumptions. This would indicate that the Iranian agricultural sector does not produce on a subsistence level, at least for the duration of the observation, and the urban demand has a significant effect on its output. This conclusion clearly rejects zero marginal productivity and thus the concept of unlimited supply of labour in the Iranian agricultural sector.

NOTES

1. Higgins, B., *Economic Development, Problems, Principles and Policies* (New York: W. W. Norton, 1968).
2. Lewis, W. A. *Economic Development with Unlimited Supplies of Labour*, The Manchester School of Economics and Social Studies, May 1954.
3. Foi, J. C. H. and Ranis, C. *Development of the Labor Surplus Economy: Theory and Policies* (Homewood, Ill., Irwin, 1964).
4. Class notes, Michaelmas, 1973, Oxford.
5. Yong Sam Cho, *Disguised Unemployment in Underdeveloped Areas, with Special Reference to South Korean Agriculture* (Berkeley, 1963).
6. Quoted by J. W. Millo, 'Toward a Theory of Agricultural Development' in Southworth, M. and Johnson, B. F. (eds) *Agricultural Development and Economic Growth* (Ithaca, New York: Cornell University Press, 1968) pp. 25–6.
7. Ibid, p. 40.
8. The national census of 1335, 1345 (1956, 1966) and the extensive research of the Institute of Economic Research of Tehran University are the major sources which are used in this section.
9. *Ministry of Agriculture's Statistics* 1339, Tehran.
10. Ibid.
11. Ministry of Agriculture's Statistics, 1341.
12. Industrial sector's income is calculated in the following way: $Ind = GNP - (Ya + oil\ exports)$.
13. Date tested covers the period 1338 to 1354 corresponding to 1959 to 1975. Population is expressed in millions, output in billions of rials, and RUY in thousands of rials corresponding to about \$13 per person per year (1959–75).

3 An Assessment of Agricultural Development Policies in Iran*

HALEH AFSHAR†

INTRODUCTION

After almost three decades of development planning Iran's industrial base remains fragile and the country has lost its earlier self-sufficiency in agriculture. This is largely because of a commitment to dualistic development policies which neglected the agrarian sector and which have resulted in increased economic dependency and in a high urban standard of living which the country cannot afford to maintain.[1]

Typically dualistic models rely on the development of selected industries within an open economy, the encouragement and growth of the private sector and the expectation that foreign investment in strategic industries would lead to a substantial growth of the economy as a whole. In Iran the oil industry was selected as the dynamic sector. Iranian planners were aware of the characteristic shortcomings of dualistic development but claimed that their policies would avoid them. They sought not to 'shift the economy's centre of gravity from agriculture to industry until agriculture became a mere appendage'[2] but to disseminate 'the growth-stimulating effects of the dynamic sector throughout the traditional sector by transforming the dynamic sector

* An earlier version of this paper appeared in World Development volume 9 number 11, 1981.

† I would like to thank Hushang Keshavarz for his considerable help in discussing post-revolutionary measures and giving me access to Ministry of Agriculture papers on the subject. Thanks are similarly due to Farhad Mehran for providing data on production, export and import of foodstuff, and to Maurice Dodson for his comments on an earlier draft of this paper.

into an engine of growth'[3] fuelled by oil revenue. Thus in contrast to the usual pattern of dualistic development the dynamic sector was not intended to be an enclave of development at the expense of the static sector. The crucial linkage between the two sectors was to be made by a 'direct transfer of financial resources ... via the public treasury'.[4] Official figures however show that government investment in agriculture was inadequate and inappropriate and the approach to agricultural development had at times some similarities to those of colonial plantations where foreign capital could use local resources and could exploit a pool of cheap local labour, which was rooted in and sustained by the subsistence sector.

As far as the direct flow of resources from the Iranian oil industry to agriculture was concerned, the 'assimilation of the dynamic sector with the rest of the economy' was not considered as 'essential' in the development strategy: 'the priority may not be very high and there may be definite limits to the inter-sectoral flows between the two sectors'.[5] These limits appear to have been critically narrow, and it is the contention of this paper that Iranian planners failed to achieve their object. In Iran as elsewhere the foreign investment in the oil industry resulted in an enclave development and the traditional sector, agriculture, did not experience many 'growth-inducing linkages' nor any marked benefit from Iran's development plans. On the contrary, agriculture which had been the major sector of the economy was relegated to a secondary position. As a result of a flow of resources from the rural to the urban areas and misconceived national planning Iran has lost its earlier self-sufficiency in food.

It is surprising that Iranians thought they could achieve a coherent development through modified dualistic policies. In the forty years preceding planned development their foreign-orientated oil industry had failed to produce any growth-inducing linkage within the economy. The oil industry was a highly developed, capital-intensive producer of unprocessed oil, mainly for consumption in the West. Oil formed an enclave of development with no backward and little forward linkage to the indigenous sector.

Before the advent of development planning in the 1950s agricultural revenue accounted for 20 per cent of total government income and was used to help finance the limited industrialisation programmes initiated by Reza Shah. After the Second World War and Reza Shah's abdication his son, Mohammad Reza, was advised by American and World Bank officials to embark on a comprehensive national development plan with a 'productive development strategy ... aimed at increasing the degree of integration between the foreign-financed export-orientated sector and the rest of the economy.[6] A series of seven- and five-year development plans followed.

THE AGRARIAN SECTOR

For the next three decades agriculture was relatively neglected to allow the expansion of the oil industry which employed less than 1 per cent of the total labour force and to promote the creation of a new capital-intensive industrial sector. The planners' assumption was that the wealth generated by oil and industry would trickle down to the agricultural sector which was thought to be backward and at a subsistence level and resistant to development:

> the majority of our cultivators ... do not have much love for labour and hard work ... and have become accustomed to unemployment or underemployment and are not willing to change their age old habits overnight ... The economic viability of holdings which has been one of the major post-land-reform pitfalls in the West is a problem that should be placed in an Iranian perspective. (Unlike) the West where people ... are traditionally brought up to be co-operative and help one another ... in Iran most people argue that if a partner was a good thing to have God would have taken one.[7]

These patronising views, which were substantially unfounded, were a result of the planners' westernised perception of the process of agricultural production and not surprisingly policies based on this misconceived analysis failed to result in a permeation of wealth and prosperity to the rural areas. The planners did not take into account that in large areas of Iran cultivation has historically been carried out communally in *boneh*, and that far from being at a subsistence level at the time agriculture was the single largest contributor to GNP, entirely financed by nationals and employing 60 per cent of the total population, even though on the whole Iran's climate and land are not well-suited for agriculture. Only 16m hectares or 8 per cent of Iran's total land area is cultivable and each year about half of that is left fallow. The average annual rainfall is almost 300mm and some 800 000 hectares are irrigated by dams and *qanats* (*qanats* are underground aqueducts which bring water from the mountains, sometimes as far as 50km, relying solely on gradient). Nevertheless, Iran was self-sufficient in all basic foodstuffs, generally produced on holdings of five to ten hectares, and remained so until the early 1970s. Moreover it had retained a favourable balance of trade in agriculture since its exports of food and fibre (particularly dry fruit, nuts and cotton) had usually been greater than its imports of food – mainly sugar, tea and vegetable oil.

Planning

Although agriculture and land taxes were a major source of government revenue throughout the 1940s,[8] Iranian development planners did not choose to extract the available income from agriculture to finance industrialisation. It is arguable that a realistic land-tax would have encouraged landowners to seek higher returns and raise the efficiency of agricultural production. In the event land-taxes were replaced by income tax and the government relied mainly on the readily-available oil revenue; this contributed to the neglect of agriculture and resulted in the industrialisation programme being dependent on revenue outside Iran's control.

The state, in what was called an 'essentially non-ideological approach',[9] extended its control and monopolised many economic activities such as oil, tobacco and communications, and held a major share in most other major concerns such as steel, copper, cement etc. In reality the government's policy of 'growth with compassion'[10] was a pale version of a centralised economy rather than one of a free market economy. The state became the active agent for development and sought to extend its control to the rural sector. This extension of centralism to agriculture was pursued through the building of an expensive infrastructure, reclamation of lands and financing farm corporations, agri-business and agricultural development policies. These measures were large-scale and were intended to change the structure of rural society, and frequently involved displacing peasants. More seriously, however, they meant that the relatively small proportion of development funds allocated to agriculture was spent on grandiose projects which were ill-conceived and ill-suited to Iranian conditions and needs.

Initially for example, the major part of agricultural investment was spent on construction of dams. Between 1957 and 1972 twelve major dams were constructed to provide irrigation, to supply and store water for urban areas and to generate electricity. But they had 'an almost undetectable influence on national agricultural output'.[11] One, the Karaj hydro-electric dam was redesigned as a water-supply dam for Tehran; others, such as the multi-purpose Dez dams in Khouzestan, failed to provide the planned quantities of water. The investment could have been spent to better advantage by supplying many pumps for irrigating small holdings; this would have been about ten times more cost-effective.[12] Moreover the gains in irrigation made by these dams were partly offset by the serious decline in the traditional method of irrigation by *qanats*. These needed constant maintenance but because of rising labour costs and rural–urban migration many were neglected and fell into disuse.

Land Reforms

Agriculture gained a brief but dramatic importance in national politics in 1962 when, after riots and political unrest a radical figure and a long standing advocate of land reform, Hassan Arsanjani, was appointed Minister of Agriculture. He was able to take advantage of the fluid political situation to rush through an ambitious programme of land reforms which were intended to distribute the lands of all large absentee landlords. The reforms, based on the traditional division of land according to *nassaq* were conceived as an effective and inexpensive means of redistributing land and wealth. (*Nassaq* is the customary form of allocating land amongst share-croppers, each cultivator has *nassaq* rights in more than one area, in poor land and good land.) Sharecroppers were entitled to buy (over a period of twelve years) the land they had worked on. The absentee landlord's income obtained from his two-thirds or three-fifths share of the produce had been generally channelled to urban areas and spent on consumption and not invested in the land. The reforms thus returned to the villages higher incomes which were reinvested in production. Their capital was to be augmented through rural co-operatives which were financed by the government with the new peasant proprietors as members.[13]

But the reforms were short-lived and in the event only 20 per cent of the peasants benefited from its provisions. Once the old political order was re-established and the landed class regained its customary control of the legislature the land reforms were fundamentally altered. The landed class and the planners based their revision of the reforms on the grounds that the peasants did not have the necessary capital for development of agriculture and that the fragmentation of holdings had made them unproductive. Indeed it was estimated that 60 per cent of the new titles were for holdings of five hectares or less.[14] Planners anticipated that this fragmentation would disrupt production and that land reform would continue to be costly. Consequently the government sought to halt the reforms and refused to provide the money requested by Arsanjani, who resigned.

Working with a Western model of development and its concepts the planners branded agriculture as 'backward' and stated that 'the major obstacle to (its) expansion ... (was) mostly organisational and structural; that is the whole spectrum of human relations governing agricultural production and marketing (was) ... thought to be incompatible and to a large extent inconsistent with non-marginal increases in agricultural output'.[15] However, as will be pointed out later, these criticisms were unfounded and in particular the fragmentation of holdings was more apparent than real. In order to bring about the 'structural' change thought necessary the government adopted a Russian-style centralist approach. A new phase of land reforms was introduced in 1966. Ostensibly its aims were:

1. The expansion of agricultural output required for the *industrial* development of the country;
2. a rise in the per capita output and standard of living of the peasantry;
3. the stabilisation of food prices by improved marketing and production techniques.[16]

In practice this phase of land reforms attempted to reverse the distribution of lands and to modernise and extend governments' control to a large part of agricultural production. Some of the distributed land was taken over by government-controlled farm corporations with displaced peasants as shareholders. By 1973 15 per cent of the total cultivable land was owned by agri-business and farm corporations who employed 3 per cent of the total rural labour force.[17] By 1976, eighty-eight corporations were formed with the land surrendered by 32 500 peasants.[18] The government also bought large tracts of land from the small peasant proprietors, consolidated these areas, and leased them to joint stock companies formed with the participation of Iranian and foreign investors. Some of these agri-business units received 80 per cent of their initial capital investment in supervised, cheap, long-term loans from the Iranian government.

A further attempt by the government to extend its control over the best agricultural land in the country by forming agricultural development poles was made in 1976; this was halted in its initial stages by the 1978 revolution.

Government Investment In Agriculture

Foreign capital was invited to invest in the modern equivalent of plantations employing dispossessed peasants. These concerns were to provide cash crops, not for the international markets, but for foreign- and Iranian-owned processing plants, some of which were built on site. Despite substantial loans, of the order of 5–6m rials (at the time £1 = 180 rials) some of the more grandiose agri-business projects failed to meet production targets. Of the four joint venture schemes started in 1969 to develop Khouzestan three were technically bankrupt by 1976 and only 13 per cent of the land allocated had been brought under cultivation. This was partly because the pool of cheap labour which was to work on these projects had dried up. About 6500 families had been moved to thirteen centres (*shahrak*) and the men were expected to work for the agri-business units as cheap casual labourers. But these people were unwilling to work for others on the land that had been historically theirs and the high urban wages enabled them to earn their living as migrant workers in urban areas or even in Saudi Arabia.[19] Poor planning was also partly responsible for the failure of these concerns; some chose unsuitable crops and all failed to anticipate the rapid increase in production costs. What happened in Kouzestan was typical of what was happening throughout Iran. The percentage of the total labour force employed in agriculture fell from 45.9 per cent in 1969 to 33 per cent in 1976.[20] The rural population during that period remained constant; clearly able-bodied men were migrating to towns leaving the dependants on the land.

Farm corporations also received a substantial part of the government's total investment in agriculture. By 1975 the eighty-five farm corporations were receiving about 2000m rials per annum or about 23.5m per year per corporation.[21] By contrast the annual 5000m rials credit earmarked for over 700 000 loans to peasant proprietors corresponded to an average annual loan of about 7000 rials each.[22] Farm corporations financed by the Agricultural Development Bank were entitled to long-term loans ranging from 5m rials to 600m rials. Peasant properties were generally entitled to short-term loans of 10 000 to 17 000 rials from the Rural Co-operative Bank; such loans were not large enough to pay for agricultural improvement and were often used for incidental expenditure.

Agricultural production

It should be noted that the performance of agriculture in Iran in the 1960s when centralised farming was still in its experimental stages was satisfactory. Throughout the 1960s agricultural growth kept pace with population growth of about 3 per cent per annum. Iran remained virtually self-sufficient in food and the cost of production of staples such as wheat, barley, sugar, fruit, vegetables, some meat and cotton compared favourably with the import price of similar products. From 1959 to 1969 the cost of living index rose by only 2 per cent and food prices by 3 per cent per annum; this included an 8 per cent increase in the price of meat, fish and poultry. The latter was partly a reflection of rising private consumption (6.9 per cent in towns and 5.7 per cent in rural areas)[23] and partly that of rising real per capita income estimated at 4.5 per cent, per annum,[24] and the resulting preference for the consumption of superior rather than staple foods. For example per capita demand for red meat increased from 8kg per annum in 1959 to 18kg per annum in the early 1970s and was increasing at 12 per cent per annum compared with an average annual increase of 9 per cent in the local production of meat.

Although production did not keep pace with the rapidly rising demand for some foods, the value of agricultural production rose steadily though less rapidly than other sectors (see Table 3.1). The slow rate of growth of agricultural production has frequently been cited as evidence of the dualistic nature of the Iranian economy. Critics cite the large percentage of planned expenditure on agriculture, ranging from

TABLE 3.1   *GNP in billions of rials*

	1959–6	1962–3	1968–9	1971–2	1974–5
Agriculture	85	97	140	172	305
Industry	45	58	130	205	464
Services	108	130	243	375	826
Oil	28	38	83	180	1635

SOURCE   'National Income of Iran', Bank Markazi.

40 per cent to 80 per cent of total for the period 1949–67 (see Table 3.2) and lament the sluggish increase in production of only 3 per cent which is frequently contrasted with the industry's average growth rate of 11 per cent.[25] Such criticism however fails to note that the bulk of the government's agricultural investment was allocated to a few capital-intensive large-scale projects which in the event did not result in the expected 'dramatic improvement in yields'. It is interesting to note that in contrast to the government-sponsored concerns production of some staples on smallholdings rose considerably faster than 3 per cent per annum. From 1961 to 1972, for example, wheat production increased by 53 per cent and rice production by 100 per cent. Other export-orientated cash crops produced on smallholdings grew faster than the average annual rate of 3 per cent (or 34 per cent in ten years); pistachios, for example, had a 46 per cent growth in ten years and a rise in exports of 262 per cent (see Table 3.3). There was however a much steeper rise in imports of staples during this period; wheat imports rose by 460 per cent – from 5 to 28 per cent of national production – and rice imports by 700 per cent – from 3 per cent to 9 per cent of national production. This is indicative of the increase in population, incomes and consumption.

TABLE 3.2   *Plan organisations' disbursements*

	Agriculture/Irrigation *(millions of rials)*	*Mining/Industry* *(millions of rials)*
First plan 1949–55	5.7 (40.4% of total)	4.1 (29.1% of total)
Second plan 1956–62	17.4 (20.9% of total)	7 (8.4% of total)
Third plan 1963–4	47.3 (23.1% of total)	17.1 (8.4% of total)
Fourth plan 1968–72	41.2 (8.1% of total)	113.1 (22.3% of total)
Fifth plan 1973–8	30.9 (6.6% of total)	84 (18% of total)

SOURCE   Bank Markazi Annual Reports.

Failure of agricultural development policies

There can be no doubt that dualistic agricultural development policies

TABLE 3.3   Production and trade of some staple and cash crops

Date	Rice—tonnes			Wheat—tonnes			Pistachio—tonnes			Almond—tonnes		
	Production	Export	Import	Production	Export	Import	Production	Export	Import	Production	Export	Imports
1959	540 000	1 170	56	2 929 000	—	9 851	7 000	3 423	—	43 000	5 670	—
1961	400 000	146	11 281	2 933 675	—	138 312	6 500	3 590	—	37 000	5 544	—
1963	573 973	1 776	933	3 468 140	—	70 900	12 000	3 395	—	31 000	3 806	—
1965	681 335	3 157	47 818	3 648 713	—	198 178	19 000	5 950	—	30 000	3 899	—
1967	640 000	1 360	10 187	3 800 000	74 463	61 805	19 900	4 849	—	32 500	1 777	—
1970	1 350 000	305	5 676	4 360 000	611	22 639	22 000	9 714	—	25 000	4 469	—
1972	1 008 000	215	91 872	4 398 000	—	771 323	37 300	12 998	—	31 100	5 672	—

SOURCE   Vezaratch Keshavarzi va Manaheh Tabiyi, Markazeh Amareh Iran. (Ministry of Agriculture, Department of National Statistics)

in Iran failed. By 1978 the country was no longer self-sufficient in food, and growth in terms of wealth and population was an urban phenomenon; contrary to planners' expectation there was little permeation of wealth downwards and little 'flow of resources from the dynamic to the static sector'.[26] Despite the rapid rate of economic growth the inequalities between rural and urban incomes were increasing with extensive dissavings in rural lower income groups and extensive positive saving in the urban higher income groups.[27] The ratio of rural to urban average household income was 1:4, the consumption ratio was 1:3 and saving ratio was 1:6.[28] This disparity of incomes was conveniently explained in terms of a temporary transfer of resources to the wealthy 'saving', classes who would be more likely to invest in production. However, the widening gap between rural and urban incomes and expenditure was eroding the base for future industrialisation as the rural sector could not provide a ready market for the goods produced by the industrial sector.[29] In order to understand the failure of the Iranian government's agricultural modernisation programme it is important not only to question the dualistic analysis of development but also the specific analysis of Iranian planners.

According to the government's analysis the rural sector was backward, suffered from extensive disguised unemployment and was short of capital. To meet these shortcomings the government chose to intervene directly by forming state-owned units and by inviting foreign capital to invest in large-scale rural concerns. As a result of these and similar measures Iran's dependency on foreign capital increased markedly in less than a decade.

The modernist approach of the planners to agriculture suffered from the typical misconceptions of westernised analysis of underdevelopment and their evaluation had scant basis in reality. These policies as expressed by the later phases of the land reforms, legitimised the position of landlords and the sharecropping system by projecting the landlords as a main source of investment and the best means of modernising smallholdings.

In the first instance the assumption that landlords would be a 'saving' class and that they would necessarily invest in agriculture is highly suspect. According to a sample survey of rural areas in 1969, in holdings owned by large landowners, agricultural income had fallen in the period 1962–9. This was attributed to the failure of landlords to invest and in particular to improve irrigation and maintain the *qanat*.[30] By contrast where ownership of the means of production was transferred to the peasants, income from the land had increased despite a fall in the sale price of wheat and alfalfa which are their main products. Since only 20 per cent of the cultivators ownership of their holdings under the land reforms the overall rural income was reduced. This reduction of incomes is consistent with a transfer of resources from rural to urban areas and a widening gap between rural and urban incomes.

A more serious misconception about Iranian agriculture however was, and still is, the notion of 'fragmentation of holdings' and the consequent need for consolidation of lands. This view fails to appreciate the structure of cultivation in Iran where with the exception of water-abundant northern regions and very arid, primarily tribal, lands of the west, cultivation has been based on small co-operative units called *boneh*.[31] Villages in central, southern and eastern regions are all short of water and water shortage has prevented the peasants from owning separate strips which would take longer to irrigate. Strips of land in irrigated parts of the village were formed into consolidated units, each entitled to twenty-four hours of water every twelve days.[32] The twelve days irrigation cycle has traditionally determined the division of holdings into *boneh* which were cultivated by groups of usually six sharecroppers using about three pairs of oxen: *joft*.[33] Although the *nassaq* holdings of these sharecroppers varied and some had greater shares than others, cultivation was carried out communally and the difference between the largest and smallest incomes of the *boneh* was not great.[34] The land reforms maintained the *nassaq* and cultivators have continued workings in *boneh*.[35] Since only *nassaq*-holding peasants were entitled to receive land and others (such as the landless *gavbandan*, those oxen-owners who did not work the land, and the *khoshneshinan*, landless labourers) were excluded the pattern of cultivation did not change. Rural underemployment was exaggerated by the planners and, despite mechanisation, in some villages there were serious labour shortages at harvest-time. These shortages were aggravated by extensive rural–urban migration.

Moreover planners misspent the inadequate funds allocated to agriculture. Their rural development plans were wrongly structured, produced the wrong crops and resulted in an increasing dependence on imported food. Had smallholdings received more help and had the government concentrated on funding traditional and small-scale irrigation projects, the rate of agricultural growth would have been significantly higher and the food shortages of the 1970s would have been averted.

Many of the inherent shortcomings of dualistic development, however, were temporarily masked by the oil-boom of the early 1970s. Because of the boom the Shah decided to catch up with the advanced European economies within the next ten years.[36] The oil boom, rising urban incomes and high elasticities, as well as rural–urban migration resulted in a steep rise in demand for food which the agricultural sector was unable to meet.[37] From 1974 the government began subsidising imports of foodstuffs to keep prices down; this in turn increased demand. Iranian farmers, however, did not benefit since the cheap-food policies resulted in an influx of imported food and an artificially low price fixed for home products. From 1970 to 1975 agricultural production costs rose by 300 per cent but farm-gate prices increased by only 50 per cent,[38] and some farmers chose to reduce production.[39]

THE FIFTH DEVELOPMENT PLAN AND THE OIL CRISIS

To meet the food shortages the revised fifth development plan which began in 1973, subsantially increased the allocation for agricultural investment. It is worth noting that the oil boom marked the end of planning in Iran in the sense of a coherent and co-ordinated programme for development and the Shah, confident that the increasing oil revenue would continue, took personal control of planning. The development budget was increased by 80 per cent and the Plan Organisation's programme was discarded and priority given to housing and communication. The allocation for agriculture was increased by 75 per cent, although the percentage of the budget of investment in agriculture fell from 7.2 to 6.6 of the total (the allocation to industry was also revised and remained about three times the agricultural investment.[40] Subsidies were made available for land reclamation and the import of livestock for breeding, but the main investment was in large-scale farming schemes. More support was given to agri-business and farm corporations and twenty development poles were introduced. The latter were to be set up in selected regions where holdings were to be consolidated into centrally controlled units of at least twenty hectares. This scheme never went beyond its initial stages.

While oil prices rose the Shah was able to pursue his frantic economic development programme, but OPEC's decision to reduce or halt oil price increases after September 1975 dealt a crippling blow to the Iranian economy. After a 200 per cent increase in foreign exchange receipts in 1974–5 oil revenues remained almost constant.[41] This drop in anticipated revenue forced major economies on the government; the planned allocation for rural improvement was substantially reduced and any hope for agricultural development ended. Matters were made worse by the low rainfall in 1976 and were not helped by the priority given to using the dams for power rather than irrigation. In addition the rapid rise in the costs of rural production and labour was jeopardising the viability of the Iranian non-oil exports. By 1978 Iran was almost bankrupt; it was estimated that there was only enough money left to meet current expenditure for five months.[42]

The deleterious effects of the development plans were important contributing factors to the 1978 revolution. It is worth noting that the revolution was a primarily urban phenomenon. Although migrant workers and rural conscripts played an important part in toppling the Shah, there was no widespread, organised rural movement against the regime.

POST-REVOLUTIONARY POLICIES

The first post-revolutionary government led by Mehdi Bazargan was liberal rather than radical. His primary aim was to meet the basic needs of the poorest section of society and his housing and welfare programmes envisaged a massive transfer of resources from the rich to the poor. But these aims were never realised since 'large vested interests still benefited from the old-style expenditure and were able to prevent change'.[43]

The land reforms proposed by the Bazargan government were a reaction against the excesses of the policies of the Shah and aimed at a balanced land distribution which would not adversely affect production. They sought to 'awaken hidden talents and to enhance the use of functional traditional methods and equipment available in Iran and to reduce dependency on foreign imports'.[44] Large-scale agricultural units and mechanised farms (which had been exempt from land reforms) were to be distributed in viable holdings, the maximum size depending on the region.[45] Some Ministry of Agriculture advisers, however had advanced more radical proposals in which the resulting smallholdings would be worked as a *boneh*. The two agricultural banks were merged and credit arrangements were rationalised, with a ceiling of 1m rials for each loan, which were made to benefit the smaller farmer.

After the fall of Bazargan, Abolhassan Bani Sadre backed a more far-reaching and egalitarian land-reform policy which was ratified by the revolutionary council in March 1980. Under the slogan 'land to the tillers' it proposed the elimination of all large private holdings and that each cultivator be allocated land. However this was considered to be impractical since it was estimated that the average per capita holding would be one hectare and individual plots would conflict with the traditional method of co-operative cultivation *boneh* prevalent in many parts of the country. In practice the maximum land holding permitted has been reduced to three times the *nassaq*.[46] In effect these reforms were not any different from Bazargan's programme since *nassaq* varies in different regions and is as much as twelve hectares of dry and irrigated land in places such as Zanjan, which would make a thirty-six hectare holding legal.

The *Majlis* appointed seven-man committees to go to the rural areas and distribute the land.[47] But there were still no real land reform policies to assist these committees. By April 1983 they were still discussing whether Islam permitted such land distribution.[48] The ensuing legal and administrative complications were so extensive that finally in January 1984 the Head of the Supreme Court sent a public letter of protest to the *Majlis*:

> The unclear and unsatisfactory land distribution regulations have not only resulted in a fall in food production and increasing antagonism between landlord and peasant, but also they have produced unsolvable legal problems ... and innumerable cases which in the absence of the necessary laws cannot be dealt with.[49]

The recent reform programmes may still be revised by *Majlis*, particularly since the religious elements have gained control. Many religious leaders have already complained that according to Islamic law, those who develop land cannot be dispossessed from it. It is worth noting that land – both rural and urban – has long been regarded as a secure inflation-proof investment. Many of the clergy as well as the merchant class, who have close links with the clergy, still own substantial agricultural lands and would resist a wholesale land redistribution.

Farm corporations and the land of many absentee landlords has been taken over by the peasants. But although many have ceased to function, agri-business units have not yet been repossessed by the previous owners and remain under the control of the government who have rented some to cultivators.

During the post-revolutionary period smallholdings appear to have flourished. Production of staples has increased, in contrast with cash crops such as cotton which have dwindled. Although with the ending of urban construction of luxury offices and houses and urban unemployment initially many casual workers returned to the land, the tide of rural–urban migration was not much affected. It is estimated that in the period 1979–82, 800 000 people moved to Tehran, many in the hope of obtaining interest-free loans for housing. To try to reduce the migration, the government announced that these loans would not be available for town-dwellers,[50] and subsequently offered cheap loans to people willing to move to small towns or villages.[51] The government also raised the minimum agricultural wage to 585 rials per day.[52] The minimum agricultural wage was 240 rials in 1973 but since inflation was then about 20 per cent per annum and is about 50 per cent now, the purchasing power of rural wages has not been restored to its former level (the increase allows for a 12 per cent annual inflation).

PRICE POLICIES

The Bazargan government raised the government's purchasing price of wheat from 12 to 18 rials per kilo, which was higher than the world price of 14 rials per kilo. In addition, the government banned imports of all non-essential food, such as citrus fruit, and raised the home price – by a factor of 5 for citrus fruit. These measures proved very effective causing a rapid fall in demand which could then be met by the national production. Such measures were, of course, inflationary and were accompanied by rising wage and salary claims (60 per cent of the Ministry of Agriculture's budget for 1978–9 was for administrative expenses including salaries).

By March 1983 the official rate of inflation was 17 per cent per annum and food prices and agricultural products were rising at 20 per cent and 19 per cent respectively. Prices of fruit, vegetables, rice, wheat, pulses, dairy products and meat were rising at about 20 per cent per annum, while farm-gate prices remained too low to meet the producers' expenses. Middlemen were reportedly making profits of 400 per cent, fruit and vegetables bought at 8–30 rials from farmers were being sold to the consumers at 30–180 rials.[53] Meat consumption was almost halved, falling from an average daily rate of 73g per head in 1980 to 43g in 1982,[54] and the government was obliged to step in and control and subsidise staples such as rice and wheat.

These subsidies, however, were once more to benefit urban-dwellers and to retain the political support of the slum-dwellers who could prove volatile. The price ceiling for farmers was so low that, according to one *Majlis* deputy, farmers were making a 10 000 rials loss per hectare of cultivated wheat.[55] Furthermore, the government was undercutting farm prices by importing cheap wheat; cheap because the import prices were calculated at the official rate of exchange which was lower than the free market rate by a factor of ten.

In 1981–2 food subsidies cost 61bn rials just 'to keep wheat prices down and bread prices cheap',[56] a level of expenditure which was hard to maintain in a war economy. As a result the *Majlis* inserted an additional clause in the 1983 Budget Bill 'requiring the government to present a bill for reduction of the public expenditure deficit caused by subsidies on foodstuffs'.[57]

Accordingly, the 1983 five-year development plan has a stated aim of removing all subsidies on consumption; this aim may prove difficult to achieve given the failure of previous attempts at floating consumer prices to remove subsidies. For example, lifting rice subsidies in 1982 had resulted in the consumers paying over 800 rials per kg for this basic staple. The farmers were at the time able to sell the rice at 500 rials per kg and naturally were entirely opposed to any government intervention.[58] However, the government still imported rice from Thailand, rationed at 3kg per adult per month and sold at 75 rials per kg. Although this rice was not liked, it was sold on the black market for 300 rials per kg.

Rationing rice failed, and in the end the government was obliged to intervene directly. In November 1983, farm-gate prices were fixed at 82 to 210 rials per kg and market-prices were to range between 83 and 250 rials; not surprisingly many farmers have decided to pull out of rice farming. As one farmer stated 'If the government kept other prices down it wouldn't be so difficult. But the cloth that used to cost 50 rials a metre last year is costing me 400 rials a metre this year; that means I have to produce two kgs of rice just to pay for one metre of cloth. It is the farmers alone who have had to bear the loss and halve their prices while expenses continue to rise.' Many northern rice-growers put their land under orchard cultivation to benefit from the relatively uncontrolled citrus-fruit prices. For example, in 1983 the Sari region which had produced 35 per cent of the total rice production in the country had 30 000 hectares transferred to orchard.[59]

SHOROHAYEH CHARIKI (THE FREEDOM FIGHTERS' RURAL COUNCILS)

The post-revolutionary government, like their predecessors, have on the whole perpetuated the unequal terms of trade between rural and urban sectors. On the other hand, there has not been any sign of an organised peasant movement emerging on a national scale, although in some mainly tribal areas such as Kurdestan, Khouzestan and Turkomansahra radical rural movements have emerged. The movement in Turkomansahra is of particular interest for land reform.

Turkomansahra is one of the richest agricultural regions in Iran and much of its land was owned by army officers. In the period 1979 to 1982 the *Fedayan*, a Marxist guerrilla group, helped the peasants to take over the land, and to do so peacefully, sometimes leaving a little for the absentee landlord. The *Fedayan* and the peasants formed 300 *Shorayeh Chariki* (The Freedom Fighters' Rural Councils) with a membership of about 15 000 peasants. The *shorayeh chariki* administered the land, obtained credit and were responsible for marketing the produce. Where the *nassaq* was clear, the peasants cultivate the land and share the produce accordingly. Where there was no clear *nassaq*, such as on mechanised lands, the land was cultivated collectively and profits shared equally. The *Fedayan*, through the *shorayeh chariki*, introduced a communal method of cultivation which respected traditional rights to the land but also enabled the peasants to consolidate their holdings, a measure which was particularly well-suited to mechanisation and the production of cash crops. The *shora* was an administrative as well as a production unit, peasant members were responsible for the management of the farms and the *Fedayan*'s members took charge of marketing and acted as brokers between the peasants and urban institutions. The *shorayeh chariki* offered a similar form of collective cultivation to *boneh*. Holdings were consolidated but production units were relatively small – the size of one village – a model which is similar to the Chinese work-team. The *shorayeh chariki* proved successful and in fact Turkomansahra was the only region in Iran where production of cash crop had increased after the revolution. It was unfortunate that in the subsequent upsurge of Islamic fundamentalism, the *Fedayan* along with all opposition parties were driven underground. In fact although the *shora*, people's council, is legally autonomous,[60] the *shorayeh chariki* was seen as a threat to the Islamic fundamentalists who with the help of the *pasdaran*, revolutionary guards, attempted to replace the *shorayeh chariki* with *shorahoyeh eslami*, Islamic councils. The Turkoman, who unlike the Shiia fundamentalist are Suni Muslims, have resorted to armed resistance.

However, despite numerous battles and a protracted armed struggle the *shorayeh chariki* were dismantled and replaced by the *shorayeh Islami* which failed to gain any local support. In Turkomanestan as elsewhere cultivators are in a state of limbo, uncertain about their rights of ownership, short of water and credits and unable to obtain maximum productivity from their land.

CONCLUSION

Since the clergy were at the forefront of the opposition to the land reforms, it is hardly surprising that they have so far failed to initiate any effective redistribution of holdings. The 1978 revolution was essentially urban and the mass of government's support is in the large cities. Thus on the whole the government has preferred to control the rural population through the establishment of Islamic rural councils rather than try to gain the support of the peasants through land reforms and favourable price policies.

There has, of course, been some *de facto* take-over of land by the peasants, but their insecurity and the political neglect of agriculture has finally resulted in serious food shortages, price escalation and extensive urban migration. In 1982, for example, over 5000 families left the Hamadan province and by the end of 1983 there were numerous deserted villages in the Qaraveh region 'where every inhabitant had migrated to nearby towns'.[61]

Although the government instituted a village reconstruction force, *Jahadeh Sazandegi*, as early as 1980, this force appears to spend more time on public relations than on reconstruction, and the rural areas remain extremely underdeveloped and starved of funds and of facilities. The government continues the Pahlavi policies of funding inefficient agri-business units, many of which have the best land and the largest losses; in Dashteh Moqan, for example, more than half the irrigated lands are owned by the agri-business unit which nevertheless continues to make substantial losses.

The seven-man land-distribution teams have proved ineffective in their two years of operation. By and large they fail to contact the peasants, who are said to be too busy to respond to the seven-man teams.[62] Where the peasants have initiated redistribution they have been opposed by massive litigation by absentee landlords with easy access to town-based judicial courts.

The acute fall in food production and large-scale migration finally resulted in a radical review of agricultural policies. The 1983 five-year development plan – the first to be formulated since the revolution – selected agriculure as the primary sector of the economy. All other sectors are to concentrate on developing inputs into agriculture and fully absorbing its output. These propositions, though promising, are unfortunately tempered by the belief that:

> the government must not extend the formulae of consumerism to rural areas. Consumerism serves only to make the peasants heavily dependent. We must encourage self-reliance and self sufficiency in rural areas. Peasants must produce for themselves whatever they need to consume.[63]

It is difficult to see any reason why self-sufficient peasants would wish to produce inputs for the economy and buy its outputs if they have no perceived needs for such products. Once more the Iranian government appears to be making public-policy statements which contradict its planned development projects.

NOTES

1. For a detailed analysis of dual resource depletion in Iran see M. A. Katouzian, 'Oil Versus Agriculture: A Case of Dual Resource Depletion in Iran', *Journal of Peasant Studies*, vol. 5, no. 3, April 1978, pp. 347–69.
2. J. Amuzegar and M. A. Fekrat, *Iran: Economic Development under Dualistic Conditions* (Chicago: University of Chicago Press, 1971) p. 147.
3. Ibid.
4. Ibid, p. 154.
5. Ibid, p. 156.
6. Ibid, p. 9.
7. J. Amuzegar, 'Chareyi barayeh halleh messaeleh eqtesadi Iran' (a solution for Iran's economic problems) *Tahqiqatch Eqtesadi* nos 21 and 22 (Spring and Summer 1349) (1970) pp. 10–11.
8. Land taxes contributed 200m rials to government in 1949 compared with 900m rials from oil. *United Nations Public Finance Information Papers: Iran*, pp. 31–3.

9. J. Amuzegar, *Economic Development* p. 128.
10. Ibid, p. 129.
11. G. B. Baldwin, *Planning and Development in Iran* (Baltimore: John Hopkins Press, 1967) p. 82.
12. Ibid p. 83.
13. See H. Afshar, *Rural Co-operatives in Iran*, mimeo (Bradford University, 1980).
14. *Report of the Seminar of Rural Development, Tehran, 1970.* For a discussion of the subsequent policies also see Pesaran in this volume, p. 23.
15. Amuzegar, *Economic Development under Dualistic Conditions*, p. 127.
16. Ibid, p. 121.
17. F. Halliday, *Iran Dictatorship and Development* (Harmondsworth: Penguin, 1979) p. 130.
18. *Bank Markazi Iran, Annual Report 1353* (1975–6) p. 83.
19. *Kayhan International*, 6 September 1972.
20. Amuzegar, *Economic Development* p. 97.
21. D. R. Denman, 'Land Reforms of Shah and People' in G. Lenczouski (ed.) *Iran under the Pahlavis* (Stanford, California: Hoover Institution Press, 1978) p. 28.
22. H. Afshar, *Rural Co-operatives in Iran.*
23. Amuzegar, *Economic Development*, p. 92.
24. Ibid.
25. Amuzegar 'Chareyi larayeh halleh massaeleh ...' p. 11.
26. Amuzegar, *Economic Development*, p. 147.
27. H. Oshima, *Income Distribution Mission Working Paper, no. II*, Employment and Income Policies in Iran, World Employment Programme (Geneva: International Labour Office, 1973).
28. F. Mehran, 'Income Distribution in Iran, Statistics of Inequality' *Income Distribution Working Paper* (Geneva: ILO, 1975) p. 21.
29. *ILO Employment and Income Policies* 'Study of Employment in Iran' (Geneva: ILO, 1972).
30. Quoted by H. Saedlou, *Massaeleh Keshavarzi Iran* (Tehran: Entesharateh Raisaq, Chapkhaneh Mihan, 1357, 1979) p. 116.
31. Individual family farming occurs in parts of the water-abundant northern regions, the arid southern belt and parts of the west. *Boneh* occurs in the central, eastern and less arid regions of the south and some of the north-western regions.
32. J. Safinejad, *Boneh* (Entesharateh Tous, Chapeh Efsat Heidars, Tehran 2535, 1977), introduction p. 34.
33. Ibid, p. 5.
34. For example 43 000–45 000 rials per annum, ibid, p. 411.
35. Safinejad in the introduction to *Boneh* laments the disappearance of *boneh* after the land reforms but both Safinejad in *Boneh* (pp. 188 and 189) Saedlou in *Massaeleh Keshavazi* (p. 104) state that after the reforms a new version of *boneh* has re-emerged. I found this to be the case in many of the villages near Saveh and Qazvin.
36. *Kayhan International*, 15 November 1973.
37. 'International Monetary Fund Staff Report on Iran', January 1975, p. 4.;

quoted by R. Graham, *Iran: The Illusion of Power* (London: Croom Helm, 1978) p. 117.

38. Ibid.
39. *Kayham International*, 11 September 1973.
40. Based on *Bank Markazi Annual Report* 1952 (1974–5) p. 34, see Table 3.2.
41. *Bank Markazi Annual Reports*.
42. Quote from Cyrus Aryanpour, Plan Organisation official interviewed August 1980.
43. Ibid.
44. Interview with Dr H. Keshavaraz of Ministry of Agriculture, August 1980 – see also 'Khotuteh Asli Hadafha, Siasatha va Sazeman Keshavarzi Iran', *Vezarateh Keshavarzi* 1357 (1978).
45. For example 40 hectares in Gonbad, or 70 hectares in Kermanshah.
46. *Layeheh Qanuni Eslaheh Qanoun Nahveh Vagozari va Ehyayeh Arazi* (*Shorayeh Enqelab*, 11 December 1958) Bandeh Jim (1979).
47. Bill for the Improvement and Distribution of Agricultural Land, Article (8).
48. Fourth seminar of seven-man distribution committees, 11 April 1983.
49. *Kayhan*, 23 January 1984.
50. *Etelaat* (August 1980).
51. *Kayhan*, 16 February 1982.
52. Many agricultural workers are not entitled to claim the minimum wage; they include workers in livestock breeding, forestry, parks and pastures, fisheries, bee-keeping, silkworms and fruit orchards. Since most arable land is already worked by peasant proprietors only a small percentage of the rural labourers would be likely to benefit from the minimum wage provisions.
53. *Kayhan*, 10 August 1982 and 15 November 1983.
54. *Kayhan* 16 February 1983.
55. Abutaleb Mahmoudi, deputy for Golpayegan speaking at the *Majlis* on 20 November 1983.
56. Report to the *Majlis*, 28 June 1983.
57. Article 39 of the 1983 Budget Bill.
58. See Chapter 10 on theocracy in this volume.
59. Report to the fourth Seminar of seven-man distribution teams, Tehran, 19 April 1983.
60. The 1979 Constitution, section VII, articles 100–6.
61. Nosratolah Hatefi Deputy for Qaraveh speaking at the *Majlis*, 20 November 1983.
62. Hojateleslam Adnani speaking to the fourth seminar of the seven-man team, 10 April 1983.
63. Mohamad Forouqi Deputy for Masjid Soleiman speaking at the *Majlis*, 20 November 1983.

4 Tribes and State in Iran: From Pahlavi to Islamic Republic

G. REZA FAZEL[1]

The revolution of 11 February 1979 brought an end to nearly fifty-five years of Pahlavi rule along with the obdurate system of monarchy in Iran. The subsequent ascendancy of the clerics has occasioned a spate of scholarly works on the evolution of the relationship between Shiism and the temporal state. Other writers have concentrated on the causal factors in an attempt to explain the revolution and the fall of the Pahlavi regime. For the most part, these contributions are historical analyses. What is conspicuously lacking is a much needed synchronic perspective on the social and cultural consequences of the revolution.

As a small step in that direction, I shall endeavour in this chapter to examine the degree of compatibility between the tribal social organisation and the ongoing post-revolutionary process of change. My main thesis is that there seems to be a greater congruence between the tribal institutions and the Islamic polity than under monarchy. Put in a dialectical sense, it may be stated that there is less structural contradiction in this area today than at any period during the Pahlavi regime. Theoretically, such structural consistency should facilitate the integration of the tribal societies with the larger national system far more effectively than before.

Pivotal in the present argument is the notion that during the Pahlavi reign institutional barriers, aggravated by myopic and often clumsy solutions to the tribal problems, rendered lasting articulation between the two social systems hopelessly elusive. Methodologically the task calls for a comparison between the past and the present modes of articulation focusing on a few crucial changes and the consequences of these for the tribal societies.

The time dimension of this comparative analysis embraces: (i) 1925–41, or the era of intense nationalism beginning with Reza Shah's accession to the throne and culminating in his abdication in favour of his son; (ii) 1942–79, a period marked by the ebb and flow of Mohammad Reza Shah's political fortune which came to a precipitous end with the 1979 revolution.

This diachronic treatment will then be followed by a look at the import of some of the post-revolutionary changes to date. Admittedly, reliable data belonging to this period are not as adequate as one wishes. The lingering climate of confusion and an interminable power struggle among the various ideological factions exacerbated by a calamitous war with Iraq have not been conducive to a dispassionate assessment of the implications of the revolution for the non-urban components of the Iranian society – the overwhelming majority of the population.

The human dimension in this context involves the pastoral–agricultural population of the south-western province of Kuhgiluyeh–Boyr Ahmad, named after two major tribal clusters: the Boyr Ahmad, the most dominant group comprising about 120 000 people, and the Kuhgilu containing roughly another 200 000 members. The region straddles an extremely rugged segment of the Zagros range which has, since time immemorial, inhibited easy incursion by external forces. For example, despite repeated and costly campaigns during the Pahlavi reign, the inaccessible pockets were only recently pacified. To achieve this end, half a dozen distinct and often mutually hostile tribal groups were amalgamated to form a single administrative unit. The central authority over the region is symbolised by the government-constructed town of Yassudj which houses the various bureaucracies and sundry services to see to the needs of some 2000 non-indigenous employees and their dependents.

Peripheral to the tribal heartland are two more market-administrative centres: Gachsaran and the historic town of Behbahan. Owing to their strategic location within the oilfields and their relative proximity to the Persian Gulf, these two urban centres have always played a significant part in the history of tribal relations with the central government and, as will be shown later, in the local intrigues of the erstwhile Anglo-Iranian Oil Company.

TRIBES UNDER REZA SHAH

All tribally-organised peoples were perceived by Reza Shah to be incompatible with national unity, and a menace to internal security. This attitude provided the moral justification for a series of measures which demanded nothing short of a complete destruction of the social, economic and political foundation of the tribal societies. In the period from 1925 to 1941, as Avery maintains, it became increasingly 'evident that tribes could be defeated and, given time, eliminated altogether' (1965, p. 286).

As elsewhere in the Middle East, the viability of pastoralism in Iran depends on free access to the summer and winter pastures through large-scale annual migrations. It is an eminently rational strategy whereby widely separated natural resources are fully exploited. The regions inhabited by pastoralists are, at best, marginally suited to agriculture. Not surprisingly, Reza Shah's initial move was the interruption of the seasonal migrations which resulted in massive losses in the nomads' herds through starvation and disease, and led inexorably to human suffering and impoverishment. His pacification policies were scarcely less pernicious. Characteristically, they began with imprisonment and summary executions of nearly all important leaders. Tribal territories were initially placed under the jurisdiction of the army but were later assigned to the *gendarmerie* whose atrocities against the poverty-stricken inhabitants continued unabated until the fall of the regime. As Upton has remarked 'it was these atrocities which caused the periodic rebellion of tribal groups goaded by desperation; rebellions were put down with extreme brutality.' Upton concludes 'All in all, the treatment of the nomadic tribes constitutes the most sordid chapter in the period of Reza Shah and inevitably casts a deep shadow on the reputations of the generals and colonels involved who must share a large measure of the responsibility' (1970, p. 80).

Official documents recently obtained in Kuhgiluyeh seem to substantiate a common belief by many informants that the military establishment had, indeed, a vested interest in promoting the hysteria of tribal menace.[2] One particular document strongly suggests that some army officers fabricated reports of fictitious rebellions and even went so far as to instigate intertribal raiding to perpetuate the myth of endemic unrest in the region. The continued military occupation of the tribal areas presumably assured the uninterrupted allocation of resources for costly operations and guaranteed premature or undeserved promotions of the commanding officers. The administration, meanwhile, paraded its accomplishments and defended its suppression of the 'recalcitrant' tribesmen in the name of national security and modernisation.

It might be relevant to point out that intertribal competition over pasture and productive human resources rarely permitted the formation of enduring coalitions against a mutual adversary. Similarly, intratribal rivalries among the political élite were hardly amenable to the ideal of unity or unanimity on how to deal with an external challenge.

TRIBES AND FOREIGN INTERESTS

Any analysis of the relationships between the state and tribes at this time would suffer without a mention of that ever-present complicating factor, the British Oil interest in Iran and its final guise, the Anglo Iranian Oil Company (AIOC). While Reza Shah exhibited a pathological concern over dynastic longevity, the British showed no less concern for a 'stable' political environment in which to continue their uncontested plunder of the nation's natural assets (cf. Elwell-Sutton, 1975, p. 67). The unholy alliance was largely sustained by a single overarching mutual interest in continuity.

To this end the repressive measures of Reza Shah against all opposition, real as well as imagined, was matched by the company's covert study of the major tribes, especially their internal politics. In the Kuhgiluyeh–Boyr Ahmad region the quasi-ethnographic intelligence information was evidently gathered by two methods: through the members of the urban upper-class in Behbahan who by virtue of their kinship ties with the tribal élite enjoyed a privileged position. The second method, and perhaps more systematic, was carried out by certain Iranian personnel of the company's public relations department, who had established a good rapport with the tribal leaders.[3] The latter channel, though probably quite profitable, never detracted from the importance of the Behbahani élite who remained the most steadfast political brokers for the AIOC until the nationalisation of the oil industry in 1951. The most prominent Behbahanis were rewarded with national political office often as *Majlis* (the lower house of parliament), deputies representing the region. Typically the economic perquisites of such positions were considerable.

The occupation of Iran by the Allied forces during the Second World War (in violation of its declared neutrality) resulted in Reza Shah's humiliating abdication in 1941. In the ensuing political vacuum the exiled sons and families of the liquidated chiefs made separate but dramatic escapes from Tehran and returned to their respective tribes. This group of educated and politically sophisticated young leaders shared an indelible loathing of the Pahlavis.

TRIBES UNDER MOHAMMAD REZA SHAH

So far as the tribes were concerned the next decade after Reza Shah's departure was a sort of interregnum. They had acquired a sizeable quantity of modern rifles smuggled across the Gulf, and by capture from the army. In 1943, for example, the Boyr Ahmad defeated and disarmed an entire battalion of Iranian troops. The availability of firearms not only intensified intratribal conflicts over succession to leadership, it led to brigandage and raiding of villages by the more destitute groups.

The provincial disturbances in this period were in part blamed on the British propensity for mischief. One may be tempted to speculate that the British recognising the tribes' unalterable antipathy toward them, on the one side, and the rise of the Marxist Tudeh Party on the c ther, were frantically working to weaken and isolate the two (cf. Cc .tam, 1964, p. 62). There is, however, little hard evidence to ascertain the extent of the British involvement if any.

In the early 1950s Prime Minister Mohammed Mossadeq's impressive success in nationalising the oil industry, and in curbing the authoritarian proclivities of the Shah brought a glimmer of hope to the tribes. Anyone who could rid them of two malevolent forces, they reasoned, certainly deserved their support (Cottam, 1964, p. 63; Upton, 1965, pp. 100–3). It would be terribly naïve, of course, to assume that their active endorsement of Mossadeq did much to diminish the general attitude of suspicion towards them. The reason is best sought in the world view of the urban Iranians reinforced by years of Reza Shah's jingoistic propaganda. It definitely transcends the tribes' purported susceptibility to foreign intrigue. Even today the conventional image of a tribesman is of a savage, marauding vagabond with questionable national loyalty.

The euphoria generated by Mossadeq's early victories was short-lived. The *coup d'état* of 1953 overthrew the nationalist government, restored the Shah's autocratic powers and ushered in another reign of terror for the tribes. In exacting vengeance the Shah was determined not to be out-performed by his father. The *coup de grâce* for tribal leadership as an institution came after the widespread riots of 1963. Certain segments of the Boyr Ahmad and the Qashqai attempted an ill-conceived and poorly co-ordinated rebellion which was ruthlessly crushed. The tribal uprising had been planned to coincide with the urban anti-government demonstrations led principally by one religious leader, Ayatollah Ruhullah Khomeini. The Shah's remarkable success in eliminating the opposition owed much to a revitalised army and the state security agency, both gifts of the United States. There is incontrovertible evidence that, at this time, at least some elements of the American intelligence-gathering community were preoccupied with counter-insurgency studies in Iran. Captain Hand's (1963) detailed statistical report on the Iranian tribes, however, suggests a much earlier interest, perhaps shortly after Mossadeq's overthrow in 1953.[4] By the end of 1963, to extirpate the potential for future tribal unification as well as intertribal alliances, chieftainship was finally abolished.

TRIBAL LEADERSHIP STRUCTURE

The central governments in Iran have always laboured under an exaggerated notion of the importance of the paramount chiefs. In fact, the viability of tribal political organisation does not necessarily depend on the administrative presence of a central leader. The ability of the major tribes to maintain their political integrity despite enormous external pressures in the past twenty years has sufficiently demonstrated the point.

The Boyr Ahmad share with most Iranian tribes an organisational structure composed of a number of sub-tribes headed by one hereditary sub-chief or *kadkhoda*. He is aided by his close agnates assigned to various sections who, in turn, oversee a number of other subordinate headmen. Each sub-tribe is thus a territorial and political unit. The paramount chief's main function was to galvanise the sub-tribes into a confederacy, albeit loose and precarious. One of the major causes of intratribal conflict was succession to political office; a problem largely complicated by procedural ambiguities and polygyny (Fazel, 1979). The ethno-history of the Boyr Ahmad, for example, is replete with cases of political assassination. It is perhaps an irony that the paramount chief was not uniformly the most powerful or influential figure; the Boyr Ahmad *khan* was frequently little more than a pawn in the hands of sub-tribal chiefs. These institutional weaknesses formed a convenient avenue for directed external manipulation. On the other hand, this type of decentralised, segmented political structure proved to be extremely adaptive under intense pressures from outside.

For this and other reasons, from 1963 on, Mohammad Reza Shah's tribal strategy assumed a multi-faceted, systemic character without any diminution in the use of the state's repressive apparatus. Whereas before the basic objective was to settle the nomadic groups and to eliminate the *khans* by undermining the economic bases of their leadership or by more drastic means, during this phase the aim was to destroy the economic and cultural foundation of tribal life altogether (Fazel, 1979). The single-minded pursuit of the settlement of nomads, however, continued to be the centrepiece of the Shah's policies.

I now turn to some of the more crucial changes introduced through the various government agencies. As noted, the focus of this analysis remains the Lur population of Kuhgiluyeh, particularly the Boyr Ahmad, but, minor exceptions aside, the generalisations derived should be applicable to other pastoral groups as well.

THE SHAH'S REFORM PROGRAMME

Beginning in 1962 the implementation of a host of social and economic changes was carried out under the aegis of the so-called 'Shah and People Revolution' otherwise known as the 'White Revolution'. Especially consequential for the pastoralists were the land reform and the nationalisation of natural resources including pastures and forests. Although the extension of the national educational system, judicial system and the state bureaucracies into the tribal societies had originated during the reign of Reza Shah, they were considerably expanded and somewhat modernised after 1963.

Despite the popular belief that the Shah's reforms had a generally salutary effect in facilitating the integration of tribal societies, the weight of the evidence seems to support the contrary.[5] The intended or inadvertent outcome was a process of economic and cultural pauperisation. The full impact was mercifully mitigated by the incompetence of government officials and the ability of tribesmen to manipulate or avoid the agencies far more effectively than was imagined possible.

LAND REFORMS

A proper analysis and evaluation of land reform is only possible when we consider the total context of social and physical environment. The tribal system of land use and tenure has evolved along fundamentally different lines compared with that which is still prevalent in most rural areas in Iran with such familiar features as: large landholdings, absentee owners, landless peasants, and insecurity of tenure (Lambton, 1953). Within the Zagros range, ecological constraints have prevented the emergence of many large landed estates by the tribal élite. Only an estimated 10 per cent of the region is actually suited to intensive agriculture; the remainder is either steep pasture lands or oak forests. The cultivable portion consists of a dozen spacious valley floors and alluvial plains coveted and fought over by rival factions. Traditionally each of these micro-environments housed several farming communities under the tutelage of a dominant lineage. The territory was defended from fortresses equipped with parapets and gun holes constructed at strategic vantage points and guarded by professional riflemen recruited from the population but loyal to the patron *kadkhoda* or *khan*. To offset his defence expenditure the patron was entitled to one-fifth of the annual produce of the farmer's land, normally wheat and barley. The point to stress is that the tribal farmer had an inalienable right to his land and could not normally be evicted, any more than he could be deprived of membership in his kinship group. The land was often worked co-operatively by a number of close patrilineal kinsmen. Each one received a certain portion of the produce, but no one had an exclusive right to the land.

Whether by ignorance or design, or both, the Shah's land reform programme injected into this system the principle of exclusive ownership by one man, recognised and sanctioned not by any descent ideology but by an arbitrary external force. Only the name of whoever happened to be working the land on the day when the land-reform officials arrived for their cadastral survey was recorded as the legitimate owner.

In the succeeding decade the real beneficiaries of land reform were the corrupt officials of the bureaucracies involved and the parasitic gendarmes. Step by step the most prized lands went to those who could offer the largest bribes, usually the relatively affluent *kadkhodas*. Thus the land reform created here precisely that which it was supposedly seeking to eradicate in the rural sector.

Approximately 50 per cent of those who relied more on farming than herding were made landless. To augment agricultural lands, desperate tribesmen began to invade the mountain pastures and the forested areas despite stiff opposition from the pastoralists. Ploughing the shallow humus layer and removing the protective vegetation led to a gradual erosion of the topsoil and precipitated widespread ecological disasters. The serious reduction in grazing resources already evident in 1970, in turn affected the overall size of the animal population forcing an ever-increasing number of herders to shift to subsistence farming. The resultant negative feedback involving pasture, animal population and human population may have already become irreversible.

To make matters worse, considerable portions of the traditional pastures were designated 'protected areas' and thus made inaccessible to the pastoralists under the nationalisation of natural resources. This, too, became another avenue for selective treatment and favouritism leading to intergroup hostility and a further step toward the destruction of the pastoral economy.

TRIBAL EDUCATION

The early 1930s witnessed the formation of an incipient tribal education system whose main objective has been to inculcate the cultural and technological superiority of the dominant society. The indoctrination, however, brings little material or technological benefits. Without denying the intrinsic advantages of literacy, it is certainly valid to ask to what extent this type of education prepares a tribal child for a productive and fulfilling life? For the most part, the education consists of endless litanies in Farsi on aspects of the urban values and material amenities. It also implants the idea of social mobility through education which means ordinarily a bureaucratic desk job in one of the nearby towns. Seduced by even less realistic hopes the parents frequently make supreme sacrifices in order to 'educate' their children. The return has to be more than a simple ability to read and write Farsi which could be acquired in a fraction of the time that it takes to earn a secondary school diploma. The most realisable goal is to become a teacher in the tribal education programme, though the rate of success is less than 5 per cent. On the other hand, the educated individuals who do venture beyond the tribal environment face either unemployment or degrading menial labour rarely accepted by their urban counterparts. Despite disillusionment they are either unwilling or more likely too poorly trained to pursue a pastoral or agricultural interest. Sadly enough, even the vast majority of those who have not succumbed to the lure of civil service feel somewhat ambivalent about the tribal lifestyle.

Male youths are by no means alone in experiencing social and psychological stress. The few girls who do become professional teachers desire marital partners in the same field. But the rules of endogamy and the traditional role of women in the domestic sphere present some insoluble problems. The viability of a pastoral household economy rests on the ability of the wife to be a full-time manager (Fazel, 1977).

To suggest an alternative to the current tribal education at this juncture, might well be an exercise in futility. Suffice it to say a rational educational programme for non-urban populations in Iran must be especially sensitive to the imperatives of human and physical environment. A responsive programme must, at the very least, effect an amelioration of social and economic conditions.

TRIBES AND THE NATIONAL LEGAL SYSTEM

No discussion of the structural contradictions between the tribal society and the former administration is complete without some mention of the impact of the westernised legal system. In a tribal society the principal mechanism of conflict resolution is mediation by a member of the community who is mutually respected by the disputants. Should the initial attempt fail, a more adroit mediator of higher status will be sought. This procedure is somewhat analogous to what is known as out-of-court settlement which is achieved primarily through negotiation and compromise by both the defendant and plaintiff (cf. Nader, 1972).

Less frequently, however, when all mediatory efforts are exhausted the dispute is resolved by arbitration. The arbitrators are recruited from the ranks of the political élite or the religious leaders, depending, of course, on the nature and magnitude of the conflict. In order to render a judicious and impartial decision, the arbitrator must not be hampered by self-interest. Normally the decision is binding and carries the threat of coercive or religious sanction.

The significant point to emphasise is that mediation and to a large extent arbitration aim to restore strained relations and thereby defuse potentially disruptive tensions, rather than establishing guilt and meting out punishment. This approach to dispute settlement is highly appropriate in an essentially kinship-based society with reticulate personal and group bonds.

To say that a radically divergent method cannot function in the same manner and therefore will not be accepted by the people is a simple truism. It is then hardly surprising that the tribesmen avoided the urban courts of the former Ministry of Justice. For the average Boyr Ahmad, for instance, neither winning a judgement nor compliance with a court decision would have meant an end to a dispute. Successful court action seldom ruled out retaliation by the losing party. Moreover, from a purely economic standpoint, namely the circuit of annual migration, the agricultural activities and labour-intensive pastoralism, to say nothing of the financial burden of the required trips to town, court litigation would have constituted an unwise allocation of precious resources. An additional obstacle was the bewildering assemblage of the procedures overlaid with an arcane legal terminology unintelligible even to those with a fairly good command of the Farsi language. These constraints reinforced by the knowledge of corruption in the court system were so compelling that gendarmes often used the ploy of serving fictitious summons to extort bribes from the unwary tribesmen.

Aside from some occasional and minor reactions to the inroads of the imposed social order, the general attitude reflected impotence but rarely submission. Armed rebellions by individuals and small groups were not unusual although seldom publicised or even acknowledged. By 1977, two years before the revolution, unprecedented collective expression of grievances in public forums began to alarm the governor and the local SAVAK. As elsewhere in Iran during this period, the Boyr Ahmad religious leaders played a major role in focusing public outcry against the abuse of power by the officials of the central government.

RELIGION IN TRIBAL SOCIETY

Frederik Barth's 1961 study of the Basseri nomads of southern Iran has been largely responsible for the enduring belief that the Iranian pastoralists are relatively lax in their observance of Islam and that their ideological system has been overshadowed by the drama of annual migrations. Empirical evidence from the Boyr Ahmad and their four tribal neighbours would not support such generalisations, however. The Iranian pastoralists may be less sophisticated in terms of the esoteric knowledge and rituals found in some urban populations, but they are scarcely less devout.

The three Boyr Ahmad religious leaders or *mojtaheds* have earned their pre-eminence through formal training in such theological centres of learning as Qum and Najaf followed by years of teaching and practice. Typifying other Lur tribes of south-western Iran (Fazel, 1978) the Boyr Ahmad clergy came from two major lineages that claim descent from the Prophet. Unlike the chiefly lineages, the clergy in general were less harshly treated provided they did not openly criticise the authorities.

In contrast to the urban-based clergy, the tribal religious leaders are fully integrated into the society's political system. They function as mediators in serious conflicts and are routinely consulted on nearly all aspects of daily life. They are equally important in regulating interpersonal, familial and community relations, as well as interpreting public mores and morals according to the laws of Islam. They provide the spiritual presence at nearly all community events. As custodians of local shrines they bear witness to oath-taking, given sanctuary and intercede on behalf of supplicants. During the Pahlavi regime they retained much of their traditional functions except the monopoly over the education and legal spheres.

From 1963 on the tribal *mojtaheds* and *mullahs* increasingly identified with the national religious figures in their opposition to the Shah, though far less assertively. That they assumed an active role in tribal politics and administration following the revolution was not unexpected.

In the foregoing discussion I have depicted only a few elements to illustrate the nature of the relationship between tribal societies and the Iranian state under monarchy. It is hoped, however, that the salient features described here have been sufficient to demonstrate how structural incongruity coupled with inane and politically motivated change thwarted the process of modernisation and integration of tribal societies into the national structure. The effects of short-sighted policies responsible for the dreadful waste of human and economic resources transcended the tribal societies. The nation also paid for a paralysed pastoral economy that even under the most favourable natural conditions could not have competed with subsidised prices of imported meat. The conversion of grazing lands into subsistence farms has set into motion a process of environmental degradation with long-range consequences for the whole region. More conspicuously in the past twenty-five years, the poverty-stricken tribesmen have been contributing to the growing population of the lumpenproletariat living in squatter settlements on the outskirts of every major Iranian city. It is impossible to escape the irony of the fact that it was this uprooted and disenfranchised population rather than organised tribal insurgency that played a decisive part in the demise of the regime.

TRIBES AND THE REVOLUTION

The tribal populations, at least those of Kuhgiluyeh and southern Iran, had a minimal part in the revolution of 1979. As the preceding argument shows, in the past the tribes were effectively excluded from the mainstream of the national political life. The fact that they were equally ignored by the liberal nationalist as well as the Marxist movements (Binder, 1964, p. 168) further suggests the extent of the tribes' disaffection. At the same time no other segment of the Iranian population was so closely scrutinised and so stringently controlled by the government. Besides, the memories of the 1953 coup and the ill-fated uprising of 1963 were too painful to forget. Consequently the clergy-led opposition which picked up momentum by early 1978 in the peripheral towns of Kazeroon, Ardekan and Behbahan was prudently ignored by the tribes. In these towns mosques were used to channel the dissemination of information and co-ordinate anti-government activities. In the tribal region this vital institution was either underdeveloped or non-existent.

The early reaction to the news of the nearby urban uprisings ranged from incredulity to a guarded optimism, but as warriors they had no illusions about the military capabilities of the Shah's army. The news of the final collapse of the regime was therefore received almost stoically in these tribal regions, in contrast to the exuberance of the urban crowds.

After the dissolution of the provincial authority structure, the urban revolutionary committees (*komiteh*) operating from the neighbourhood mosques gradually assumed responsibility for the internal security and the regulation of social, political, and commercial activities. However, as noted, since the mosque as an institution of social protest was much less crystallised here, the tribes came under the jurisdiction of the urban-based *komiteh*. Perhaps the most important contribution of the clergy at this time was to mediate between the well-armed rival factions who were jockeying for power in the new political arena.

Another problematic area related to the strident demands for expeditious rectification of inequities in civil service employment and in the distribution of other economic and political resources. By early 1980 practically all the Boyr Ahmads who had occupied relatively high-ranking posts in the previous regime were dismissed. A few who were accused of collaboration with security agencies were arrested and imprisoned along with the *kadkhodas* who became large landowners through the land reform often at the expense of other tribesmen.

The present guidelines for the distribution of government-controlled resources derive from proven loyalty to the Islamic Republic, knowledge and observance of Islamic tenets, and to some extent proximity to the current nucleus of power: the religious leaders and the revolutionary guards. More significantly, the institutionalisation of the clergy's local authority followed the anticipated Islamisation of the country's judicial system. Although it is still to early for any definitive statement, it might be safe to assume that much of the mediatory procedures described above, will be incorporated into the Islamic adjudicative framework.

The tribal education stripped of its previous budgetary independence has also experienced fundamental transformations including extensive curricular modifications and the abolition of co-educational class-rooms. The *paksazi*, 'cleansing' of the schools of a large number of experienced teachers by forced retirement is apt to affect the quality of education. On the whole, the Islamisation of schools has been met with either approval or indifference. If the question of relevancy is once again invoked, the new changes can claim little improvement over the old approach. Nevertheless, the present emphasis on the traditional Islamic precepts in the school textbooks might have more appeal than the ones which recounted the imperial munificence *ad infinitum*.

The extent to which Luri history and literature may be included in textbooks, will depend solely on the role of the tribal intelligentsia in shaping the political future of their people. To be realistic, however, the current official penchant for submerging all cultural heritage in favour of doctrinal teachings does not leave much room for optimism. For the more pessimistic prognosticator, this factor alone portends an eventual return to the type of relationship between the state and the tribes reminiscent of the *ancien régime*.

The legacy of the Shah's land reform under the present substantially weakened state conrol is perhaps the most potentially disruptive factor in this region.[6] There has been little attempt by the authorities to disturb the *status quo* for fear of political repercussion. Not unlike the occurrences among the Turkomans and the Kurds, there is some evidence that kinship groups and territorial factions have been trying to redress what is perceived as the injustice of the land reform, through self-help. Notwithstanding the tacit approval of the authorities, the escalation of this method will surely increase the likelihood of state intervention.

A noteworthy change especially welcomed by practically every tribal producer is the abolition of usury. It has seriously affected the town merchants who provide the tribesmen with credit often at 100 per cent compounded annually. The credit thus obtained is applied toward the purchase of manufactured goods and consumable items from the same merchant at prices substantially above the normal market level. What contributed to the tribesmen's perpetual indebtedness were the former government's subsidised imports such as meat, cereals, and legumes which had depressed the prices of pastoral and agricultural products thus making the hope for investment and economic expansion unattainable. For the average producer the rational solution to these market pressures was to join the migrant workforce. The resultant manpower drain, on the other hand, was seriously eroding the economic viability of the large herd-owners.

A few months after the revolution, the new regime began to raise support prices for grains, meat and other pastoral and agricultural products purchased by the government. This timely policy substantially improved the producers' income and created a tangible economic incentive (cf. Paul, 1982, p. 22). Other factors such as high urban unemployment, a rising inflation rate, the availability of interest-free government agricultural loans have combined to generate an added incentive to increase production and at the same time resist the temptation of purchasing non-essential commodities.[7]

CONCLUDING REMARKS

The preceding analysis is predicated on the fundamental premise that seemingly insurmountable barriers – to varying extents still present today – have isolated the tribal enclaves from the national structure. The obstacles are legion, they span the whole gamut of cultural, political and economic life. They are, moreover, implicit in the cognitive domain of the technologically and militarily dominant urban sector.

Misguided policies and blunders during the so-called era of 'nationalism' had rendered the integration of tribal people into a cohesive national system a virtual impossibility. The tribes were elaborately portrayed as elements inimical to the goals of nationalism. The systematic vilification served to justify their unconscionable treatment by the state. In the latter part of this era the tribes became the passive recipients of another series of egregious and paternalistic changes whose central purpose was, as before, to transform the pastoral nomads into subsistence peasants irrespective of the human suffering or the economic cost to the nation.

The pertinent question is whether the present socio-political order will replicate the mistakes of its predecessor. Will the future policies and programmes also emanate from a self-serving distrust or, will they show a genuine concern for these segments of the Iranian society?

Despite insufficient post-revolutionary time, a few general statements might be permitted. Judged by some basic similarities in the overall cultural premises, the early signs seem to point to a greater degree of conformity and structural accommodation between the present administration and the tribal societies in south-western Iran. The local institutional structures and values governing adjudication, interpersonal and familial relations, commercial transactions and the normative basis of education – if not its pragmatic relevance to social and economic exigencies – all seems to articulate remarkably well with those envisaged for the nation. If this argument is logical enough as well as empirically defensible, it might be possible to predict a gradual process of integration of tribes into the national system.

However, this should not be construed to imply that there are no disparities in other areas, nor that the integration will be smooth. Additionally, it would be unrealistic to assume that all tribal groups would exhibit the same natural affinity with the Islamic State. For example, the three major tribal populations, namely, Turkomans, Kurds and Baluchis, comprising roughly 5 million people who belong to the Sunni sect of Islam have felt, almost from the early days of the Islamic Republic, an increasing sense of alienation from the Shiia ruling majority. The Shiia-biased constitutions and the ferocity with which political opposition and some legitimate demands have been suppressed are cited by them as clear evidence of their subservient status. If the claim is true, then one can hardly expect disgruntled minorities to contribute toward nation-building.

Finally, two qualifying points need to be stressed: first, the analysis of the dialectics of the Iranian State and the tribal entities under post-revolutionary conditions is kept relatively independent of ideological preference. Second, normative projections concerning the future character of the integrated whole will do little to promote an elucidation of the observable phenomena. Neither the apocalyptic prophecies nor the promise of a theocratic utopia have much relevance in the present context. In four short years, much of the previous social order has disappeared in an ever-expanding vortex of the revolution. In an attempt to create a new social order, many drastic and far-reaching changes have been proposed and in some instances forcefully implemented. There is, however, an uncomfortable hiatus in objective information regarding the magnitude and effects of these changes. To assess the results of the revolution, therefore, a great deal of intensive research is needed in both the urban and the rural tribal sectors.

NOTES

1. This chapter is based on data collected in the course of several field studies covering a period from 1968 to 1979. I am grateful to the National Institute of Health for the initial grant and to the University of Massachusetts, Boston for a subsequent support. I would also like to thank my colleague Professor Lucille Kaplan for having read the first draft of this chapter and for her helpful comments. Responsibility herein is entirely mine.

2. During the 1977–9 research in the Boyr Ahmad and the Persian Gulf tribes of Dashtestan I was fortunate enough to acquire a substantial quantity of official and semi-official documents spanning a period from 1921 to 1970. The acquisition included a considerable number of highly illuminating pieces of personal correspondence of the tribal leaders and one meticulously-composed memoire by a Boyr Ahmad ethno-historian. All this material is part of work in progress.

3. This method of information-gathering is exemplified by Mahmoud Bavar's book (1944). More accurately the work might be termed a *Khan nameh* or an account devoted almost exclusively to the leadership class. Not surprisingly, it deals primarily with the Boyr Ahmad, militarily the most dominant and potentially troublesome tribe in the region.

4. Captain Hand's 200-page study bears a curious resemblance to Bavar's book mentioned earlier in that both concentrate almost wholly on the tribal élite. The details include names of leaders, their ages, social background, aspects of personality and potential successors or contenders. The figures on population and other demographic features are roughly estimated with absolutely no discussion of methodology. I might add, however, that Bavar's book is far superior as an ethnographic source than Captain Hand's report.

5. For a fuller discussion of the rural conditions prior to and after the Shah's land reform see Lambton (1953 and 1969) and Richards (1975).

6. In late 1979 the Ministry of Agriculture submitted a modest land reform programme to the Revolutionary Council. In 1981 the *Majlis* ratified the programme but the Council of Guardians rejected it on grounds that it was

incompatible with the tenets of Islam. In late 1981, however, Ayatollah Khomeini declared that only the *Majlis* had the power to decide the fate of the bill (cf. Paul, 1982, 22).

7. Many dire predictions regarding the deteriorating conditions in farming communities have been little more than armchair analysis. On the other hand one also finds perhaps excessively glowing official accounts by the new regime of efforts to resuscitate the agricultural economy and improve the quality of life in the countryside. Recent observers tell of rural electrification projects, clinics, development of water resources for irrigation and consumption, construction of roads to make villages accessible to market towns, all, however, on limited scale and more often in communities close to urban centres. The government claims that strict price control and the nationalisation of export and import trades will in the long run create favourable markets for the farmers' products.

REFERENCES

Avery, P. (1965) *Modern Iran* (London: Ernest Benn) p. 286.

Barth, F. (1961) *Nomads of South Persia: The Basseri Tribe of the Khamseh Confederacy* (New York: Humanities Press) pp. 147–53.

Bavar, M. (1944) *Kuhgiluyeh and its Tribes* (Iran: Aqbal) (in Farsi).

Binder, L. (1964) *Iran: Political Development in a Changing Society* (Berkeley: University of California Press) p. 168.

Cottam, R. W. (1964) *Nationalism in Iran* (University of Pittsburgh Press) pp. 62–3.

Elwell-Sutton, L. P. (1975) *Persian Oil: A Study in Power Politics* (Westport, Connecticut: Greenwood Press) p. 67.

Fazel, G. R. (1973) 'The Encapsulation of Nomadic Societies in Iran', in C. Nelson (ed.) *The Desert and the Sown: Nomads in the Wider Society* (Berkeley: University of California Press) pp. 129–43.

Fazel, G. R. (1977) 'Social and Political Status of Women Among Pastoral Nomads: The Boyr Ahmad of Southwest Iran', *Anthropological Quarterly*, vol. 50, no. 2 pp. 77–90.

Fazel, G. R. (1978) 'The Lur', in R. V. Weekes (ed.) *Muslim Peoples: A World Ethnographic Survey* (Westport, Connecticut: Greenwood Press) pp. 231–7.

Fazel, G. R. (1979) 'Economic Bases of Political Leadership Among Pastoral Nomads: The Boyr Ahmad Tribe of Southwest Iran', in M. B. Leons and F. Rothstein (eds) *New Directions in Political Economy: An Approach from Anthropology* (Westport, Connecticut: Greenwood Press) pp. 33–49.

Hand R. P. (Captain) (1963) *A Survey of the Tribes of Iran* (United States Army Special Warfare School: Counter-insurgency Department).

Helmut, R. (1975) 'Land Reform and Agri-business in Iran', *MERIP Reports*, no. 43, pp. 3–18.

Lambton, A. K. S. (1953) *Landlord and Peasants in Persia* (Oxford: Oxford University Press).

Lambton, A. K. S. (1969) *The Persian Land Reform 1962–1966* (Oxford: Clarendon Press).

Nader L. (ed.) (1972) *Law in Culture and Society* (Chicago: Aldine).
Paul, J. (1982) 'Iran's Peasants and the Revolution: An Introduction', *MERIP Reports*, no. 104, pp. 22–3.
Upton, J. M. (1963) *The History of Modern Iran: An Interpretation* (Cambridge: Harvard University Press) pp. 100–3.

5 Iran's Petroleum Policy: How Does the Oil Industry Function in Revolutionary Iran?

FEREIDUN FESHARAKI*

INTRODUCTION

The Iranian Revolution of February 1979 brought about fundamental changes in national and foreign policy. One of these fundamental changes concerned energy policy and particularly oil policy. Indeed, it may not be an exaggeration to argue that oil had been the central theme in the struggle to overthrow the Shah. Ever since the discovery of oil in Masjid-e-Soleiman in 1908, oil has played a major role in shaping the destiny of Iran. Iranian politics and nationalistic sentiments have for long been driven by the struggle against foreign domination of the Iranian oil industry. That the 1953 US-backed coup which brought the Shah back to power had been motivated by Western interest in Iran's oil, was a factor that plagued the Shah for twenty-five years, denying him legitimacy as a political leader.

When the anti-Shah demonstrations started in 1978, the oil workers were the first group to go on strike. Their strike was particularly effective. Not only did it destroy the image of the Shah's invincibility, it also paralysed the economy, and sent a message abroad that the Shah could no longer be relied upon as a stable ally, who could deliver oil to the international economy.

The Shah's hawkish attitude towards oil prices in 1971 and 1973 had been forgiven by his Western allies as the price they had to pay for a

*This chapter draws heavily on access to unpublished sources and the author's own experiences in Iran. For this reason, there are no footnotes in this chapter.

secure source of supply from a stable regime. In fact, the Western thirst for Iranian oil and the Shah's grandiose plans for economic development through industrialisation, were a perfect match. It required little or no pressure to persuade the Shah to run the oilfields at maximum capacity. When OPEC was formed in 1960, Iran had been the smallest producer in the organisation. By 1970, Iran had risen to the rank of the second-largest producer in OPEC and the second-largest exporter of oil in the world after Saudi Arabia. The expansion in productive capacity required large investments by the oil companies, with the encouragement of their parent-countries. Indeed, investments in Iran's oil industry came at the expense of other Middle East producers, particularly Iraq. The Western world found it preferable to have oil production expanded in Iran and Saudi Arabia, who seemed to enjoy long-term stability. However, it must be borne in mind that except for Iraq, few oil-producers had the potential to expand production beyond 4m barrels per day.

By 1978 Iran's productive capacity had risen to 7m barrels per day, of which 6.2m was located in the southern oilfields of Khouzestan. This capacity was considered peak capacity which could be sustained with heavy gas injection investments for eight years before an inevitable decline would set in. In the period 1974–8, Iran's actual production ranged between 5.2 and 6.0m barrels per day, leaving over 1m barrels of shut-in (spare) capacity which could be relied upon in an emergency. This large expansion in the rate of production and the capacity of a supposedly stable country made the world extremely vulnerable to interruptions in the supply of Iranian oil when the Shah fell.

This chapter focuses on the resilience of the oil industry in revolutionary Iran; specifically, on how the industry has been able to function as the major source of foreign exchange in Iran, despite the massive outflow of highly trained Iranian expertise, departure of expatriates, war with Iraq and the difficulty of access to specialised equipment and technology.

We will examine: (i) Iran's oil resource base and production potential; (ii) the fate of incomplete projects abandoned after the revolution and their impact on Iran's production potential; (iii) investment requirements of the oil sector; (iv) Iran's export strategy and her position in OPEC, and (v) oil sector and revenue potential for the Iranian economy.

OIL RESERVES

Iran's reserves of oil-in-place are estimated at 347bn barrels, 320bn barrels of which are located in the Southern Khuzistan region and 27bn barrels in other parts of the country. This figure which includes all possible and probable reserves is, of course, far larger than the proven reserves, which are estimated today at 59bn barrels. This implies a 17 per cent recovery factor (347bn barrels × 17 per cent = 59bn barrels).

Generally speaking, Iran's proven reserves figures must be treated with caution. No one in the country is convinced of the reliability of reserve figures. This is also true of other Middle East oil-producers' estimates of reserves. Iraqi and Kuwaiti reserves, for instance, are widely believed to be inaccurate. The problem stems from lack of co-ordinated and regular reporting by the oil companies. Unlike the US, UK and Canada, the oil companies in the Middle East were never required to undertake such systematic reporting.

Iran, like many other OPEC members, does not officially report its estimates of reserves. Such figures are obtained from trade journals and even within the Iranian government, trade journal figures form the basis of various computations. There are a number of reasons why the proven reserves figures are suspect:

1. The reserves figure reported at 75bn barrels in the 1960s has steadily fallen to 59bn barrels in 1979. Although there is no linear relationship between price and reserves, it is hard to believe that the increase in price from $1.80 per barrel in 1970 to $30.00 per barrel in 1980 had no impact on reserves.
2. By the early 1970s, all new discoveries with costs of production of more than 25 cents per barrel were excluded from estimates of proven reserves because they were regarded as being uneconomical or too small. Even today such fields are not counted.

Since proven resources imply reserves which are recoverable under current technical and economic conditions and these conditions have significantly changed over the past decade, the reserve figures must be adjusted upwards. Iran's proven reserves may be realistically assessed by adding three new factors to the proven reserve figures: already discovered but shut-down fields (Dasht-e-Moghan, Qom, etc.) expected additional discoveries and the increased recovery factor through secondary recovery (gas injection). Exploratory activity which during the 1970s was inadequate and disappointing is now significantly reduced. Between 1972 and 1977 only 175 exploratory oil and gas wells were drilled in Iran, less than 2 per cent of the number of wells drilled in the US during 1977 alone. Though no exact figures are available on the already discovered, high-cost oilfields (not included in proven reserves figures) it is generally believed that they may amount to around 5 per cent of published reserves estimates. The largest addition to oil reserves is likely to come from secondary recovery. This technique is expected to raise the recovery factor from 17 per cent to at least 25 per cent or 87bn barrels. This activity, as we shall see later, has nearly been brought to a halt after the revolution.

Since the developments in host-country–oil-company relations in the 1970s led to large increases in government take and relatively steady oil-company take (except for 1974 and 1979) there was little incentive on the part of the oil companies to undertake costly reserve appreciation activities. However, the oil exporters' economic rent increased from 80 cents per barrel in 1970 to over $30 per barrel in 1980 and there are major incentives for them to invest in activities which increase their reserves. In the case of Iran, little was done. Reserve estimation is now the duty of the government, particularly since such estimation will form the basis of its future economic strategy. When the author proposed a revision in Iran's oil reserves during 1976–7 so that Iran's reserves would be shown at alternative costs of production, neither the Prime Minister and Cabinet Ministers nor the Shah himself were aware of the possibilities that this approach would offer in terms of economic planning. Despite the backing of a number of ministers, the NIOC empire managed to suppress the proposal on the grounds that it would undermine Iran's bargaining position on the international level. The urgency of the issue has remained unchanged even under the new regime in Iran.

Productive Capacity

Iran's productive capacity was projected in 1973 to reach 8m barrels per day within five years. Eventually, it became clear that such capacity and rate of production was unrealistic and the figures were revised downwards. By 1977, the productive capacity had reached 6.9m barrels per day, 6.2m of which was located in the oil-rich Khouzestan province. Such productive capacity could not be maintained over a long period because of the decline in the gas lift pressure of the oil fields. With the application of secondary recovery techniques, it was hoped that capacity could be maintained at this level through 1985, and then decline gradually. The slow start-up of the gas injection programme which was nearly two years behind schedule when political flare-ups started in 1978, would have made it improbable that capacity could be maintained even if the former regime had survived. After the revolution, capacity began to decrease because of the decline in pressure as well as lack of effective service and maintenance programme. Currently, capacity stands at around 3.5m barrels per day. Whether capacity will decline further is a matter of conjecture. Some US intelligence reports indicate a decline in capacity of 2.9m barrels a day in the next year or so. This estimate seems to be on the low side and it is likely that a capacity of 3–4m barrels per day can be maintained over the next two years without expatriate help, barring any major accidents, assuming some service and maintenance is carried out by the Iranians, and spare parts are made available to them.

Relations with Foreign Oil Companies

Iran's most long-standing relationship was with the Consortium, consisting of the eight largest oil companies in the world as well as a few independents. The relationship with the Consortium was changed in 1973 under the Purchase and Sales Agreement. The Consortium was replaced by the Iran Oil Participants Ltd. (that is, the former Consortium) which owned the Oil Services Company of Iran (OSCO). OSCO became a contractor to NIOC, and in effect carried out the same functions as the Consortium in the South. However, as a contractor OSCO charged NIOC with the expenses. The OSCO contract, originally for five years (1973–8) was about to be renewed by the Shah when the revolution started. Under the 1973 Agreement, control of production and sales were given to NIOC, but little else changed in substance. Still over 90 per cent of Iran's oil was produced by OSCO and the former members of the Consortium, which effectively controlled OSCO, bought the lion's share of Iran's crude. When the demand for oil fell in 1975, the trading companies refused to lift their 'nominated' volumes. As a result, NIOC began to step up its direct sales. By 1977, the Purchase and Sales Agreement had effectively died through non-compliance by both sides. Negotiations for a new agreement had started and except for a few minor points, a new agreement permitting the former Consortium members to lift 3.3 million barrels per day of Iran's oil could have been reached. The revolution with its strong anti-oil company tone forced the Shah to postpone final ratification. The 1973 Agreement also included two other important points. First, a sales agreement of twenty years (1973–93) and a provision guaranteeing that Iran's oil income per barrel would not fall below similar crudes in the Gulf ('balancing margin principle').

After the revolution, OSCO was abolished and the twenty-year sales contract was cancelled. Given the tight petroleum market which existed after the revolution and the shortening of supply contracts (which is likely to prevail in the 1980s), long-term sales agreements did not mean very much. But the abolition of OSCO as a service company and the handing over of its responsibilities to NIOC may prove troublesome in view of the sophisticated nature of OSCO's operations in Iran. OSCO's main duties were: (i) exploration; (ii) production; (iii) secondary recovery; (iv) repair and maintenance; (v) terminal link; (vi) gas processing/separation and delivery of LPG and (vii) equipment purchase. The last task was carried out through Iran Oil Services Company (IROS) which handled all purchase of equipment for Iran's oil industry – a multi-billion dollar operation infested by corruption and kickbacks. IROS, now under direct NIOC control and renamed *Kala*, still operates from its old offices in London.

NIOC's past experience with exploration and production has been extremely limited. It has also undertaken very little work on repair and maintenance and gas-processing. Furthermore, it has no experience dealing with secondary recovery, which by virtue of its sophisticated nature and the difficult geological condition of Iran's oilfields must be handled by foreign expertise not widely available in the world even to the major oil companies (see the section on Secondary Recovery). This makes it extremely difficult for NIOC to handle OSCO's duties. However, the lower production target of the Iranian oil industry has made it possible for Iran to cope with these problems so far but the cost in terms of future potentially recoverable oil is thought to be heavy.

Iran's relations with other oil companies was through a number of service contractors and joint venture partners (see Table 5.1). Of six joint ventures, four (SIRIP, IPAC, MINICO, and LAPCO) had been producing crude since the early 1960s. The combined production of the four joint ventures was 550 000 barrels per day in 1977 or 10 per cent of Iran's crude production. The four joint ventures by the late 1970s had come to the conclusion that their chance for new discoveries were exhausted. Also, their potential for expanding the capacity of the existing fields was extremely limited. This meant that their production would be stable for a number of years and then gradually decline.

TABLE 5.1   *Foreign oil companies in Iran*

Company	Owners	Percentage share
Companies Associate with NIOC		
Iran Oil Participants, Ltd	British Petroleum	40
(i.e. the Consortium)	Royal Dutch Shell	14
	Compagnie Française des Pétroles	
	(CFP)	6
	EXXON	7
	Gulf Oil	7
	Mobil Oil	7
	Standard Oil of California	7
	Texaco	7
	Iricon Agency Ltd, consisting of:	
	Atlantic Richfield Company	1.66
	American Independent Oil Company	0.83
	Getty Oil Company	0.83
	Charter Oil Company	0.83
	Continental Oil Company	0.41
	Standard Oil Company of Ohio	0.41
Service Contractors to NIOC		
Oil Service Company of Iran	Iran Oil Participants Ltd	100
AGIP Iran Petroleum Company	AGIP	100
DEMINEX Iran Oil Company (Two contracts, each for a different area, signed 30 July 1974)	Deutsche Erdolversorguns-gesellschaft mgH (Deminex)	100
EGOCO (European Group of Oil Companies) (Contract effective from 26 June 1969)	ERAP	32
	Hispanica de Petroleos SA (Hispanoil)	20
	Petrofina	15
	Oesterreichischt Mineral-oeverwaltung (Oemv)	5
LAR Exploration Company (LAREX) (Contract signed 20 August 1974)	Ashland Oil Company	n/a
	Pan Canadian	n/a
Philiran (Phillips Oil Company of Iran) (Contract effective from 29 September 1969)	Phillips Petroleum Company	50
	Continental Oil Company	25
	Cities Service	25
SOFIRAN (Contract effective from 13 December 1966)	Entreprise de Recherches et d'Activités Pétrolières (ERAP)	40
	Mitsubishi Oil Development Company	40
	Société Nationale de Pétroles d'Aquitaine	20
TOTAL Iran (Contract signed 27 July 1974)	CFP	100
Ultramar Iran Oil Company (Contract signed 7 August 1974)	American Ultramar Ltd (Wholly owned by Ultramar Company Ltd, of the UK)	100

Company	Owners	Percentage share
NIOC Joint Ventures		
SIRIP (Société Irano-Iraliène des Pétroles) (Agreement	NIOC	50
effective from 27 August 1957)	AGIP	50
IPAC (Iran Pan American Oil Company) (Agreement effective	NIOC	50
from 5 June 1958)	AMOCO Iran Oil Company	50
IMINOCO (Iran Marine International Oil Company	NIOC	50
(Agreement effective from) 13 February 1965)	AGIP	16.66
	Phillips Petroleum	16.66
	Oil and Natural Gas Commission of India	16.66
LAPCO (Lavan Petroleum Co.) (Agreement effective from	NIOC	50
13 February 1965)	Atlantic Richfield	12.5
	Murphy Oil	12.5
	Sun Oil	12.5
	Union Oil	12.5
INPECO (Iran Nippon Petroleum Company) (Agreement effective	NIOC	50
from 5 January 1972)	IRAPEC (Owned by Teijin Ltd, North Sumatra Oil Development Corp, and other firms)	33.33
	Mobil Oil	16.66
HOPECO (Hormuz Petroleum Company) (Agreement effective	NIOC	50
from 5 January 1972)	Petrobras	25
	Mobil Oil	25

The other two joint ventures, INPECO and HOPECO, did not have much success. INEPCO drilled nine holes and although gas-fields were discovered which will be used in the future by NIOC and NIGC, no oil was found. INEPCO is reported to be about to be dissolved. HOPECO met with some success on its acreage in the Straits of Hormuz but was unable to reach agreement with NIOC over amendments which would be required in their basic operating agreement.

Of eight service contracts, all except SOFIRAN and DEMINEX have ceased operations or have been dissolved because of their failure to find commercial oil. SOFIRAN, the pioneer in service contracts in the Middle East, took twelve years to reach the production stage. It planned to produce 50 000 barrels per day in the third quarter of 1978 and was expected to increase production to 90–100 000 barrels per day. The revolution effectively halted any flow of oil from SOFIRAN. DEMINEX found some low gravity oil on the Abadan Plain and was unsure whether it would be worthwhile to develop the reservoir.

The fate of the Iran Oil Participants and OSCO was decided immediately after the revolution. They were taken over by NIOC without any announcements about compensation. A new company, NIOC Fields, was established to take over OSCO's activities. The fate of the joint ventures and service contractors initially remained unclear with no official announcements by NIOC. However, it was understood that the Revolutionary Council had decided that all such companies would be dissolved. The companies have not been notified of this decision and all their activities have been taken over by NIOC.

Operating joint venture and service contract activities by NIOC is going to prove just as troublesome as taking over OSCO's duties – if not more so. Unlike the Southern Khouzestan oilfields which have been producing crude oil for decades, the activities of joint ventures and service contractors were confined to difficult, low production, high cost areas. Some were operating in offshore areas for which NIOC has had little or no practical experience. The likely impact of the take-over on the future of crude production from these areas will be negative. While the four operating joint-venture areas may continue to produce oil, the production rate is likely to decline. During 1981 production from joint ventures stood at 200 000 barrels per day or 40 per cent of pre-revolution production, thanks to the advanced automation facilities. However, it is understood that even small accidents, which are not unusual, could drastically cut production without expert help. Areas operated by INPECO and HOPECO are likely to be closed down for the time being. SOFIRAN's two small fields in the Straits of Hormuz will probably not produce much, if any, in the next few years and DEMINEX's Abadan discovery is likely to be left aside.

NIOC's own activities in the past decade, apart from supervision and control of production and exports, have been confined to producing about 18 000 barrels per day from the 45-year old Nafte-Shah oilfield on the Iraqi border. NIOC exploration activity, which expanded rapidly between 1975 and 1978, was only possible with the help of foreign contractors. With the expulsion of expatriates, it will be a very difficult task for NIOC to handle all such activities on its own. Indeed, the only real possibility of increased production or new discoveries would be through inviting the foreign companies back to Iran and offering additional acreage for exploration. So far the exploratory activity has suffered serious setbacks, not only because the expatriates have left, but also because NIOC's capital budget for 1980–1 has been cut by 50 per cent, with exploration activities suffering the largest cutback. Until September 1978, OSCO had fourteen rigs in onshore exploration and other companies had ten rigs in offshore exploration. By the last quarter of 1979, NIOC had only one rig operating offshore and eight rigs onshore, two of which were in use on workovers and the other six (owned by SEDCO-SEDIRAN) on exploration and delineation. Another SEDIRAN rig was used for development. By early 1980 even this meagre drilling activity had significantly slowed down. Indeed, the only discovery of oil after the revolution was reported in March 1980. This was a field near Dezful of 40m barrels of light crude and potential production of 4500 barrels per day. Most of the exploratory work on the field had been carried out before the revolution.

SECONDARY RECOVERY AND THE FATE OF INCOMPLETE PROJECTS

The secondary recovery project mentioned earlier has been the most difficult and ambitious project facing Iran in the 1970s. The revolution has only postponed its implementation and has slightly reduced the sense of urgency of the operation. But the problem is still there.

Until 1973 when Iran took over the overall control and supervision of the oilfields, the former Consortium members were responsible for running the Khouzestan oil industry. Some time in the late 1960s, signs of declining gas pressure in the oilfields became evident to the Consortium which decided to ignore it for reasons related to its own commercial objectives. When responsibility was handed over to Iran in 1973, NIOC realised that the decline of pressure could, in a few years, lead to sharp declines in productive capacity. Thus, to build up pressure in the oilfields, a gas-injection secondary recovery programme was instituted in 1974. The secondary recovery programme was expected to achieve two objectives: first, to stabilise capacity at 6.5–7m barrels per day (6–6.2m barrels for the Khouzestan area) for five to ten years, and second, to increase the recovery factor from 17–18 per cent to 25 per cent, adding more than 25bn barrels to Iran's oil resources. (Indeed, every 5 per cent increase in Iran's recovery factor would equal all North Sea reserves.)

The implementation of the programme required a great deal of gas, a resource with which Iran is well endowed. Initially, it was estimated that the optimum level of gas injection by 1982 would be 12.8bn cubic feet per day (cfd) or thirteen times Iran's pre-revolution gas exports to the Soviet Union. Later, the requirement was scaled down to 8bn cfd at a minimum. At the time Iran's gas production stood at 5.5bn cfd of which nearly half was flared. This was associated gas produced with oil, most of which came from Khouzestan. It was thus clear that the associated gas, constituting around one-half of Iran's gas reserves, was insufficient for this programme. As a result, NIOC decided that gas fields of Pars *C* structure, near Bushehr, should be developed for reinjection.

Initial studies considered the need for reinjection into seven large fields: Agha Jari, Ahwaz-Asmari, Marun, Gachsaran, Haft Kel, Bibi Hakimeh and Pars. Haft Kel was chosen as the first experimental field where 300m cfd from the gas cap at Nafte-Sefid would be injected in 1975, later being augmented with associated gas. By late 1976, injection was to begin at Gachsaran and Agha Jari, using associated gas produced by themselves as well as dome gas from the Pazanan field. In 1977, the Pars field was expected to receive 300m cfd of Nafte-Sefid dome gas. From 1978 onwards, it was hoped that additional fields would be included in the programme as more non-associated natural gas became available, and eventually fields producing as little as 30 000 barrels per day would be included as individual engineering studies became available.

The secondary recovery programme entailed three stages: gas gathering, gas processing and NGL (natural gas liquid) recovery, and the actual injection of gas. If politics do not allow re-establishment of close ties with the oil companies, Iran could go to the international market for expertise and get it. The Iranian leaders feel that asking for expatriate help weakens their argument for political and economic independence. They would not feel badly about it if they were to look across the border to see the Soviets and even Chinese seeking American and European technology for secondary and tertiary recovery of oil. The Islamic leaders' contempt for Western technology may lead to losses of oil which is colossal in terms of Iran's national interest.

INVESTMENTS IN THE PETROLEUM SECTOR

An analysis of the proposed and actual investments in the petroleum sector provides a good indication of the change of direction in the Iranian oil industry and the likely bottlenecks in the future. Table 5.2 shows the planned investments during the Fifth, Sixth and Seventh Development Plans, while Table 5.3 shows the actual investments between 1976 and 1980 and the planned investment during 1980–1.

Table 5.2 shows that Iran had planned to spend \$11.7bn during the

TABLE 5.2 *Iran's planned investment in the petroleum sector (billions of US $)*[a]

	Fifth Development Plan[b] (1973/4–1977/8)			Sixth Development Plan[c] (1978/9–1982/3)			Seventh Development Plan[c] (1983/4–1987/8)		
	Development budget	NIOC funds	Total	Development budget	NIOC funds	Total	Development budget	NIOC funds	Total
Exploration and production	2.3	7.4[d]	9.7	3.2	6.6[e]	9.8	3.3	4.2	7.5
Refining	1.0	—	1.0	3.3	—	3.3	3.9	—	3.9
Domestic Transport and distribution	1.0	—	1.0	2.0	—	2.0	2.6	—	2.6
Total	4.3	7.4	11.7	8.5	6.6	15.1	9.8	4.2	14.0
Annual average investment	0.9	1.5	2.4	1.7	1.3	3.0	2.0	0.8	2.8

Notes:
[a] Capital expenditure only. Excludes current expenditures.
[b] By the time of the Revolution two-thirds of investments had actually been made.
[c] Proposed plans, now defunct.
[d] Includes $1.7b investment by SIRIP, LAPCO, IMINOCO and IPAC.
[e] Includes $780m in supplier's credit.

SOURCE Plan and Budget Organisation of Iran: 'Oil Outlook in the Next Ten Years'. 1978 (Unpublished).

TABLE 5.3   *Iran's investments in the oil industry (millions of US $)*[1]

	1356 (1977–8)	1357 (1978–9)	1358 (1979–80)[3]	1359 (1980–1)
Exploration and production	980	1885	1051	n.a.
Refining	377	218	235	n.a.
Transport and distribution	284	198	143	140
Import duties[2]	n.a.	(214)	n.a.	n.a.
Total[4]	1641	2301	1429	500–700

Notes:
[1] Capital costs only. Excludes current expenditures.
[2] The value of foregone import duties due to exemptions. Not included in the totals.
[3] About half the outlays are believed to have been actually spent.
[4] Figures for 1356 and 1357 are final and for 1358 projected, 1359 figures estimated by the author. Rials are converted to the US dollar: 70 rials = US $1.00.

SOURCE   The National Budget of Iran 1358.

Fifth Plan in the petroleum sector, $9.7bn of which was earmarked for exploration and production. NIOC's own funds together with investments from joint venture partners made up 63 per cent of the total investments. For the Sixth Plan a total investment of $15.1bn was envisaged, again the largest share allocated for exploration and production. In the Sixth Plan, NIOC's own funds would make up 44 per cent of the total investment. In the Seventh Plan, total investment would decline to $14.0bn of which less than half would go to exploration and production. The structure of the proposed investment plans clearly shows Iran's expectation under the Shah. First, the large allocations for exploration and development mainly reflected the secondary recovery projects, increasing cost of services and maintenance and exploratory activity in high cost areas. However, by the mid-1980s it was thought that the level of investment would gradually decline as most of the high-cost projects were completed. Second, Iran's need for refining facilities would grow at a very high rate necessitating a tripling of investment in the Sixth Plan and further increases in the Seventh Plan. Third, investment in the domestic transport and distribution would rise from $1bn in the Fifth Plan to $2bn and $2.6bn in the Sixth and Seventh Plans, again reflecting the growing domestic need for petroleum products, and fourth, the government had planned a tightening of control over the NIOC budget, through increasing the allocations for the petroleum sector and reducing the size of NIOC's own resources. This accounts for the declining contribution of NIOC's internal resources to the investments. The plans also tell us that average annual investments in the petroleum sector were planned at $1.7bn for the Fifth Plan, $3.0bn for the Sixth, and $2.8bn for the Seventh Plan.

A comparison of Tables 5.2 and 5.3 shows the current problems. During 1977–8 and 1978–9, investments were roughly according to plans. In the first year after the Revolution, total investments fell by 38 per cent. This reflects the low activity in secondary recovery projects. In fact, for 1979–80 the actual expenditures are thought to have been no more than $700–800m, or one-third of the investments in the previous year. For 1980–1, the capital expenditures fell to around $500m or one-quarter of the pre-Revolution investments. The decline reflects the near-stoppage of secondary recovery projects and little exploration and maintenance work. Although the present regime's lack of desire to maintin pre-Revolution productive capacity requires a scaling-down of investments in production and exploration, such a rate of reduction is clearly dangerous for the fields. Annual expenditures of $1–1.5bn are required for exploration and production at the minimum during the period 1980–5. Also, refining and distribution investments planned by the previous regime must be followed exactly by the Islamic regime to avoid interruptions in supplying the domestic market with its petroleum needs. The current level of investment in these areas is far below the required needs. Without a major reversal to perhaps three times the 1980–1 levels, not only will some recoverable oil be lost forever, but also domestic distribution of oil products and low export levels cannot be maintained.

OPEC AFFAIRS

Before the Revolution, OPEC affairs in Iran were handled by various organisations which competed for power and influence and undertook little co-ordination of their activities. While NIOC had an office of OPEC Affairs and Iran's OPEC Governor and National Representative came from NIOC, the Ministry of Finance and Economic Affairs had a greater say as the Minister was the head of Iran's delegation to OPEC. Often NIOC chiefs were not informed of what went on at the meetings and NIOC's OPEC office had to fight hard to find out what was going on. After the Revolution, it was decided to centralise all OPEC affairs at NIOC under the control of the

Minister of Oil, with the understanding that one Finance Ministry representative should be included in the OPEC team. Despite this sensible move, some of the old problems are still there. As before, Iran has one of the weakest OPEC teams, with members of the delegation rotating every time. At least two important OPEC positions in the Secretariat in Vienna which could have gone to the Iranians went to other nationals because of internal in-fighting and indecisiveness. Indeed, unlike what might be expected, little work or research is going on within Iran, beyond short-term policies regarding the country's OPEC position. NIOC must be one of the few oil companies in the world which does not have a well-established economics department.

Iran's pre-Revolution attitude toward OPEC was solely determined by the Shah, with some small flexibility left for the head of Iran's delegation. The Shah's hawkish attitude during the period 1970–5 was determined by his desire for larger oil revenues to pay for his grandiose plans and sophisticated weaponry as well as his thirst for international recognition and stature. When he realised that this attitude was costing him support in the industrial countries, particularly the US, he decided to moderate his attitudes. As the 1975 recession came about and Iran's exports fell by 12 per cent, he leaned toward a passive OPEC position. He instructed his OPEC officials to keep a very low profile and vote with the moderate forces.

After the Revolution, Iran's position within OPEC significantly affected the power structure within the organisation. Iran's hawkish attitude strengthened the hard-liners and isolated Saudi Arabia – Iran's former ally in price moderation – as the lone (though very powerful) voice for lower prices. Unlike the pre-Revolution period, when Iran and Saudi Arabia, together produced one-half of the OPEC output and forced the other members to follow suit, this time Saudi Arabia had to increase its output and stand out as the single 'swing' producer to balance demand with supply. Despite the Saudi's attempt to keep prices from rising, the changes in Iran's production policy led to a doubling of price between 1979 and 1980. As the impact of higher prices began to be reflected in massive conservation as well as a recession in the OECD countries, demand fell by 7 per cent in 1980 and by a further 7 per cent in 1981. This led to a decline in demand for OPEC oil from 30m barrels per day in 1979 to around 23m barrels per day in 1981. The decline in demand for OPEC oil – which came as a surprise to all oil analysts – effectively neutralised the radicalism that the Iranian revolution had brought to OPEC. Surprisingly enough, while radicals in OPEC

(Algeria, Libya, Nigeria, and Iraq) understood the realities of the market situation, Iran's OPEC team continued to insist on higher prices. This insistence was the result partly of the government's ignorance of the oil market and partly of the need for officials to try to score political points at home by showing that Iran was the most radical of all OPEC nations. Thus, by misjudging the oil market and by trying to impose high prices and hard contract terms at a time of glut, Iran lost both money and political influence. Although the hostage crisis and the two way Iran–US oil embargo had some impact on the decline in lifting of Iranian oil – the main factors behind the decline were higher prices and the unreliability of crude deliveries by the Iranian government. This is demonstrated by the fact that the lifting of the US embargo and release of the hostages did not lead to increased liftings of Iranian crude. As the glut continued into 1981, Iran had to begin to offer discounts and officially shave prices. At the OPEC conference on 29 October 1981 in Geneva, Iran reduced prices by over $3 per barrel and in the OPEC meeting on 9 December 1981 in Abu Dhabi, Iran further reduced its heavy crude prices to become the lowest-priced seller of heavy crude in the Persian Gulf. Very little domestic publicity was given to the OPEC meetings in the autumn of 1981.

In 1982, Iran continued its discounting of oil. By mid-1982, Iranian prices were $4–6 per barrel below the official OPEC price. Iran insisted that because of the revenue needs resulting from the war with Iraq, a 'price advantage' was necessary. Although many OPEC Ministers were agreeable in principle to such an advantage, they wanted a smaller price differential and production discipline by Iran. By late 1982 and early 1983, Iran had undergone a major change of attitude. The political leadership had accepted the fact that without OPEC, Iran would be significantly worse off. Nearly four years after the revolution, Iran became an OPEC insider again – working hard for the stability of the organisation and accepting production limits. At the OPEC meeting in March 1983, Iran agreed with the Saudis that the price of oil should be reduced to $29 per barrel for the so-called Arabian Marker Crude. Iran also accepted a quota of 2.4m barrels per day and gave firm guarantees to adhere to the production ceiling. Other OPEC nations agreed to give Iran an official price advantage of $1 per barrel at $28 per barrel. Since then Iran has behaved in a responsible manner. As the second largest oil-producer in OPEC, Iran has stayed well within the OPEC price and production formula.

PRODUCTION, EXPORT AND REVENUES IN THE 1980S

Iran's need for oil revenues will be a factor in determining production and exports. But more importantly the political climate of the country will decide production levels. It is highly unlikely that production will ever exceed 3.5–4m barrels per day even if such capacity exists. To what extent it will be below that ceiling is the matter under consideration. Today, the Iranian planners feel confident that a $18bn oil income in 1983 would be quite adequate to meet their needs. Of course, government policies may require more funds, but the above figure should be a reasonable target.

In 1980–1, Iran's oil revenues were around $12bn. By 1983, Iran's oil revenues rose to $18bn – close to pre-revolution levels in nominal terms. As indicated by Table 5.4, until 1985, oil revenues are forecast to be stable but will rise to $28 in 1990. In the 1990s, the Iranian oil reserve base could easily sustain an oil production of 3.5–4m barrels per day; however, rising domestic oil demand will probably result in exports of no more than 2m barrels per day in the year 2000.

TABLE 5.4   *Iran's production, exports, and oil revenues in the 1980s (thousands of barrels per day and billions of US $)*

	1983	*1985*	*1990*
Production[1]	2.4	2.4	3.5
Domestic demand	0.6	0.7	1.0
Exportable crude	1.8	1.9	2.5
Oil revenues[2] (billions of nominal US dollars)	18.0	19.0	28.0

Notes:
[1] Assumes constant production level of 2.4m barrels per day throughout 1985. Assumes production rise to 3.5m barrels per day by 1990 with re-start of some gas re-injection projects.
[2] Assumes current prices to 1985 and a 2 per cent nominal increase between 1985 and 1990.

Just after the revolution, Iran pushed itself into a financial bind by mismanagement of the economy. Foreign exchange reserves of over $15bn before the revolution were nearly exhausted by the end of 1981. By early 1984, the situation was reversed; foreign exchange reserves of around $10–12bn are now estimated to be held by the Central Bank of Iran.

CONCLUSION

That the Iranian petroleum industry seems to have been able to withstand so many problems and still continue to survive is not necessarily due to the sound management and expertise of the Islamic regime in Iran. The oil industry has faced major troubles because of the lack of skilled manpower, equipment and maintenance. It has continued to tick along because of its strong infrastructure which has developed over the past thirty years. Many of the oilfields have downward flows through the pipelines to the Kharg export terminal (without pumps). However, the level of 'free flow' is below 2.0m barrels a day and the lack of equipment and maintenance of pumps can create a ceiling to Iran's exports. At the same time, Iran's oil industry, has traditionally attracted high levels of Iranian expertise, with continuous sound training programmes. This is the reason why, unlike other government organs, there is still a certain level of skills in the industry – despite the departure or dismissal of the higher level experts. The Iranian oil industry, resembles a high quality car, driving at a fast speed, which has run out of fuel. It does not immediately come to a halt, but the slowdown and damages are visible. The eventual stop is inevitable, without expert help.

The biggest damage to the Iranian oil industry has been inflicted on the oilfields. Iranian engineers in the southern oilfields estimate an *irreversible* loss of one billion barrels between 1979 and 1981, equal to $34bn in 1981 prices. The losses accelerate as time goes by. If the regime did not change its attitude toward Iranian and foreign expertise, the losses might have increased further.

The sobering realities of the oil market have pushed the Iranian regime toward adopting more rational policies. By early 1984 some 1000 Italian, Japanese, British and German expatriates were working in the Iranian oil industry – a far cry from the original declarations that the Islamic regime would never again rely on foreign labour. This author is aware of at least a dozen American oil experts who have visited Iran at the invitation of the Iranian government. In the latter half of 1983, Iran's oil exports to the United States reached 180 000 barrels per day, a sixfold increase over the 1982 level and larger than Venezuela's exports to the US.

The regime in Iran has turned full circle – without giving up its political rhetorics. Like many other revolutionary or radical governments, the Iranian regime has learned to cope with capitalist realities of the free market. The signs of realism are apparent in many sectors of the economy – although perhaps not as much as in the oil sector. The oil revenues – the lifeblood of the country – necessitated dealing with the oil market in a fashion acceptable to the market. Iran was forced to learn that she had to change her policies and attitudes to benefit from the market. In doing so, Iran adopted oil policies which have moderated the very structure of the revolutionary government.

Part II
Politics of Dissent
and the Armed Forces

Part II
Politics of Dissent
and the Armed Forces

6 The Crowd in Iranian Politics, 1905–53*

ERVAND ABRAHAMIAN

George Rudé's observation that 'Perhaps no historical phenomenon has been so thoroughly neglected by historians as the crowd'[1] is especially true of the Middle East. While European journalists have invariably portrayed oriental crowds as 'xenophobic mobs' hurling insults and bricks at Western embassies, local conservatives have frequently denounced them as 'social scum' in the pay of the foreign hand, and radicals have often stereotyped them as 'the people' in action. For all, the crowd has been an abstraction, whether worthy of abuse, fear, praise or even humour, but not a subject of study.

This chapter has three aims. First, it will discuss the role of the crowd in modern Iran. The subject will be limited exclusively to political crowds, for to have included all public disturbances – such as bread riots, demonstrations against taxes, 'collective bargaining by riot', and communal conflicts – would have meant undertaking a task as formidable as that of Rudé: perhaps even more formidable, since the street has played a more important role in Iran than in England and France. Second, it will attempt to portray the 'faces in the crowd', comparing the social composition of pre-industrial demonstrations with those of the semi-industrial. Third, it will make some general comparisons with European public disturbances by contrasting the conclusions found here with those drawn by Rudé.

*World Copyright: The Past and Present Society, Corpus Christi College, Oxford, England. This chapter, 'The Crowd in Iranian Politics, 1905–53', is reprinted with the permission of the Society and the author, from *Past and Present: A Journal of Historical Studies*, no 41 (December 1968).

THE ROLE OF THE CROWD

Absolutism in nineteenth-century Persia had more in common with the Tudor form of government in England than with the 'oriental despotism' described by Karl Wittfogel.[2] The Qajar dynasty based its power not on a standing army, nor on an extensive bureaucracy, for it had neither, but on the readiness of the magnates, the *ulama* (religious authorities), the judges and the guild masters to enforce the Shah's will, and the disposition of the subjects to submit to his authority. Public dissatisfaction was channelled through petitions, meetings, strikes, and the taking of *bast* (sanctuary) in holy places, in the royal palace, and in telegraph offices where the protesters had access to the Shah. Those who took their protest outside these bounds were brought to heel not by the state machinery, but by subjects who were willing to enforce the royal writ.

The impact of the West undermined this form of government. Military defeats, the collaboration of the royal family with the imperial powers, the granting of concessions, monopolies, and privileges to 'the heathen', the inability of the government to help Persian merchants against European traders, the failure to protect home industry from foreign competition, and the introduction of the subversive doctrine of the 'Rights of Man' create an acute crisis of confidence. The Qajars ceased to be God's appointed protectors of His people and the bulwarks against social dissolution and instead became an ineffective and a corrupt family joining in the plunder and the destruction of the country.

The *ancien régime* was still intact at the end of the nineteenth century, although its foundations had received a drastic jolt in a major political earthquake during the Tobacco Crisis of 1891–2.[3] It began to crumble in 1905. The upheaval started in April with a petition drawn up in Tehran against the European official in charge of the Customs. When the petitioners failed to obtain a response from the government they called for a general strike and took sanctuary in the Abdul Azim Mosque outside the capital.[4] A week later the Shah agreed to examine the matter, and the assembly dispersed. However, he failed to take any meaningful action and consequently nine months later when the Governor of Tehran tried to lower the price of sugar by victimising a few prominent merchants, the events of April were repeated, but with greater intensity. A general strike was organised, one group of protesters took sanctuary in a mosque in Tehran, and a procession of two thousand made its way to Abdul Azim. They remained there until the Shah accepted their main demands: the removal of the European Customs official, the dismissal of the Governor, and the creation of a 'House of Justice'. Again they were fooled, for as soon as they returned to work the promises were forgotten. All seemed quiet on the surface until July 1906, when an attempt to arrest a prominent anti-government preacher sparked off another crisis, this time even more intense than the preceding one. A large and angry crowd tried to release the victim, the police fired, killed another cleric and fled in face of the threatening throng. For two days the streets of the capital were taken over by demonstrators while a thousand protesters took sanctuary in the holy city of Qum outside Tehran, and fifty fled to the British Legation. Within eight days this fifty had increased to fourteen thousand. This time the protesters were not satisfied with royal pledges and with a 'House of Justice'. They demanded a written constitution and an elected parliament. They camped on the Legation grounds for three weeks, until the Shah capitulated.

The revolutionaries had obtained their constitution, but they had not yet secured it on a firm foundation. The court had lost its absolute power, but it was not yet willing to accept the new order. The struggle between the two continued for the next three years, with the former attempting to preserve what it had won, and the latter striving to regain what it had lost. For both the streets were a vital weapon in the conflict. When the Shah procrastinated over the parliamentary elections, there were strikes and demonstrations in Tabriz for ten consecutive days. When he delayed over the signing of the final draft of the Fundamental Laws, there were protest rallies in most towns; in Tabriz armed volunteers prepared to defend the city while a multitude of twenty thousand vowed to 'remain away from work until the Laws were signed'.[5] Their strike continued for a whole month. When the conservatives in Tabriz tried to undermine the constitution, the radicals organised continuous mass demonstrations until their opponents left the city. When it became apparent that the Shah's chief minister was plotting against the radicals, a general strike was organised in Tehran demanding his resignation, and when he was murdered fifteen thousand gathered to pay their respects to the dead assassin and to pledge their support for the revolution.

In the meanwhile the court had not remained idle. It had mobilised its supporters, and by December 1907 it was able to show its strength by assembling ten thousand menacing royalists in the expansive Artillery Square at the centre of the capital. The constitutionalists responded by collecting outside the Parliament Building. For three days the two sides faced each other until the Shah dispersed his supporters. However, this was only a tactical retreat, for six months later these events were repeated, but with a different conclusion. First the Cossack Brigade, the only effective military force on the royalist side, bombarded the Parliament Building, and then a group of monarchists pillaged the Chamber. Martial Law was decreed and all public meetings, even Passion plays, were prohibited. The conservatives had won in the capital, but the capital was not the whole of Persia. In the provinces the struggle continued: protest meetings were organised, strikes were called, and arms were displayed. By July 1909, only thirteen months after the Shah's successful coup, active resistance reappeared even in the capital. A general strike was organised while a force of volunteers from Rasht and an army of tribesmen from Isfahan converged upon Tehran. The Shah was deposed and his throne was given to his twelve-year-old son. The Civil War was over.

During the next twelve years the conflict between the royalists and the constitutionalists was replaced by the struggle between the imperial powers and the Persian nationalists. The issues that brought the masses into the streets were no longer those dealing with constitutional rights, but those touching national integrity.[6] During the Civil War Russian troops had moved towards Tabriz to 'prevent anarchy'. Mass demonstrations throughout the country failed to stop their advance, and gradually during the next few years they expanded their occupied territory in the north. In the south, British troops arrived in October 1911 and proceeded to Shiraz to safeguard British 'lives and property'. The climax came in November 1911, when the Russian government sent an ultimatum to the Persian cabinet demanding payment for the army that had been despatched south and forbidding the cabinet to hire foreign advisers without the consent of the two great powers. The government was willing to submit, but the deputies, encouraged by massive demonstrations outside the Parliament Building, refused to capitulate. The ministers, caught between the devil and the deep blue sea, between the imperial powers and the angry public, chose the former. The volunteers and the tribesmen, who had saved the constitution only two years earlier, now forcibly closed parliament, sent the deputies packing, and declared Martial Law. However, nineteen months later parliament was reconvened because of 'threats' of demonstrations and strikes.[7] The country continued to be occupied throughout the First World War, and it was not until the Russian Revolution that the danger from the north ceased. Instead, the threat from the south increased. The Anglo-Persian Agreement of August 1919, drawn up by Lord Curzon, intended to reduce Persia into a vassal state. What destroyed these plans was the public, using its chief weapon, the streets. Curzon was informed by a British General in Persia: 'the feeling grew that Great Britain was a bitter foe who must be rooted out of the country at any cost'.[8] Again, the cabinet had fallen between two opposing forces, between the outraged public and the British who continued to occupy the country. This led to a twenty-month period of acute political instability during which the premiership changed hands nine times.

It was in this atmosphere of insecurity that an unknown colonel by the name of Reza Khan marched into the capital with a brigade of unpaid Cossacks and installed a new administration. He proceeded to calm the nation by annulling the Anglo-Persian Agreement, and to pacify Curzon by appearing as the 'man on horseback' who was going to save the country from Bolshevism. During the next three years he was the power behind the throne, making and unmaking deputies, ministers and premiers. By March 1924 he felt confident enough to attempt the elimination of the two-thousand-year-old monarchy and the establishment of a republic. A Bill proposing such a change was introduced into a packed parliament, and its smooth passing into law seemed guaranteed. Again, the public stepped into the scene and ruined the act. Some thirty thousand monarchists besieged the Parliament Building while a small group of republicans collected nearby.[9] The Bill was hastily withdrawn, and eventually a compromise was reached: the Qajar dynasty was constitutionally deposed, but instead Reza Khan became Reza Shah.

Between 1925 and 1941 the new king ruled with an iron hand. Basing his power upon the modern army and bureaucracy, both of which he vastly expanded by using the increasing revenues from oil, he was able to control not only the ministers, the deputies and the press, but also the public. 'Oriental despotism' was gradually introduced into Iran in these years in the form of westernisation and modernisation. As a result of this change, the crowd ceased to be a factor in politics. With the exception of two May Day Parades and three religious outbursts, all of which were promptly dispersed by the army, demonstrations disappeared from the scene and became an historical phenomenon belonging to the 'anarchistic' past.

The crowd returned with a vengeance after August 1941, when the Allied invasion crushed Reza Shah's army, forced him to abdicate in favour of his son, and freed the public of his absolutism. It was not until August 1953 that the court, supported by an army which had been re-equipped, re-trained and enlarged, was able to depose the cabinet, re-establish autocracy and again control the streets. In the intervening twelve years the crowd was a major element in politics, and although many tried to mobilise the masses and to use the streets as a weapon, only two organisations had notable success: the Tudeh Party and the National Front.[10]

The Tudeh Party's first major showing in the streets came on 21 October 1943, when it held a rally to celebrate its second anniversary and to start its election campaign for parliament. The response surprised most observers, perhaps even its organisers. The party press probably inflated the figures when it claimed that over 40 000 attended the meeting, but it did not exaggerate when it described the crowd as 'the largest in Tehran's history'.[11] In the same year, Tudeh demonstrators in Isfahan proved so 'decisive' that the Governor had to escape from the city.[12] In the autumn of 1944, the Tudeh Party organised meetings throughout the country to protest against a cabinet that had refused to negotiate an oil agreement with the Soviet Union. The United States' Minister in Tehran described the rally of 35 000 outside the Parliament Building as 'orderly'.[13] When the same government resigned, *The New York Times* correspondent reported that these mass demonstrations were 'largely responsible for the overthrow of the cabinet'.[14] The peak of Tudeh Party activity came in 1945–6. On Constitution Day, in August 1945, it held mass celebrations in over twenty towns. One non-Tudeh journalist estimated the crowd in the rally in Tehran to be over forty thousand.[15] In February 1946, it held a memorial service at the grave of Dr Arani, the 'spiritual father' of the party and a Marxist who had died in one of Reza Shah's prisons; fifteen thousand packed into the cemetery.[16] On May Day, parades were held in twenty cities: in Isfahan the meeting attracted 40 000; in Tehran 50 000;[17] and in Abadan, according to both *The Times* and the Tudeh Party press, 80 000.[18] All records were surpassed in October 1946, when 100 000 took part in its fifth anniversary celebrations in Tehran.[19]

The Tudeh Party was suppressed after December 1946, and the streets remained relatively deserted until the autumn of 1949, when the National Front began its campaign for free elections and for the nationalisation of the oil industry. The new era began in October 1949, when a small group of anti-court politicians, led by Dr Mossadeq, staged a minor demonstration in the palace grounds protesting against royalist interference in the parliamentary elections. Within a year Mossadeq had the support not only of a few politicians, but also of the

masses in the streets. As a militant nationalist and a staunch constitu-
tionalist, he was determined to bring the oil industry under Iranian
ownership and to force the Shah out of politics completely. After a
campaign of petitions, strikes, demonstrations and rallies, the National
Front forced a reluctant parliament and an antagonistic court to accept
Mossadeq as Premier and to pass the oil nationalisation bill into law.

Mossadeq had come to power by the streets; he continued to remain
in office by the same manner. Every time the opposition reared its head,
whether in parliament or in the court, he would make a direct appeal to
the public, and would rely on demonstrations to bring his opponents
'under his influence'.[20] The royalist Speaker of the House cried in
exasperation:

> Is this man a Prime Minister or a mob leader? What type of a
> statesman says, 'I will speak to the people' every time there is a
> political issue to be solved? I have always considered this man to be
> unreliable, but, in my wildest nightmares, I never imagined that an
> old man of seventy could be a demagogue, a rabble rouser who
> would not hesitate to surround the Parliament building with thugs.[21]

The ultimate use of the crowd came in July 1952, when the Shah
refused to discard his unconstitutional custom of appointing his own
nominees to head the War Ministry. Mossadeq resigned as premier,
and appealed directly to the people. His 'charisma' again proved
successful: National Front and Tudeh Party demonstrators poured
into the streets, and after three days of bloodshed, the Shah was forced
to recall Mossadeq and to hand over to him the Ministry of War. The
crowd had defeated not only the court and the politicians in parliament, but also the armed forces of the state.

The July 1952 uprising was the combined effect of both the National
Front and of the Tudeh Party, but the thirteen months following the
victory saw the gradual weakening of the former and the steady
strengthening of the latter. One Iranian observer wrote: 'if in the
nationalistic rallies before 1952 one-third of the participants were
Tudeh Party members, and two-thirds were National Front supporters,
after 1952 the roles were reversed'.[22] This trend was conspicuously
apparent at the anniversary of the July uprising. The two held their
own separate rallies in Parliament Square: the Tudeh Party meeting
attracted as many as a 100 000, and outnumbered the National Front,
for some of its supporters now turned to the Shah for protection
against the 'red menace'. On 18 August, the day before the generals

struck against Mossadeq, there were Tudeh Party demonstrations throughout the country, 'even in tuberculosis hospitals', while National Front supporters were nowhere to be seen.[24] On 19 August, the army cleared the streets of demonstrators while royalist groups systematically pillaged the homes and offices of their opponents.[25]

Thus, the crowd was not just a factor in politics; it was a major factor. It was instrumental in carrying through a Constitutional Revolution and in winning the Civil War, in struggling against the Imperial Powers and in defeating the Anglo-Persian Agreement of 1919, in preserving the Monarchy and in preventing the establishment of a Republic in 1924; and between 1941 and 1953 it was the main weapon of the Tudeh Party and of the National Front, providing them with a lever by which they could put pressure upon the decision-makers.

THE FACES IN THE PRE-INDUSTRIAL CROWD, 1905–25

In the traditional economy the *bazaar* was more than a market-place; it was the granary, the workshop, the bank and the religious centre of the whole society. It was there that landowners sold their crops, craftsmen manufactured their wares, traders marketed their goods, those in need of money raised loans, and it was there that businessmen built and financed mosques and schools. Moreover, the *bazaar* was not an amorphous mass of merchants, traders, craftsmen, moneylenders, pedlars and *mullas*, but was tightly structured into guilds. Each craft, each trade, and each unskilled occupation had its own organisation, hierarchy, traditions and sometimes even its own secret dialects.[26] In 1926 there were over a hundred different guilds for craftsmen, some seventy for traders, and forty for those without skills or financial resources.[27]

The Constitutional Revolution was a movement of the *bazaar*. Its rank-and-file came from the guilds, its financial backing from the merchants, its moral support from the religious authorities, and its theorising from a few westernised intellectuals.

The initial crisis of April 1905 was instigated by the moneylenders and the cloth-dealers of Tehran. The former were protesting at the failure of the Treasury to meet its financial obligations. The latter were criticising the policies of the European Customs Official. One of the organisers of the demonstration informed a newspaper correspondent that the merchants in the crowd were protesting against the new tariffs which favoured Russian companies against Persian traders: 'We must encourage home industry, even if its quality is not as good as foreign imports. The present trend of increasing imports will inevitably lead to the destruction of our industry and trade'.[28] The strike organised by these protesters closed down the cloth-dealers' market, the moneylenders' arcades and the inns. The procession that made its way from Tehran to Abdul Azim was led by a prominent shopkeeper and a scarf-seller. Their followers were members of the cloth-dealers' and of the moneylenders' guilds. They also had the support of the religious authorities, for they had circulated a photograph of the Customs Official masquerading in clerical clothes. Although the demonstrators failed to obtain their main objectives, five months later the Ministry of Finance conceded to the merchants an advisory council through which they could express their views on tariffs and customs.

The assembly that took sanctuary in a mosque in Tehran during December 1905 was formed of wealthy traders protesting against the bastinadoing of two prominent sugar merchants, one of whom had built three mosques. They were supported by the *bazaar*, which went on a general strike, and by a group of religious leaders, who took *bast* in Abdul Azim with their families and theology students. Their one-month stay in Abdul Azim was financed by a wholesale dealer and by a few prominent merchants.

The intensity of the crisis in July 1906 was generated by the active participation of all the craft and trading guilds, who until then had limited themselves mostly to organising sympathy strikes for the merchants and the *ulama*. The three-week protest of the fourteen thousand in the British Legation was organised by the Society of Guilds, a recently-formed association of all the guilds in the bazaar. Those participating in the crowd were mostly craftsmen and traders with their apprentices and journeymen. One observer wrote: 'I saw more than 1500 tents, for all the occupations, even the cobblers, the walnut-sellers, and the tinkers, had at least one tent'.[29] The British Minister reported to the Foreign Office:

The crowd of refugees was organised by the heads of the guilds, who took measures to prevent any unauthorised person from entering the Legation grounds . . . No damage of wilful character was done to the garden, although, of course, every semblance of a bed was trampled out of existence, and the trees still bear pious inscriptions cut in the bark. Discipline and order were maintained by the refugees themselves.[30]

The protesters permitted some students from the Technical College, the Military Academy, and from the Agricultural School to join their ranks. Outside the garden walls, in the streets of Tehran, the wives of the protesters held periodic demonstrations, and in Qom 1000 religious leaders and theology students staged a concurrent *bast*.

The importance of the *bazaar* in the revolutionary movement can be seen in the First Electoral Law of 1906.[31] The electorate was divided into six categories: the Princes and the Qajar tribe; the landowners; the nobles; the Doctors of Divinity and the theology students; the merchants; and the guilds. Tehran, with a total representation of sixty delegates, was apportioned four seats for the *ulama*, ten for the merchants, and thirty-two for the guilds. Of all the deputies elected to the First National Parliament, 26 per cent were guild members, 20 per cent were *ulama*, and 15 per cent were merchants.[32]

The *bazaar* continued to be the bastion of the constitutional movement throughout the Civil War. At critical periods it was regular practice for the religious leaders, the merchants and the guild masters to call for strikes and demonstrations, for the workshops, stores and markets to close, and for the bazaar community to congregate at the designated street square. Between July 1906 and July 1909 this procedure was carried out in Tabriz in response to at least eight separate issues. When the streets were too dangerous the protesters would go directly to a place of safety. After the bombardment of Parliament, the British Minister reported that in Isfahan a crowd of some 200 persons, 'mostly small shopkeepers', tried to enter the Legation grounds.[33] At one point in Kermanshah, 'the whole of the trade and employment of the town down to the porters', took sanctuary in the Telegraph Office.[34] When a show of force was needed, volunteers would arrive with their own rifles and ammunition, indicating that the hard-core militants were affluent enough to possess a weapon that was too expensive for the majority of the population.[35]

The social composition of these radical crowds is also reflected in the backgrounds of the revolutionaries who were executed in Tabriz.[36]

Among the thirty martyrs whose profession are known, there were five merchants, three religious leaders, three government employees, two shopkeepers, two arms dealers, two pharmacists, one carpenter, one tailor, one baker, one coffee-house keeper, one jeweller, one auctioneer, one musician, one journalist, one barber with his apprentice, one painter, one preacher and one school principal. Another four were hanged for being related to prominent revolutionaries: two of them were sons of a merchant who had organised the Social Democrat Party in Tabriz, and the other two were nephews of Sattar Khan, a horse-dealer who had become the commander of the local volunteer force.

The history of the Constitutional Revolution has been written mostly by liberal activists who have glossed over the popular appeal of the reactionary side, and have dismissed the royalist demonstrations as mobs of 'ruffians', 'hooligans', and of *lutis*.[37] Even the few writers who have admitted that the court had some popular appeal have failed to explain and account for the phenomenon.[38]

The royalist crowds can be explained by the presence of three different elements who sympathised with the reactionary cause. First, there were those who had economic ties with the court, and therefore had a vested interest in preserving the old order. Second, there were various religious leaders who feared that the constitution was only the first step towards 'anarchism', 'nihilism', 'equality', 'socialism', and the 'Babi heresy'.[39] The participation of this religious element converted the pro-Shah demonstrations into 'Islam and Shah' crowds. Third, there were occasionally 'the poorest of the poor', the *sans-culottes*, who had a strong dislike for the wealthy in the *bazaar* and who had gained nothing from this revolution of shopkeepers, moneylenders, and merchants.

The Qajars, with their vast family wealth and their generous income from the state, controlled a network of patronage. They granted gifts and pensions to their favourites, offices and salaries to their faithful administrators, and provided employment for thousands of household servants, stable-hands, labourers and craftsmen hired in the royal palaces, stables, farms and workshops. Moreover, many of the magnates, both in the capital and in the provinces, imitated the royal way of life. Thus, when the parliamentary regime, in its first year, proposed a budget which trimmed the court allocation, eliminated the revenue of the Crown Prince, cut off some 2000 pensioners and courtiers, and planned to collect the tax arrears of landowners, it threatened not only the social power of the royal family and the aristocracy, but also the economic livelihood of those in their service. The Household Treasury, which until the revolution had made a special point of meeting promptly all its commitments even when the State Treasury was in dire difficulties, now delayed over its remittances, and informed those on its pay-roll that their salaries and wages could not be paid because of the budget.[40] As was intended, these retainers flocked to royalist rallies. One veteran of the Civil War wrote:

In those days, a common method of abuse was to describe someone as having 'the character of a groom', or 'the mentality of a footman', for these and other lackeys had been pampered by the court, and as a result had become the meanest, the most backward, and the most fanatical advocates of absolutism in the whole population of Tehran.[41]

These retainers provided the reactionary demonstrations with a faithful nucleus; the presence of religious figures supplied them with an ideological content. Although most of the *ulama* had close ties to the mosques and the religious schools located in the *bazaar*, there were some whose salaries, fiefs and appointments linked them to the Shah and the state, rather than to the business community. Thus the religious hierarchy, even before the Constitutional Revolution, was sharply, but unevenly, divided between the few who expressed the views of the court and the many who sympathised with the *bazaar*. Initially, the latter by far outnumbered the former, but as the revolution progressed, and as the radicals made their aims clear – demanding the equality of all citizens, irrespective of their religion, the building of state schools independent of the religious establishment, and the imitation of the European mode of life – some of the liberal *ulama* deserted the cause for the safety of the old order: 'No Absolutism, No Islam'. In July 1907, one of the leading religious figures in Tehran declared himself against parliament, and together with some seventy theology students took sanctuary in Abdul Azim. Ahmad Kasravi, the anti-clerical historian of the Constitutional Revolution, writes: 'this was the first defection from the masses'.[42] Three months later, a larger group of 500 took *bast* in the same place, and declared that the religious law was in danger. Kasravi comments that this had a strong demoralising effect on the radicals, for the religious figures who led the protest were highly 'respected by the people'.[43]

The ranks of the 'Islam and Shah' crowds were also, at times, swelled by the participation of the 'lower classes'. Their role can be accounted for by the issues of bread and the right to vote, and by their allegiance to the orthodox Shiite faith.

In the early stages of the revolution the rebels had succeeded in attracting the poor to their side by championing the cause for cheaper bread, and by waging a war against the government over the question of high food-rices. Thus, the *petite bourgeoisie* of *bazaar* and the poor of the slums had been able to work together against the court. The two parted company when the regime changed, and when it became apparent that the new administration was no better than the old in its promise to lower food-prices. The breach was further widened by moneyed interests in parliament who advocated a free market in agricultural goods, and an end to the traditional policy of stabilising bread prices by government interference in the sale of wheat.[44] This conflict between the poor and the radicals over the issue of bread broke into the open in Tabriz. In June 1907, the pro-constitutional Town Assembly was besieged by an angry crowd demanding cheaper bread, and one of its prominent members, a wealthy corn-merchant, was lynched in the outburst. Two years later, the British Minister reported to the Foreign Office that the constitutionalists in Tabriz were in a 'critical situation', and that 'they feared a popular rising from the starving poor'.[45] Kasravi comments:

> In Tabriz during the Constitutional Revolution, as in Paris during the French Revolution, the *sans-culottes* reared their heads. The driving force of these men was towards anarchy. First, to overthrow the despotic order, and then to turn upon the rich and propertied classes. It was with the backing of these men that Danton and Robespierre rose to power. In Tabriz no Danton and Robespierres appeared, but if they had we also would have had a 'reign of terror'.[46]

In Isfahan such leaders did make a brief appearance. A peaceful procession of women presenting a petition to the President of the Municipality asking for cheaper bread, turned into a riot when they were given 'an obscene answer'. They chased him through the streets and eventually killed him, sacked the government offices, and opened the city prison. By the time the Governor ordered the troops to fire, the bread riot had turned into a political movement led by the 'reactionary clergy'.[47]

The revolution failed not only to lower the price of bread, but also to provide the poor with the right to vote. The Electoral Law disqualified all landowners who owned less than £200 worth of land, merchants who did not occupy 'a definite office', craftsmen and traders who did not belong to 'a recognised guild' and who were not in possession of a shop 'of which the rent corresponded with the average rents of the locality'.[48] In the first election in Tehran only one hundred and five guilds were permitted to participate.[49] The lowest-paid groups, such as coolies, carpet-weavers, dyers, bricklayers, labourers, muleteers and camel-drivers, were not recognised as constituting valid associations, even though many of them paid guild taxes. Moreover, these occupations not only gained nothing from the revolution, but also suffered economic hardship from the frequent general strikes which lowered the demand for labour and further raised prices. These factors caused strains in the movement, even during the early days of the revolution when no defections had yet occurred. One of the participants in the venture into the British Legation has written:

> I clearly remember the day when our Propaganda Section was informed that the reactionaries were sowing discontent among our ranks, especially among the young carpenters and the illiterate sawyers. The former were angry at being taken away from their work, and demanded to know what they had to gain from the whole escapade. The latter were even more difficult, for they refused to accept any logic. If these irresponsible groups had walked out of the Legation our whole movement would have collapsed, and there would have been an open conflict between the various guilds. Fortunately, we succeeded in persuading them to vow that they would continue to remain in sanctuary with the others.[50]

Religion also played a role in attracting the poor towards the royalist side. While the lower classes tended to be staunch advocates of the orthodox Shiite faith, many of the Westernised intellectuals in the constitutional movement held anti-clerical opinions, and some of the wealthy in the *bazaar* were tempted by the Sheikhi heterodoxy and the Babi heresy. Thus, when the royalist *ulama* raised the banner of 'Islam in Danger' they were able to undermine the mass basis of the constitutionalists.

The participation of the different groups in royalist demonstrations can be seen both in Tabriz and in Tehran. Throughout the Civil War, the city of Tabriz was geographically divided between the monarchists entrenched in the northern precincts, and the radicals holding out in the southern districts. The court and the orthodox *ulama* found their adherents in the poor areas of Davache and Sarkhab; the constitutionalists and the Sheikhi leaders drew their support from the prosperous parishes of Khiaban and Amirkhizi. The slum precincts were bulwarks of reaction, and centres of royalist riots; the middle-class regions were hotbeds of political discontent, and staging-grounds for radical rallies. In the capital, the social bases of monarchism could be seen at the Artillery Square meeting of December 1907. In the crowd, there were religious leaders with their theology students from the conservative Society of al-Mohammad, courtiers with their retainers, footmen, grooms, camel-drivers, muleteers and craftsmen from the royal palaces, labourers from the Shah's stud farm outside Tehran, *lutis* in the pay of the court, and the 'poorest of the poor' who had no reason to be on the same side as the wealthy constitutionalists of the *bazaar*.

With the invasion of Persia by the Russians in November 1911, the royalist and the radical demonstrators merged into one large nationalistic crowd. In Tabriz, the *bazaar* went on a general strike, and the conservative *ulama* led the protest procession. At Mashad, the Russian artillery bombarded the shrine in which 'an enormous mob' had taken sanctuary.[51] The *bazaar* at Enzeli closed down and when some Tsarist officers attempted to open the food stores, a pea-seller assaulted one of them with a stool and so sparked off a riot in which twenty-two civilians were killed. In Shiraz, the whole population refused to buy British goods, withdrew its savings from the Imperial Bank and declined to sell supplies to the British garrison. His Majesty's Minister complained that the attitude of the local *bazaar* was 'scandalous'.[52] The strongest revulsion against the invasion occurred in Tehran. During the parliamentary debate on the ultimatum, 300 women marched into the public gallery, 'with pistols under their skirts or in the folds of their sleeves',[53] and threatened to shoot any deputy who was willing to submit to the Russians. Outside, the Belgium-owned tramway was deserted on the mere suspicion that Russians had shares in the company; 'crowds of youths, students, and women filled the streets, dragging the occasional absent-minded passenger from the trams, smashing the windows of shops which still displayed Russian goods, and seeing that no one drank tea because it came from Russia'.[54] The crowds became even larger when parliament was forcibly closed, and the deputies had no alternative but to take their case to the streets. In Parliament Square, 'the largest rally up to that point in Persian history'[55] assembled shouting 'Independence or Death', while in the poorer sections of the city the *sans-culottes* took to the streets demanding cheaper bread. However, unarmed demonstrators were powerless against Western troops; extensive strikes and boycotts hurt the *bazaar* more than they scandalised the foreign representatives; and expressions of public outrage had no influence on imperial governments located in far-away St Petersburg and Westminster. The boycotts fizzled out, the rallies disappeared, and what resistance remained moved from the cities into the desert. It was not until after 1918, when St Petersburg had vanished and Westminster was in disarray, that the same nationalist crowds reappeared in Persia.

The conservative and the radical crowds regained their separate identities during the republican crisis of 1924, but they were not the same 'Islam and Shah' nor the same revolutionary rallies of the earlier period. The old faces were now demonstrating under a new banner, and fresh faces were shouting novel slogans.

Three days before the republican majority in parliament was scheduled to introduce a Bill proposing the abolition of the monarchy, some 8000 royalist guild-leaders in Tehran flocked to the main mosque in the *bazaar*, where they heard preachers extol the divine authority of the crown. Recent events in Turkey, where the elimination of the Sultanate had been preceded by the eradication of the Caliphate and by an attack upon the *ulama*, had convinced the religious establishment that Monarchy and Islam stood and fell together. In the mosque, a petition was drawn up, signatures were collected, and each of the guilds elected their own representatives to present their plea to parliament. The following day this delegation obtained a hearing in the House, but the hostile reception it received, and the rumours that its leader had been physically assaulted by one of the deputies, caused an uproar in the *bazaar*. On the morning the Bill was read, the stores and workshops closed, and an angry procession, shouting 'We want to keep the religion of our fathers, we don't want a republic, we are the people of the Koran, we don't want a republic', made its way from the *bazaar* to Parliament Square. The demonstrators broke through the police barriers and flooded the square, where they remained peaceful until one of the army officers used his horse-whip on a religious leader who had played an important role in the constitutional movement and was now advocating the conservative cause. Missiles were hurled, Reza Khan was punched, a number of heads were broken, and 1000 demonstrators were arrested, before the Speaker of the House intervened and informed the army commanders that it was an inalienable right of the people to express their views in the sanctuary of Parliament Square. Reza Khan disappeared into a back room with the religious and the *bazaar* leaders, and announced that since the nation had shown itself to be against republicanism he was willing to bow to the will of the people and to forget the whole issue. Two days later, he set off on a religious pilgrimage to prove to the public that he was a good Muslim.

While this huge demonstration of monarchists was sabotaging the republican plans, some 300 'red shirts' were staging a counter-demonstration on the other side of Parliament Square. This rally was sponsored by the secularist Modern Party and by the reformist Socialist Party, and was helped by the left-wing Trade Union Council and by the Communist Party. Those participating were mostly militants from the recently formed trades unions, teachers, telegraphists, pharmacists and workers from the printing shops, bakeries, public baths and shoe factories. They were joined by civil servants who had been given a day off in order to 'express' their republican sympathies.

This republican demonstration can be considered the first 'modern' crowd in Persian history, for it was organised by political parties and its participants were members of the new classes. The fact that it was so small, while its rival was so large, is an indication of the economic and social, as well as the political backwardness of the country in 1924.

THE FACES IN THE SEMI-INDUSTRIAL CROWD 1941-53

Two factors made the crowds of post-Reza Shah's Iran different from those of pre-Reza Khan's Persia. One was the changed social structure caused by modernisation and industrialisation. The other was the spread of socialism, an ideology that attracted not only the modern working class and segments of the new intelligentsia, but also the traditional wage-earners of the *bazaar*. The new class-consciousness alienated the journeyman from the master, the apprentice from the craftsman, the employee from the employer, and thus broke asunder the old guild-system which had proved so effective during the Constitutional Revolution and the republican crisis of 1924. In the past, there had been strains within the guilds, but they had been overcome; there had been desertions to the opposition, but they had occurred *en masse*, and the individual guilds had preserved their traditional unity between masters and journeymen. Now, the latter were no longer willing to follow the political policies of the former, and instead demanded 'associations which would represent their class interests'[56] and would protect their wages during periods of spiralling inflation. Many left the guilds and formed their own trade unions. Those who remained no longer complied with the wishes of their masters. Moreover, they were no longer swayed by the words of the *bazaar ulama*, who continued to be closely associated with the business community, but instead searched for more radical spokesmen. As a Western correspondent reported: 'the masses are being stimulated to think and act politically for the first time'.[57] A pre-electoral survey of the traditional guilds in Tehran, conducted for the Prime Minister in 1949, indicates that in few of them would the employers and the employees vote for the same candidates; in most, the former favoured the conservative and the religious contestants, while the latter preferred secular radicals sponsored by the Tudeh Party.[58]

The changing environment is strikingly apparent when one compares the somewhat ridiculous turnout of the republicans in 1924 with the mammoth rallies organised by the Tudeh Party. Their sizes were extremely disparate, but their social composition was not. Both were formed predominantly of the modern middle class and of the working class. Most Tudeh Party meetings were co-sponsored by the Central Council of United Trades Unions (CCUTU), which at its height in 1945, claimed a total membership of 400 000.[59] Although the CCUTU was, for the most part, an organisation for the modern working class – for factory, communications and oil workers – it also had many members among the traditional wage-earners in the *bazaar*, and numerous professional affiliates, such as the Union of Office Employees, the Union of Teachers, the Association of Lawyers, the Syndicate of Engineers and Technicians and the Society of Doctors.

At the memorial meeting by Arani's grave in 1946, which 15 000 attended, twenty-eight different organisations were represented: eleven factory syndicates, four trades unions from the bazaar, five student groups, The Society of Women, and seven party branches.[60] At the party's fifth anniversary rally, 100 000 participated. One reporter estimated that the bulk of the crowd (some 70 per cent) were wage-earners, and some 17 per cent were students, office-workers and intellectuals.[61] The proletarian element was even more pronounced in industrial centres such as Abadan and Isfahan. A British Labour MP who visited the oil fields wrote:

> With the spread of communistic literature, the ignorant, if I may say so, the semi-literate Persian workers began to listen to this ideology and for four years they organised themselves in an underground way into some sort of trade union entity ... and took into their ranks persons with communistic ideology as their leaders. On May Day, in 1946, the union came into the open, and paraded in Abadan 81 000 strong; 81 000 who are intent on serious business is an industrial force to be reckoned with.[62]

The fact that they were serious was apparent when 120 unions in the oil industry and twenty in the *bazaar*, involving a total of 50 000 workers, called a general strike. The oil company's attempt to break the strike by hiring blacklegs caused violent riots in Abadan and Ahwaz, where a total of 196 workers were killed.[63] The situation was similar in Isfahan, the Manchester of Iran. The local Tudeh Party derived its strength mostly from the trade-union movement in the nine large textile mills, which employed 11 000 workers, and to a lesser extent from the 35 000 wage-earners in the *bazaar*.[64] In July 1943, only eighteen months after the introduction of trade unionism into the city, the Iranian labour movement achieved its first major victory: the left-wing unions obtained the closed shop, the right to collective bargaining, and recognition from the mill-owners and from the government.[65] The next three years were, in the words of a British Army Officer who was stationed there, 'a struggle between management and labour'.[66] When the factory owners attempted to form their own 'yellow unions', the struggle was taken outside the plant gates into the streets, and the local authorities were faced with 'a workers revolt'.[67] The unions took over not only the factories and their granaries, but also the whole city. The propertied classes were horrified: 'the concept of private property has been violated'.[68]

The social composition of those attending Tudeh Party rallies is reflected in a published list of 167 demonstrators arrested after Peace Partisan meetings in Isfahan, Abadan and Shiraz, during 1951–2. Among the twenty-eight detained in Isfahan, there were twenty-three workers, one journalist, one office employee, one religious leader, one student and one unemployed worker.[69] Of the 110 imprisoned in Abadan, thirty-five were students from an industrial school, sixteen were workers' apprentices, fifteen were workers, fifteen were high-school students, another fifteen were office clerks, ten were teachers, three were engineers, and one was a tradesman.[70] In Shiraz twenty-nine were seized: ten students, six teachers, three workers, three journalists, three clerks, one artisan, one artist, one farmer and one agricultural labourer.[71]

The working class and a segment of the modern middle class formed the bases of the Tudeh Party. The traditional middle class of the *bazaar*, and the section of the modern middle class that considered the Tudeh Party too sympathetic towards the Soviet Union and too radical in its social policies constituted the bulk of Mossadeq's nationalist movement.

The first time Mossadeq proved that he had a following in the streets was in March 1945, after a speech in parliament in which he denounced his fellow members as 'corrupt' and described the House as 'a den of thieves'. The following day the whole *bazaar* came out on strike in his support, and a throng of law students carried him from his home to

Parliament Square. The police tried to prevent them entering the square, and in the process killed one student and wounded three others.[72]

During the oil crisis, Mossadeq's two pillars of strength within the National Front were the Iran Party and the Mojahedin Islam Society. The former had started as an engineers' association, and although it had transformed itself into a national party, it continued to be predominantly an organisation of the salaried middle class: engineers, lawyers, doctors, teachers and civil servants. Its rallies were well-attended by undergraduates, high-school students, and white-collar workers. The latter was a loosely-knit society of merchants and clergymen, and was led by Ayatollah Kashani, a prominent religious figure. His activities were centred in the mosques and the traditional schools of the *bazaar*, and his followers were mostly *mullas*, shopkeepers, traders and workshop owners. Even his proclamations calling for demonstrations made a special point of appealing directly to 'the merchants, the traders and the guilds of the *bazaar*'.[73] Kashani was, in fact, the heir of the early constitutional leaders, but with the significant difference that he had lost the traditional rank-and-file, the wage-earners of the old economy.

The three days that shook the world and returned Mossadeq to power were the combined effort of the Tudeh Party and of the National Front, both of whom were brought together by the government's declaration of war on communism and on *mullas* who meddled in politics. The revolt broke out in Tehran as soon as the news reached the *bazaar* that Mossadeq had been forced to resign. An angry assembly of 'traders and guildsmen' fought with the security forces and made their way to Parliament Square.[74] The National Front deputies, encouraged by this enthusiasm, called for a general strike. Their call was answered the following day by the *bazaar* where 'not a single store was open'.[75] At this point the Tudeh Party joined the movement, and summoned its supporters to join the strike and to demonstrate in the streets. The effectiveness of this proclamation was apparent when the whole economy ground to a halt and demonstrators took over most of the capital. An anti-communist intellectual wrote: 'it must be confessed that the Tudeh Party played the most important role in this popular uprising, and that the National Front held only a secondary part'.[76] After a whole day of bloodshed, at the end of which there were signs of defections within the army, the government capitulated.

The heaviest fighting had taken place in four different areas: in the *bazaar*, especially in the market places for the drapers, the vegetable-sellers and the metal crafts; in the working-class districts, near the factories in the eastern section of the city, and by the railway repair shops near the station, *en route* from the university to the Parliament Building, where a procession of students had been intercepted by the army; and by Parliament Square, the traditional rallying point for protest meetings. The worst slum districts in the southern parts of the city were significantly quiet.

A list of those declared missing as a result of these riots in Tehran provides a sample of the social background of the demonstrators. Among the twenty-six whose occupations are given, there were six factory workers, four pedlars, three drivers, three students, three apprentices, two craftsmen, one office-worker, one labourer, one farmer, one coffee-house keeper and one unemployed worker.[77]

The revolt in the provinces followed a similar course. It began with strikes and riots in the bazaars of most towns. It snowballed into general strikes and mass demonstrations as the working class joined the protest. In Abadan, the refinery workers stopped work, and a crowd of 40 000 assembled outside the Telegraph Office. In Isfahan, all the guilds marched in protest, but the textile workers were prevented from joining the demonstration by a network of machine guns placed around the mills.[78]

The semi-industrial environment was noticeably different from the pre-industrial, not only because of the expansion of the radical secular crowds, but also because of the shrinking of the 'Islam and Shah' riots. In 1924 the republicans had seemed ridiculous; now it was the monarchists who appeared pathetic. Through most of this period, the scene was devoid of any major royalist demonstrations, and it was not until 1 March 1953 that a public expression of sympathy for the Shah occurred in the streets of Tehran. On that day, the court leaked the rumour that the Shah was planning to go into exile because of Mossadeq. A throng of some 300 royalits, led by two prominent clergymen, and composed of axed army officers, soldiers dressed in civilian clothes and members of the Fascist Sumka Party, assembled outside the palace.[79] In the same week, a minor royalist riot broke out near the Prime Minister's home. The disturbance was led by some *chaqou-keshan,* the *lutis* of the earlier period.[80]

The monarchist demonstration that appeared on the last day of Mossadeq's administration was more substantial, but it was by no means a major crowd. One Western observer gave it a generous estimate of 3000.[81] Moreover, it played no important role in the crisis, but merely provided an acoustical diversion while the army officers executed their military *coup d'état*. The composition of this riot has been a subject of much political controversy. In the eyes of the present regime, the demonstrators represented 'the people'. To the opposition, they represented nothing but a handful of 'thugs' and reactionary *mullas* hired by the American CIA. The truth is closer to the second version than to the first, but with the important qualification that some individuals from the slum population also participated in the riot. It is not certain whether they were rewarded for their show of enthusiasm towards the Shah, but it is obvious that 'the poorest of the poor' had few ties with the radical movement, that they were hurt by the rising cost of living and the increasing unemployment; they were thus suitable material for the royalist *ulama* and *chaqou-keshan*. As the demonstrators made their way from the southern slum areas, through the *bazaar*, into the centre of the capital, they were joined by policemen and soliders,[82] and by 800 armed peasants who had been supplied with army rifles and had been transported to the city in military trucks.[83]

SOME COMPARISONS WITH THE EUROPEAN CROWD

Many of the conclusions drawn by Rudé for France and England also apply to Iran. In all three societies, the crowd was a means, often the only means, of expression for the masses. Before the Constitutional Revolution, demonstrations were recognised forms of protest and accepted methods for checking the arbitrary powers of the monarch. In 1906 the propertied classes obtained the vote, but the vast majority of the population remained outside the political system. Universal male suffrage was introduced in 1919, but because of the economic relations existing between the landowners and the peasants, and because of increasing government interference in the voting, elections did not guarantee true representation. Between 1919 and 1953, 57 per cent of the deputies were landowners, 20 per cent were senior bureaucrats, 10 per cent were wealthy merchants, and only one per cent were from the 'lower classes'.[84] As far as the discontented were concerned, the right to vote in elections was meaningless, while the right of vote with their feet in the streets was all-important.

Similar faces appeared in the crowds of all three societies. Those who attacked the Bastille, took part in the Gordon Riots, and participated in political rallies in Iran, were not riff-raff, thieves, criminals, vagrants nor the professionally unemployed, but were sober and even 'respectable' members of the community. During the pre-industrial period in Iran, merchants, shopkeepers, traders, craftsmen, apprentices, journeymen, clergymen and students from the traditional schools formed the bulk of the crowd. As the country industrialised, factory workers, clerks, teachers, undergraduates and high-school students joined the ranks. In Tehran, as in Paris and London, the main centres of radical activity were not the slums, but the regions of industry, crafts and trade.

In both Europe and Iran, the conservative and the religious elements – the 'Church and King' riot and the 'Islam and Shah' demonstration – shrank as society developed and as secular radicalism took the place of loyalism and orthodoxy.

In Iran, as in Europe, bread shortages and high prices often acted as a stimulus in driving people into political movements that were not solely concerned with economic issues. The public disturbances of 1905–13 and of 1919–21 took place in years of bad harvests and bread shortages; those of 1941–6 and of 1951–3 in periods of acute inflation. Only the crisis of 1924 was purely ideological.

Moreover, in all three countries, crowds were not fickle, irrational nor blood-thirsty except when faced with starvation. On occasions when rioters indulged in destruction, their violence was directed more at property than at people. Blood was shed frequently by the authorities, rarely by the demonstrators.

So much for the similarities. Three main differences can be seen. First, public disturbances in Iran broke out only in the towns, while in Europe they occurred as frequently in the villages as in the cities. Second, the Iranian crowd was more successful than its French and English counterparts. Third, in Europe there was a transition from riot to strikes, organised demonstrations and rallies, as the economy developed; in Iran this change did not take place, for general strikes, public meetings and organised protests were as much features of the pre-industrial economy as of the semi-industrial society.

Rural tranquillity can be explained by peasant passivity. During the turbulent years of 1906–13, when there were frequent disturbances in the towns, there were only three recorded incidents of peasant ferment. Near Rasht peasants refused to pay taxes and took sanctuary in the town mosque.[85] Near Talish they attacked the house of the Governor.[86] In one mass action against heavy taxation, they captured the town of Yazd.[87] In the twelve years between 1941 and 1953, there were only four incidents of rural agitation of any significant size. In 1941, after the flight of the authorities from the advancing Soviet army, a number of villages in Azerbaijan appropriated the grain set aside for their landowners.[88] Near Tabriz, in 1945, a mob of peasants lynched a landlord.[89] In August 1946, there were widespread fears of a 'war breaking out between peasants and their masters' in the areas south of Tehran.[90] And in 1952–3 armed villagers in Kurdestan fought their landowners.[91] However, these incidents were rare; the peasant continued to be apathetic, his political activity limited to being shepherded to the polls to vote for the local magnates. Political scientists and historians have failed to explain this phenomenon of rural passivity. The answer will probably be found by social psychologists.

Rudé gives two factors which determine whether the crowd succeeds or fails: the attitude and strength of the armed forces, and the policy of the ruling class. In Iran, the crowd, much of the time, functioned in favourable conditions. Until Reza Shah, the troops at the disposal of the government were few and unrealiable. In the crisis of July 1906, when 14 000 had taken sanctuary, the Commander of the Tehran regiments made the 'fatal announcement' that his troops would not fight against the protesters.[92] As one observer noted: 'what can the Shah do with his unarmed, unpaid, ragged starving soldiers, in the face of the menace of a general strike or of a riot'.[93] After Reza Shah, the army was better armed and paid, but it was not always willing to obey commands. During the general strike in the oil industry in 1951, the local soldiers refused to fire.[94] In the dramatic events of July 1952, there were dissensions in the ranks. Moreover, demonstrators often received political help. During the Constitutional Revolution, the British and even some courtiers gave them protection. In 1924, the Speaker of the House intervened on their behalf. And throughout the period between 1941 and 1953, many politicians had a vested interest in preserving the freedom of the streets, for they realised that the suppression of the crowd would result in the re-establishment of court autocracy. When these factors were missing, the Iranian crowd proved as ineffective as its European counterparts.

Riots are the product of spontaneity; strikes, rallies and demonstrations that of organisational premeditation. In Europe, through the long duration between the decay of the traditional guilds and the rise of modern trade unionism, there were few organs that could represent popular interests and mobilise the working man into effective pressure-groups. Thus, public dissatisfaction was expressed often through outbursts of unplanned rioting, rarely through organised protest. In Iran, the transitional period between the decay of the guilds and the birth of unionism did not take centuries, but a mere fifteen years. As a result, the crowd in Iran, even more so than in Europe, was rarely a 'mob', but was usually a demonstration or a rally.

NOTES

1. G. Rudé, *The Crowd in History, 1730–1848* (New York, 1964), p. 3.
2. Karl Wittfogel, *Oriental Depotism* (New Haven, 1957).
3. For the Tobacco Crisis see N. Keddie, *Religion and Rebellion in Iran* (London, 1966).
4. Information on the crowds during the Constitutional Revolution and the Civil War has been obtained from: A. Kasravi, *A History of the Iranian Constitution* (in Farsi) (Tehran, Chap-i Amir Kabir, 1961); A. Kasravi, *An Eighteen-Year History of Azerbaijan* (in Farsi) (Tehran, Chap-i Amir Kabir, 1961); Y. Doulatabadi, *An Autobiography* (in Farsi) (Tehran: Chap-i Chahar, 1961), vols i and ii; M. Malekzadeh, *A History of the Constitutional Revolution in Iran* (in Farsi) (Tehran, Ketab-i Khaneh-i Suqrat, 1962), vols. ii and iii; the newspaper *Hablu'l Matin*; M. Khurasani, *The Genesis of the Constitution in Iran* (in Farsi) (Meshed, Chapkhaneh-i Khurasan, 1953); M. Taherzadeh, *The Revolt in Azerbaijan during the Constitutional Revolution* (in Farsi) (Tehran, Sherat-i Eqbal); British Government, *Correspondence Respecting the Affairs of Persia, December 1906–October 1913* (London, HMSO May 1911–April 1914).
5. Kasravi, *A History of the Iranian Constitution*, p. 336.
6. Information on the crowds during the struggle against the Imperial Powers has been obtained from: the newspaper *Kaveh*; British Government, *Persian Affairs*; *Documents on British Foreign Policy, 1919–39*, 1st ser. (London, 1963), vols iv and xiii; M. Shuster, *The Strangling of Persia* (New York, 1920).
7. British Government, *Correspondence Respecting Affairs of Persia*, vol. iii, no. 2, p. 134.
8. *Documents on British Foreign Policy*, xiii, p. 586.
9. Information on the crowds during the Republican Crisis have been obtained from: H. Makki, *A Twenty Year History of Iran* (in Farsi) (Tehran, Chapkhaneh-i Majlis, 1945) vol. ii, pp. 319–49; H. Mustaufi, *An Account of My Life* (in Farsi) (Tehran, Ketab-i Furush-i 'Alami, 1947) vol. iii, part 2, pp. 410–30; Doulatabadi, *An Autobiography* vol. iv; M. Hedayat, *My Memoirs* (in Farsi) (Tehran, Ketab Furush-i Zavar), p. 363.
10. Information on the crowds of the period from 1941 until 1953 has been obtained from newspapers of diverse political views. Those most relied upon have been: *Mardom, Zafar, Rahbar, Ettelaat, Keyhan, Jebeh, Democrati- Iran, Ra'ad Emruz, Emruz va Farda.*
11. *Mardom*, 22 October 1943.
12. N. Fatemi, *Oil Diplomacy* (New York, 1954) p. 216.
13. US, Dept. of State, *Papers Relating to the Foreign Relations of the US* (Washington, D.C.: US Government Printing Office) vol. v, 1944, p. 461.
14. *The New York Times*, 17 March 1945.
15. *Tofeq*, quoted in *Rahbar*, 6 August 1945.

16. *Mardom*, 2 February 1946.
17. *Zafar*, 3 May 1946.
18. Ibid, and *The Times* (London) 30 July 1946.
19. *Rahbar*, 8 October 1946.
20. *Ettelaat-i Haftegi*, 20 June 1951.
21. M. Fateh, *Fifty Years of Iranian Oil* (in Farsi) (Tehran, Sherkat-i Saham-i Char, 1956) p. 58p.
22. Ibid, p. 653.
23. *The New York Times*, 23 July 1953.
24. Ibid, 19 August 1953.
25. Information on the royalist crowd of 19 August 1953 has been obtained mostly from: R. Cottam, *Nationalism in Iran* (Pittsburg University Press, 1964) pp. 38, 155, 226; The Central Committee of the Tudeh Party, *Concerning 19 August* (in Farsi) (1953); Aresh, *The Revolution for the Monarchy* (in Farsi) (Tehran, Chapkhaneh-i Majlis, 1954).
26. M. Hussein-Khan, *The Geography of Isfahan* (in Farsi) (Tehran, Tehran University Press, 1963).
27. Iranian Government, *Parliamentary Debates*, The Sixth Majlis, The Fortieth Meeting, 11 December 1926.
28. *Hablu'l Matin*, 19 June 1905.
29. Quoted in Kasravi, *The History of the Iranian Constitution*, p. 110.
30. British Government, *Persian Affairs*, i, no. 1, p. 4.
31. The Electoral Law of 1906, E. Browne, *The Persian Revolution of 1905–9* (Cambridge University Press, 1910) pp. 354–61.
32. Z. Shajeehi, *The Members of Parliament* (in Farsi) (Tehran, Tehran University Press, 1965) p. 176.
33. British Government, *Persian Affairs*, 1, no. 2, p. 46.
34. Ibid, i, no. 1, p. 27.
35. Taherzadeh, *Revolt in Azerbaijan*, vi, p. 47.
36. Information has been obtained from: Kasravi, *An Eighteen-Year History of Azerbaijan*; Taherzadeh, *Revolt in Azerbaijan*, Malekzadeh, *Constitutional Revolution*, vol. vii.
37. *Lutis* were muscular athletes from the Houses of Strength that existed in the various precincts. Many of them worked as pedlars, and some were prosperous enough to own shops, but most were willing to put their physical abilities in the service of an employer, so long as their assigned task did not conflict with their strong religious beliefs. They were to be found on both sides during the Civil War.
38. M. A. Bahar, *A Short History of Political Parties* (in Farsi) (Tehran, Chap-i Rangin, 1943) writes: 'During the revolution, the upper and the lower classes supported absolutism, and only the middle class advocated constitutionalism' (p. 2).
39. A proclamation of the conservative *ulama* published in Karavi, *A History of the Iranian Constitution*, p. 415.
40. Ibid, p. 488; Taherzadeh, *Revolt in Azerbaijan*, iv, p. 59; Malekzadeh, *Constitutional Revolution*, ii, p. 93.
41. Taherzadeh, *Revolt in Azerbaijan* iv, p. 59.
42. Kasravi, *A History of the Iranian Constitution*, p. 226.
43. Ibid, p. 386.

44. *Hablu'l Matin*, 23 September 1907.
45. Great Britain, i, no. 2, p. 97.
46. Kasravi, *A History of the Iranian Constitution*, p. 355.
47. Great Britain, ii, no. 2. p. 65.
48. The Electoral Law of 1906, Browne, p. 356.
49. *Hablu'l Matin*, 12 November 1906.
50. Khurasani, *Genesis of the Constitution*, p. 50.
51. Great Britain, ii, no. 4, p. 88.
52. Ibid, ii, no. 3, p. 117.
53. Shuster, *The Strangling of Persia,* p. 198.
54. Ibid, p. 184.
55. 'Demonstrations and Meetings in Iran' (in Farsi), *Ettelaat-i Haftegi*, 26 April 1951.
56. A quotation from a trade union pamphlet, *Rahbar*, 31 January 1944.
57. *The New York Times*, 17 March 1945.
58. 'An Electoral Survey' (in Farsi) *Khandani-ha*, vol. xvi, no. 53, 23 January 1966.
59. World Federation of Trade Unions, 'Report on Iran', *Report on the Activities of the WFTU* (1949) pp. 105–70.
60. *Mardom*, 1 February 1946.
61. *Rahbar*, 6 October 1946.
62. J. Jones, 'My Visit to the Persian Oil Fields', *Royal Central Asian Journal* (January 1947) vol. xxxiv, part 1, p. 60.
63. *Zafar*, 15 June 1946.
64. *Rahbar*, 4 March 1945.
65. *Rahbar*, 18 June 1944.
66. Major E. Sykes, 'Isfahan', *Journal of the Central Asian Society*, xxxiii (January–October 1946) p. 312.
67. Fatemi, *Oil Diplomacy*, p. 216.
68. A quotation from Sheif-Pour Fatemi, a local magnate, *Ra'ad Emruz*, 2 May 1944.
69. *Besuyeh-i Ayandeh*, 15 October 1951.
70. *Besuyeh-i Ayandeh*, 2 March 1952.
71. *Besuyeh-i Ayandeh*, 21 April 1952.
72. H. Key-Ostovan, *The Politics of Negative Equilibrium in the Fourteenth Parliament* (in Farsi) (Tehran, Taban Press, 1946) i, p. 290.
73. *Etelaat*, 10 July 1952.
74. *Etelaat*, 19 July 1952.
75. *Etelaat*, 20 July 1952.
76. A. Arsanjani, *The Thirtieth of Tir* (in Farsi) (Tehran, Chapkhanehi Atesh, 1956) p. 4.
77. *Etelaat*, 30 July 1952.
78. *Bakhtar-i Emruz*, 20 July 1952.
79. *Etelaat-i Haftegi*, 5 March 1953; *Besuyeh-i Ayandeh*, 5 March 1953.
80. Ibid.
81. S. Margold, 'The Streets of Tehran', *The Reporter*, 10 November 1953, p. 15.
82. Ibid.
83. *Etelaat-i Haftegi,* 28 August 1953.

84. Shaje'ehi, *Members of Parliament*, p. 177.
85. Great Britain, i, p. 26.
86. Ibid, p. 43.
87. Ibid, p. 144.
88. J. Moose, 'Memorandum on Azerbaijan' (unpublished report sent to the State Department in October 1941, filed in the State Department, no. 740.0011 EW).
89. H. Faboud, *L'Evolution Politique de l'Iran* (Lausane, 1957) p. 206.
90. *Khandaniha*, 13 September 1946.
91. *Etelaat-i Haftegi*, 19 September 1952.
92. British Government, *Persian Affairs*, i, no. 1, p. 4.
93. Browne, *Persian Revolution*, p. 137.
94. *Etelaat-i Haftegi*, 19 April 1951.

7 The Guerrilla Movement in Iran, 1963–77*

ERVAND ABRAHAMIAN

One crisp morning in the winter of 1971, thirteen young Iranians armed with rifles, machine guns, and hand-grenades, attacked the gendarmerie post in the village of Siakal on the edge of the Caspian forests. Killing three gendarmes, they tried to release two colleagues who had been detained a few days earlier, and, failing to find the prisoners in the gendarmerie post, escaped into the rugged mountains of Gilan. Unknown both to the participants and to the outside world, this famous 'Siakal incident' sparked off eight years of intense guerrilla activity and inspired many other radicals, Islamic as well as Marxist, to take up arms against the Pahlavi regime. But despite the importance of the guerrilla movement, its history is being rapidly distorted, misused and misinterpreted: partly because almost all the original leaders have been killed, partly because their followers are more interested in making history than in writing history, and partly because the new regime, like its predecessor, is eager to dismiss and denounce the revolutionaries as 'terrorists', 'atheists' and 'foreign agents'.

Between February 1971, when the Siakal incident occurred, and October 1977, when the Islamic Revolution began to unfold in the streets of Tehran, the regime, notably its secret police SAVAK, killed 341 members of guerrilla organisations and political parties advocating armed struggle.[1] 177 of these died in gun battles; ninety-one were executed – some without trial, others after secret military tribunals; forty-two were tortured to death; fifteen 'disappeared'; seven committed suicide to avoid capture; and nine were shot 'trying to escape'. After the revolution the jailers confessed that they had killed these nine in

*Ervand Abrahamian, 'The Guerrilla Movement in Iran, 1963–1977', *MERIP Reports*, No 86 (March/April, 1980) pp. 3–15. *MERIP Reports*, Box 1247 (New York, NY 10025, USA).

cold blood. In these years the regime also tortured to death seven political prisoners not associated with armed organisations; two prominent left-wing intellectuals who were executed for 'plotting to kidnap the royal family'; two clerical leaders, two members of the communist *Tudeh* Party, and one activist from the Confederation of Iranian Students in Europe. Countless others were imprisoned and tortured for suspected 'anti-state' activities. In his annual report for 1974–5, Martin Ennals, Secretary-General of Amnesty International, declared that 'the Shah of Iran retains his benevolent image despite the highest rate of death penalties in the world, no valid system of civilian courts, and a history of torture which is beyond belief'.[2]

In terms of class background, almost all the guerrillas came from the ranks of the young intelligentsia. Guerrilla organisations and next-of-kin have provided information on the occupation of 306 of the 34[ ] dead. Of the 306, 280 (91.5 per cent) can be described as members of the intelligentsia. They included 139 college students, thirty-six engineer[s], twenty-seven teachers, twenty office employees, twenty professiona[l] (such as architects, professors, accountants, lawyers, and librarians[ ]), fourteen housewives (all married to university graduates), eight hig[h] school students, six doctors, five intellectuals (poets, novelists, an[d] translators), and five college graduates conscripted into the army. Th[e] other 26 (8.5 per cent) consisted of twenty-two factory workers, thr[ee] shopkeepers, and one low-ranking clergyman. At time of death, on[ly] ten of the 306 were over 35 years old. Among the total 341 dead, the[re] were thirty-nine women – they included fourteen housewives, thirte[en] college students, nine schoolteachers, two doctors, and one off[ice] employee.

The growth of the guerrilla movement in no way correlated with a[ ] decline in the economy. On the contrary, the movement developed a[t a] time of middle-class prosperity, rising salaries, employment opportu[ni]ties for college graduates, and a sixfold expansion in univers[ity] enrolment. In fact, almost all the dead guerrillas had been able to go [to] university either because they had won state scholarships or becau[se] their upwardly mobile middle-class families could afford to pay t[he] tuition fees. They took up arms as a result of social, moral and politi[cal] indignation, rather than of economic deprivation.

The guerrillas can be divided into five political groupings:

1. The *Sazman-i Cherik-ha-yi Fedd'-i Khalq-i Iran* (The Organisati[on] of the Guerrilla Freedom Fighters of the Iranian People), known as the Marxist *Fedayi*.

2. The *Sazman-i Mojahedin-i Khalq-i Iran* (The Organisation of the Freedom Fighters of the Iranian People) – generally referred to as the Islamic *Mojahedin.*

3. The Marxist offshoot from the *Sazman-i Mojahedin-i Khalq-i Iran.* From 1975 to 1979, this organisation was known as the Marxist *Mojahedin.* After the revolution, it adopted the title of *Sazman-i Paykar dar Rah-i Azad-i Tabaqeh-i Kargar* (The Fighting Organisa- tion on the Road to Liberating the Working Class). It is now known simply as *Paykar* (Battle).

4. Small Islamic organisations often limited to one town – such as the *Gorueh-i Abu Zahr* (The Abu Zahr Group) in Nahavand, *Gorueh-i Shi'-iyan-i Rastin* (The Group of True Shi'is) in Mashad, *Gorueh-i Allah Akbar* (The Allah Akbar Group) in Isfahan, and the *Gorueh-i Al-Fajar* (The Al-Fajar Group) in Zahedan.

Small Marxist organisations, including independent groups, such as the *Sazman-i Azadibakhsh-i Khalq-ha-yi Iran* (The Organisation for the Liberation of the Iranian Peoples), the *Gorueh-i Lurestan* (The Lurestan Group), *Sazman-i Arman-i Khalq* (The Organisation for the People's Ideal), and the *Razmandegan-i Azad-i Tabeqeh-i Kargar* (The Fighters for the Liberation of the Working Class), as well as cells associated with such political parties as the *Hizb-i Demokrat-i Kurdestan-i Iran* (The Kurdish Democratic Party of Iran), the pro- Chinese *Sazman-i Inqelab-i Hizb-i Tudeh* (The Revolutionary Orga- nisation of the *Tudeh* Party), and the New Left-styled *Gorueh-i Ittehad-i Komunistha* (The Group of United Communists). Mor- eover, in 1976–9 some *Fedayis* affiliated with the *Tudeh* Party, which is the orthodox, pro-Soviet Communist Party of Iran.

Of these five categories, the Marxist *Fedayi* and Islamic *Mojahedin* re by far the largest. Between 8 February 1971 and October 1977, l guerrillas lost their lives (see Table 7.1); of these 172 (50.4 per cent) onged to the *Fedayi*; 73 (21.4 per cent) to the Islamic *Mojahedin*; 30 7 per cent) to the Marxist *Mojahedin*; 38 (11.3 per cent) to the small irxist groups; and 28 (8.2 per cent) to the small Islamic groups.

RIGINS (1963–71)

ne origins of the guerrilla movement reach back to the summer of 1963, when the regime used massive violence to crush peaceful demonstrations organised by the opposition. The Shah's determination to use massive force, the army's willingness to shoot down thousands of unarmed demonstrators, and SAVAK's eagerness to root out the underground networks of the *Tudeh* and the National Front, all combined to compel the opposition, especially its younger members, to question the traditional methods of resistance – election boycotts, general strikes, and street demonstrations. Not surprisingly, in the next few years, militant university students formed small secret discussion groups to explore new methods of resistance, to translate the works of Mao, Che Guevara and Fanon, and to learn from the recent experiences of China, Vietnam, Cuba and Algeria. In the words of one such group: 'The bloody repression of 1963 was a major watershed in Iranian history. Until then, the opposition had tried to fight the regime with street protests, labour strikes, and underground parties. The 1963 bloodbath, however, exposed the bankruptcy of these peaceful methods. After 1963, militants, irrespective of their ideology, had to ask themselves the question 'What is to be done?' The answer was clear: 'guerrilla warfare'.[3]

This period of study produced a number of small Marxist and Islamic groups advocating armed struggle, but most of them were dismantled by SAVAK before they could initiate any armed actions. In 1965, fifty-five youngsters, many of them high-school students, were arrested in Tehran for buying weapons and forming a secret *Hizb-i Mellat-i Islami* (Party of the Nation of Islam). In 1966, another group of religious students were picked up for collecting money to buy arms and forming a *Jebe'eh-i Azadibakhsh-i Mell-i Iran* (The Front for the Liberation of Iran). In 1969, some 200 *Tudeh* members, dissatisfied with their party's decision to avoid political violence, formed a *Sazman-i Inqelab-i Komunist-ha-yi Iran* (The Revolutionary Organisation of Iranian Communists) and robbed a bank in Isfahan to finance future guerrilla operations. The whole group, however, was arrested before it had the chance to launch any such operations. Similarly, in 1979 eighteen young professors and university students – some of whom had been in the *Tudeh* or in the *Jam'ieh-i Sosyialistha* (Society of Socialists) the Marxist wing of the National Front – were arrested as they tried to cross the Iraq border to join the PLO. The sentences meted out to these activists were relatively mild, since none had physically assaulted the authorities. The rank-and-file members received prison terms varying from one to ten years, the leaders' terms varying from ten years to life imprisonment. The flood of death sentences was to come soon with the emergence of the *Fedayi* and the *Mojahedin*.

THE FEDAYI

The *Fedayi*, which did not adopt its name until March 1971, was formed of three separate groups that traced their origins back to the mid-1960s.[4] The first group had been established as early as 1964 by five Tehran University students: Bezhan Jazani, 'Abbas Sourki, 'Ali Akbar Safa-i Farahani, Muhammad Ashtiyani, and Hamid Ashraf. Jazani, the circle's central figure, was a student of political science and had been in and out of prison since the mid-1950s. Born in 1937, he had completed high school in his home town, Tehran, and had been active in the youth section of the *Tudeh* before leaving the party and forming his own secret group. In later years, he wrote for the *Fedayi* a series of pamphlets including *Nabard Ba Diktator-i Shah* (*Struggle Against the Shah's Dictatorship*), *Tarikh-i Siy Saleh-i Iran* (*Thirty Year History of Iran*), and *Chehguneh Mobarezeh-i Maslehaneh Tudeh-i Meshavad* (*How to Transform the Armed Struggle into a Mass Struggle*). Sorouki, also a student of political science and a former *Tudeh* member, had grown up in Mazandaran before moving to Tehran to enter the university. Safa'i Farahani, a student of engineering, was a native of Gilan but had met the others in Tehran University. In later years, he wrote for the *Fedayi* a handbook entitled *Ancheh Yek Inqelabi Bayad Bedanad* (*What a Revolutionary Must Know*). Ashtiyani, the oldest, was a student of law who had been born in Tehran in 1934. He had completed his military service and was therefore able to train his colleagues in the use and upkeep of light arms. Finally, Ashraf, the youngest among them, was a student of engineering. Born in Tehran in 1946, he joined the Society of Socialists as a high-school student, and in 1964 entered the university where he met the others. All five, as well as many other students who joined them, came from middle-class homes.

Three years after the group was formed, SAVAK infiltrated it and arrested fourteen members, including Jazani and Sourki. Ashraf, however, managed to escape and gradually found enough recruits to keep the group alive. Meanwhile, Farahani and Ashtiyani escaped to Lebanon, established contact with the *Tudeh*, and, after spending two years with al-Fatah, returned home to rejoin Ashraf.[5] Jazani, Sourki, and five others were kept in prison until April 1975, when they were shot 'trying to escape'. Although Jazani did not actually organise the *Fedayi*, he can still be considered its 'intellectual founder'.

The second group that formed the *Fedayi* was led by two university students who had come to Tehran from Mashad. Mas'oud

TABLE 7.1   *Dead guerrillas*

	Fedayi	Islamic Marxist Mujahidin	Other Mujahidin	Other Marxist	Islamic
Killed fighting	106	36	16	11	8
Executed	38	15	10	12	16
Tortured to death	10	18	1	9	4
Missing	6	1	1	6	
Suicide	5	1	1		
Murdered in prison	7	2			
Total	172	73	30	38	28

TABLE 7.2   *Occupations of guerrillas who died*

	Fedayi	Islamic Mujahidin	Marxist Mujahidin	Other Marxist	Other Islamic	Total
College students	73	30	15	14	7	139
High school students	1				7	8
Teachers	17	5	3	1	1	27
Engineers	19	14	2	1		36
Office workers	7	4		1	8	20
Doctors	3			3		6
Intellectuals	4			1		5
Other professionals	11	6	2	1		20
Housewives	8	3	2	1		14
Conscripts	5					5
Shopkeepers		2			1	3
Clergymen		1				1
Workers	12	2	1	7		22
Not known	12	6	5	8	4	35
Total	172	73	30	38	28	341
(Women)	(22)	(7)	(8)	(2)	(0)	(39)

Ahmadzadeh, the main personality, came from an intellectual family well-known in Mashad for its support of Mossadeq and its opposition to the Pahlevis since the mid-1920s. While at high school in Mashad, Ahmadzadeh created an Islamic Student Club and participated in religious demonstrations against the regime. But while studying mathematics in Aryamehr (Industrial) University in Tehran, he turned towards Marxism, and in 1967 formed a secret circle to discuss the works of Che Guevara, Debray and Carlos Marighella, the Brazilian communist who developed the theory of urban guerrilla warfare. In 1970, Ahmadzadeh wrote one of the main theoretical works of the *Fedayi*, entitled *Mobarezeh-i Aslehaneh: Ham Estrategi Ham Taktik* (*Armed Struggle: Both a Strategy and a Tactic*). Amir Parvez Poyan, his close colleague, had a very similar background. Born in Mashad in 1946, he studied in the local high school and participated in religious organisations. But while studying literature in the National University in Tehran during the mid-1960s, he was drawn to Marxism and especially to Fidel Castro's example, and wrote a work entitled *Zarurat-i Mobarezeh-i Maslehaneh va Rad-i Teor-yi Baqa* (*The Need for Armed Struggle and the Rejection of the Theory of Survival*).

The third group was located in Tabriz and had been formed in 1965 by a group of intellectuals led by Behrouz Dehqani, Ashraf Dehqani, and 'Ali Reza Nabdel. Behrouz Dehqani, a village teacher, had been born in 1938 into a poor family in Tabriz. His father, a construction worker, had been active in the *Tudeh* labour movement during the 1940s. Winning state scholarships, Behrouz Dehqani had studied English in Tabriz, where he had met Samad Behrangi, a radical writer well-known throughout the rest of Iran as well as Azerbaijan. Together they published a five-volume work on Azerbaijani folk tales. Dehqani also wrote a book on the relationship between literature and society, and translated works of Maxim Gorki and Sean O'Casey. Through Behrangi and his literary circle, Dehqani met Poyan and thereby forged the first links between Tabriz and the Ahmadzadeh group in Tehran. Behrangi, however, did not live to see the formation of the *Fedayi*, for he was said to have drowned in 1968 in the Aras river. Ashraf Dehqani, Behrouz Dehqani's younger sister, had a very similar background to her brother. Born in Tabriz, she studied there and taught in a village school near her home town. Nabdel, another young teacher, had also been born and raised in Tabriz, but had gone to Tehran to study literature. Graduating from Tehran University in 1963, he had returned home to teach and write poetry. Although he wrote in both Persian and Azeri Turkish, only his Persian poetry was printed since Azeri had been banned from the publishing houses. To publicise the plight of the Azeri language under the Pahlavis, Nabdel wrote for the *Fedayi* a pamphlet entitled *Azerbaijan va Masaleh-i Melli* (*Azerbayjan and the National Question*). Like the Dehqanis, his own father had been active during the 1940s both in the *Tudeh* and in its local ally the Democratic Party of Azerbaijan.

The three groups began to merge in 1970. In the spring of that year, the Tabriz and the Ahmadzadeh groups amalgamated and carried out their first armed attack – the robbery of a Tehran bank to finance their future operations. In the autumn of the same year, these two merged with the other Tehran groups to create a unified organisation with three cells: an 'urban team' formed mostly of Ahmadzadeh's followers; a 'publication team' formed predominantly of the Tabriz intellectuals; and a 'rural team' headed mostly by survivors from Jazani's circle.

In negotiating the mergers, the groups hammered out a joint strategy which Ashraf summed up as follows:

After much deliberation we reached the conclusion that it was impossible to work among the masses and create large organisations since the police had penetrated all sectors of society. We decided that our immediate task was to form small cells and mount physical assaults on the enemy so as to destroy the repressive 'atmosphere' and to show the people that 'armed struggle' was the only way to liberation.[6]

Similarly, Poyan declared:

The defeat of the anti-imperialist movement in Iran has enabled the reactionaries to establish a fascist state, destroy the opposition organisations, and co-opt opportunistic elements. In a situation where there are no firm links between the revolutionary intelligentsia and the masses, we are not like a school of fish in water, but rather like isolated fish surrounded by threatening crocodiles. Terror, repression, and absence of democracy have made it impossible for us to create working-class organisations. To break the spell of our weakness and to inspire the people we must resort to a revolutionary armed struggle ... To liberate the proletariat from the stifling culture, to cleanse its mind from petty bourgeois thoughts, and to equip it with ideological ammunition, it is necessary to shatter the illusion that the people are powerless.[7]

Ahmadzadeh further elaborated the *Fedayi* strategy:

How can the masses become conscious of themselves, their interests, and their formidable power? Persistent suppression, lack of leadership, constant government propaganda, and the omnipotent presence of the bayonet – all have combined to erect a huge barrier between the people and the masses and between segments of the masses. How can this barrier be destroyed to release the swelling torrent of the masses? The only way is armed struggle ... To defeat the enemy, the broad masses must be drawn into the struggle. To smash the enemy's army, there must be a people's army. To create the people's army, there must be a prolonged guerrilla war. A guerrilla war is necessary not only for military victory, but also for mass mobilisation. On the one hand, the mobilisation of the masses is the condition for military and political victory. On the other hand, mobilisation of the masses is not possible without the armed struggle. We have learnt this not only from the experience of Cuba but also from those of China and Vietnam ... As Debray has stressed, 'Under present conditions the most important form of propaganda is successful military action'.[8]

In formulating a strategy, the *Fedayi* developed critiques of other political organisations. They dismissed the National Front as a 'petty bourgeois' and 'anachronistic' paper organisation still preaching the false hope of free elections.[9] They accuse the pro-Chinese groups, especially the Revolutionary Organisation, of 'mechanically' applying Mao to Iran, of dogmatically refusing to accept the fact that during the last decade Iran had been transformed from a feudal society to a dependent capitalist society, of permitting SAVAK to infiltrate their top ranks, of uncritically accepting the notion that the Soviet Union rather than American imperialism was the major threat to Asia, Africa and Latin America, and of talking much about 'armed struggle' but invariably postponing such a struggle on the grounds that first a viable political party had to be formed.[10]

The *Fedayi*'s criticism of the *Tudeh* was even more extensive. While praising the *Tudeh* for organising the working class during the 1940s and producing many national martyrs during the 1950s, they accused the party of 'blindly following' the Soviet Union, of hastily denouncing Stalin, and of underestimating the 'nationality problem', especially in Azerbaijan and Kordestan. The *Fedayi* asserted that the *Tudeh* had held back the peasant movement in the 1940s, had overestimated the importance of the Iranian *bourgeoisie*, and thereby expected the forthcoming revolution to be 'national democratic' rather than 'people's democratic'. Above all, claimed the *Fedayi*, the *Tudeh* favoured a political struggle over an armed struggle, organisational survival over heroic action, 'parliamentary reformism' over revolutionary socialism.[11] The *Tudeh* retorted that all socialists had the 'duty' of supporting the Soviet Union and that the talk of quickly transforming a 'bourgeois democracy' into a 'people's democracy' smacked of Trotsky's notion of 'permanent revolution'. The *Fedayi*, they said, underestimated the Iranian *bourgeoisie* and consequently misunderstood the true nature of the forthcoming revolution. According to this analysis, the *Fedayi* also underestimated the class-consciousness of the industrial proletariat, and thereby overlooked the possibilities of waging a political struggle. Most important of all, the *Tudeh* viewed the guerrillas as having more in common with Bakhunin and the nineteenth century Narodniks who cried 'Long Live Death' and 'Propaganda by the Deed' than with Marx, Lenin and the Bolsheviks, who always stressed that an armed struggle would fail unless it was waged by a disciplined political party and the objective conditions were ripe.[12]

Once the *Fedayi* had formulated their strategy, they made preparations for the armed struggle. Their first major decision was to send the 'rural team' to the forested mountains of Gilan to live with the local shepherds, establish contact with the villagers and generally lay the groundwork for future operations. They chose this area partly because the rugged mountains were inaccessible to heavy armour; partly because the forests, called *jangals*, provided thick cover against air attacks; and partly because the Gilan peasantry had a history of radicalism reaching back not only to the early 1920s when local rebels known as *Jangalis* had set up a Soviet Socialist Republic, but also to the 1850s when mass uprisings had swept through the Caspian provinces.[13] In the original plans, the *Fedayi* intended to spend a full year making preparations. But these plans had to be scrapped in early February 1971 when the gendarmes in the village of Siakal arrested two of their sympathisers. Afraid that torture would be used to extract vital information, the *Fedayi* made the fateful decision to attack the gendarmerie post. As soon as news of the attack and successful getaway reached Tehran, the Shah reacted with full force and sent his brother to head an expeditionary army of commandos, helicopters and SAVAK agents. After a massive manhunt which lasted a full three weeks and left thirty soldiers and two guerrillas dead, the military authorities announced the capture of eleven *Fedayi*. Of the eleven, ten faced firing squads, and one, Farahani, died under torture without revealing information about the other teams. For the *Fedayi* the whole affair was a military failure but a great propaganda success, since it proved that a small group of determined revolutionaries could shake the foundations of the Pahlevi regime. Not surprisingly, *Bahman 19 (February 8)*, the day of the Siakal incident, has gone down in history as the birth of the Iranian guerrilla movement.

As if to confirm the importance of the Siakal incident the regime followed up the executions with a series of dramatic measures. It waged a major propaganda war against the guerrillas, accusing them of being 'atheists', '*Tudeh* agents', and 'tools of the PLO, Baghdad, and Arab imperialism'. It arrested fifty-one left-wing dissidents – none of whom had any *Fedayi* connections, granted a week's unscheduled vacation to the universities of Tehran, and 'outlawed' the Confederation of Iranian Students in Europe and America as an 'international communist conspiracy'. It also increased government salaries, decreed the current year to be the 'Civil Servants Year', raised the minimum wage, and declared that in future 1 May would be celebrated throughout Iran as 'Worker's Day'.

During the nine months after Siakal, SAVAK, in a series of armed encounters, managed to arrest and kill almost all the founding members of the *Fedayi*. Nevertheless, the survivors, notably Hamid Ashraf and Ashraf Dehqani, were able to continue and intensify the struggle. They found eager recruits, established new cells, especially in Tehran, Tabriz, Rasht, Gurgan, Qazvin, and Enzeli (Pahlavi), started two underground newspapers – *Bahman 19 (February 8)* and *Nabard-i Khalq (People's Struggle)* – and helped to organise a number of university strikes and demonstrations to coincide with the first anniversary of Siakal. They also carried out a series of armed operations, holding up five banks, assassinating two police informers, a millionaire industrialist and the Chief Military Prosecutor, and bombing the embassies of Britain, Oman and the United States, the offices of International Telephone and Telegraph, Trans-World Airlines, and the Iran–American Society, and the police headquarters of Tehran, Tabriz, Rasht, Gurgan, Mashad, and Abadan.

By late 1975, it was clear that the struggle between the regime and the *Fedayi* had reached a stalemate. The former had succeeded in hunting down the guerrillas, waging an aggressive propaganda war against 'atheistic terrorists', and, most important of all, containing the movement to the university intelligentsia. The latter, on the other hand, had succeeded in replenishing its heavy losses, harassing the authorities and carrying out heroic feats. But despite five years of struggle, they had failed to ignite a 'people's revolution'. In debating how to end the stalemate, the *Fedayi* divided into two factions. The majority faction – headed by Ashraf Dehqani and Hamid Ashraf until his death in mid-1976 – insisted on continuing the armed confrontations until they sparked off a mass uprising. The minority faction, however, argued in favour of avoiding armed confrontations, increasing political activity, especially among factory workers, and establishing closer links with the *Tudeh* Party. In mid-1976, this group affiliated with the *Tudeh*, denounced the theory of 'Propaganda by the Deed' as an aberration of Marxist–Leninism,[14] and formed the *Gorueh-i Munsh'eb Az Sazman-i Cherik-ha-yi Fedayi Khalq Vabasteh Beh Hezb-i Tudeh-i Iran* (The Group Separated from the *Fedayi* Guerrilla Organisation and Attached to the *Tudeh* Party of Iran) – known in short as the *Fedayi Munsh'eb*.[15] Of course, both factions kept their weapons, and, therefore, once the revolution began, were able to surface as experienced organisations eager to challenge directly the armed might of the Pahlavi state.

THE MOJAHEDIN

The *Mojahedin*, like the *Fedayi*, had its origins in the early 1960s. But whereas the *Fedayi* developed mostly out of the *Tudeh* and the Marxist wing of the National Front, the *Mojahedin* evolved predominantly from the religious wing of the National Front, especially from the *Nahzat-i Azad-i Iran* (The Liberation Movement of Iran). This organisation had been formed in 1961 by two staunch supporters of Mossadeq, Mehdi Bazargan and Ayatollah Taleqani. The former was a French-educated engineer and a highly devout Muslim who served in Mossadeq's cabinet and continued to help his National Front even though the Front's secular outlook increasingly alienated the religious establishment. The latter was unique among the religious leaders – unlike most *ayatollahs*, he came from a poor family, advocated socialism, openly criticised his colleagues for being fearful of the modern world, and remained loyal to Mossadeq to the very end.

In creating the Liberation Movement, Bazargan, Taleqani, and their circle of French-educated technocrats, sought to bridge the gap between the National Front and the modern salaried middle class on one side and the religious establishment and the traditional propertied middle class on the other. They intended to break the clerical monopoly over religion and develop a new Islam that would synthesise the mild features of European socialism with the progressive ideals of early Iranian Shiism, and the advantages of industrial technology with the cultural values of their own traditional society. In short, they aimed at formulating a lay-dominated religion that would be acceptable both to the Anti-Shah clergy, especially to the junior clergy, and to the modern-educated middle class, particularly the discontented intelligentsia. Although the Liberation Movement formulated entirely new goals, it continued to rely on traditional non-violent means to 'liberalise' the regime.

Just as the Liberation Movement was getting off the ground, the 1963 crisis erupted, causing a group of young and more militant activists to leave the organisation to form their own secret discussion circle. This group was led by nine recent graduates of Tehran University: Muhammad Hanifnezhad, Sa'ed Mohsen, Muhammad Bazargani, Muhammad Asgarizadeh, Rasoul Moshkinfam, Ali Asghar Badi'zadegan, Ahmad Reza'i, Naser Sadeq, and Ali Mehandoust.[16] Hanifnezhad, the oldest, was an agricultural engineer from Tehran University. Born in 1938 into a clerical family in Tabriz, he completed high school in his home town and then moved to Tehran to enter the Agricultural College. There he formed an Islamic Club, joined the Liberation Movement, and, as a result of the 1963 demonstrations, spent a short spell in prison where he met Ayatollah Taleqani. After his release, Hanifnezhad graduated from the university, volunteered for military service and spent a year in the Isfahan garrison reading as much· as he could on the recent revolutions in Algeria, Cuba and Vietnam. Finishing national service in 1965, he returned to Tehran, gathered together some of his former classmates, and laid the foundations of the *Mojahedin*.

Bazargani, a brother-in-law of Hanifnezhad, was also a native of Azerbaijan who had come to Tehran to enter the University. While in the Business College, he joined first the Liberation Movement and then Hanifnezhad's circle. Mohsen, a civil engineer, was another Azerbaijani who had studied in Tehran University. From an impoverished clerical family in Zanjan, he won a state scholarship to the Engineering College where he joined religious clubs and the Liberation Movement. Spending eight months in prison after the 1963 riots, he finished his degree and entered the army to do his military service. Asgarizadeh, a graduate of the Business College, was one of the few *Mojahedin* who came from a working-class family. Born in Arak in central Iran, he grew up partly in his home town and partly in Tehran. Completing his degree, he worked in Tehran and Tabriz for a machine-manufacturing company. Moshkinfam, an engineer trained in the Agricultural College, came from a middle-class family in Shiraz. Graduating from Tehran University, he was drafted into the army and sent to Kordestan where he learned Kurdish and secretly compiled a detailed report on the impact of capitalism on the local peasantry which was later published by the *Mojahedin* under the title of *Rusta va Ingelabi-i Sefid* (*The Countryside and the White Revolution*).

Badi'zadegan, a junior professor of chemistry, came from a middle-class family in Isfahan. Graduating from Tehran University, he was conscripted into the army and stationed in the main arms-manufacturing factory in Tehran. Reza'i, the group's main intellectual, was one of the few *Mojahedin* leaders who had been born in Tehran. From a small merchant family living in northern Tehran, he joined the Liberation Movement while in high school, met Hanifnezhad while in military service, and entered his secret group while teaching in a high school in Tehran. SAVAK later killed him as well as his two younger brothers and his 18-year old sister, all of whom were members of the *Mojahedin*. Sadeq, an electrical engineer, came from a lower middle-class family in Shiraz. As a college student, he attained national fame by winning a number of gymnastic competitions. Finally, Mehandoust, also an electrical engineer, was born in Qazvin but educated in Tehran University. After graduating from the University, he moved to Isfahan, but kept in touch with his former classmates in Tehran.

Beginning with this nucleus of nine, the group gradually expanded not only in Tehran but also in the provinces. Mehandoust formed a cell in Isfahan, Sadeq in Shiraz, and Asgarzadeh in Tabriz. At the same time, Bazargani, Badi'zadegan, Moshkinfam, and three new recruits went to Jordan to receive guerrilla training from the PLO. What is more, the discussion group, especially Hanifnezhad and Reza'i, followed the Liberation Movement's footsteps in reinterpreting Islam, eventually reaching the conclusion that true Shiism stood not only against despotism, but also against capitalism, imperialism, and conservative clericalism. In a book entitled *Nahzat-i Hosseini* (*Hossein's Movement*), Reza'i argued that the *Nezam-i Towhid* (*Monotheistic Order*) the Prophet sought was a commonwealth fully united by virtue of being 'classless' and striving for the common good as well as by the fact that it worships only one God. Reza'i further argued that the banner of revolt raised by the Shiia Imams, especially Ali, Hassan, and Hossein, was aimed against feudal landlords and exploiting merchant capitalists as well as against usurping Caliphs who had betrayed the true cause of *Nezam-i Towhid*. For Reza'i and the *Mojahedin* it was the duty of all Muslims to continue this struggle to create a 'classless society' and destroy all forms of capitalism, despotism, and imperialism. The *Mojahedin* summed up their attitude towards religion in these words: 'After years of extensive study into Islamic history and Shiia ideology, our organisation has reached the firm conclusion that Islam, especially Shiism, will play a major role in inspiring the masses to join the revolution. It will do so because Shiism, particularly Hossein's historic act of resistance, has both a revolutionary message and a special place in our popular culture.'[17]

The theme that Shiism preached social revolution was further refined during the late 1960s when the *Mojahedin* helped set up a lecture hall named *Hosseinieh-i Ershad,* and invited Dr Ali Shariati—who later became known as the *Fanon* of Iran – to give a series of lectures on Islam. For Shariati, as for the *Mojahedin*, the Prophet planned to establish a 'classless society', Imam Hosein exemplified man's inalienable right of resistance, and true Muslims had the duty to fight against despotic rulers, foreign exploiters, greedy capitalists and false clergymen who used Islam as an opiate to lull the masses into subservience. In his own words, the history of mankind since Cain and Abel was a history of class struggles. On one side stood the oppressed – the people. On the other side were the oppressors – 'the governors, the wealthy, and the clerics *(mullahs)*'.[18] It was the duty of contemporary Muslims to expose the false teachings of the clergy and to inspire the masses to rise up against 'world imperialism, international Zionism, colonialism, exploitation, oppression, class inequality, cartels, multinational corporations, racism, cultural imperialism and the blind worship of the West'.[19] The ideas of Shariati and the *Mojahedin* were so close that many concluded the former had inspired the latter. In actual fact, the *Mojahedin* had formulated their ideas by 1965 – two years before they discovered Shariati and invited him to the *Hosseinieh*. Whatever the exact relationship between the two, it is clear that in later years Shariati indirectly helped the *Mojahedin*: his taped lectures and numerous pamphlets – which totalled over sixty at the time of his fatal heart attack in the late spring of 1977 – circulated widely throughout Iran, especially among college and high-school students.

The *Mojahedin* began their military operations in August 1971, some six years after Hanifnezhad had formed his secret discussion group. Their first operations were designed to disrupt the extravagant celebrations for the 2500th anniversary of the Iranian monarchy. After the group bombed the Tehran electrical works and tried to hijack an Iran Air plane, the police arrested nine *Mojahedin*, one of whom under torture gave information that led to the detention of another sixty-six members. In the subsequent months, the *Mojahedin* lost the whole of its original leadership through executions or in shootouts. Despite these losses, the *Mojahedin* survived and found new members. They published an underground paper named *Jangal* (*Forest*), sent five volunteers to help the Dhofar rebels in Oman, and, in the next four years, carried out a succession of violent acts. These included the robbing of six banks, the assassination of a US military adviser as well as the Chief of the Tehran Police, the attempted assassination of a US General, and the bombings of Reza Shah's mausoleum and the offices of El Al, British Overseas Airways, British Petroleum and Shell. By mid-1975, fifty *Mojahedin* had lost their lives. Over 90 per cent of them came from the intelligentsia.

Although the membership of both the *Mojahedin* and the *Fedayi* was drawn from the younger generation of the intelligentsia, there were nevertheless subtle differences in their composition. Most *Mojahedin* – with the notable exception of their founders – came from the central provinces, especially Isfahan, Fars and Hamadan. Most *Fedayi*, on the other hand, came from the northern cities, particularly Tehran, Tabriz, Rasht, Gurgan, Qazvin, and Mashad. Many *Mojahedin* were sons of religious-minded merchants, *bazaar* traders, clergymen, and other members of the traditional middle-class. Many *Fedayi*, however, were children of secular-minded civil servants, teachers, professionals, and other members of the modern middle class. All the *Mojahedin* had been born into Shiia families; a few of the *Fedayi* came from non-Shiia backgrounds – from Sunni, Armenian and Zoroastrian families. The *Mojahedin* dead contained only seven women; but the *Fedayi* dead as many as twenty-two women. The *Mojahedin* recruited predominantly from students of the physical sciences, especially from Tehran Polytechnic, the Engineering College, the Agricultural College and the Aryamehr University. The *Fedayi*, by contrast, drew their members mostly from the arts, humanities and social sciences, particularly from the Colleges of Art, Literature, Economics, Law and Political Science, and Teachers' Training. Furthermore, whereas the *Mojahedin* failed to recruit among the lower classes, the *Fedayi* found a few members among the industrial proletariat: the *Mojahedin* dead included only two workers, the *Fedayi* as many as twelve.

Even though the *Mojahedin* was Islamic, its revolutionary interpretation of Islam produced an ideology not very different from that of the Marxist *Fedayi*. It argued that Iran was dominated by imperialism, especially American imperialism, that the White Revolution had transformed Iran from a feudal society to a bourgeois one heavily dependent on Western capitalism, and that cultural imperialism, as well as economic, political, and military imperialism, were threatening the existence of the country. The Pahlavi regime, it asserted, had little social support outside the comparador bourgeoisie, and ruled mainly through terror, intimidation and propaganda. The only way to shatter the 'atmosphere of terror' was through heroic acts of violence. It also argued that once the regime collapsed the revolutionaries would carry out radical reforms, ending the dependence on the West, building an independent society, giving a free voice to the masses, redistributing wealth, and, in general, creating the 'classless' *Nezam-i Towhid*. In fact, these ideas were so close to those of the *Fedayi* that the regime labelled the *Mojahedin* as 'Islamic Marxists' and claimed that Islam was merely a cover to hide their Marxism. The *Mojahedin* retorted that although they 'respected Marxism as a progressive social philosophy' their true culture, inspiration, attachment, and ideology was Islam.[20] In a pamphlet entitled *Pasokh Beh Etamat-i Akher-i Rezhim* (*An Answer to the Regime's Latest Slanders*), the *Mojahedin* summed up their attitude to both Marxism and Islam:

The Shah is terrified of revolutionary Islam. This is why he keeps on shouting a Muslim cannot be a revolutionary. In his mind, a man is either a Muslim or a revolutionary; he cannot be both. But in the real world, the exact opposite is true. A man is a true Muslim only if he is a revolutionary. A Muslim is either a revolutionary or not a true Muslim. In the whole of the Koran, there is not a single Muslim who was not a revolutionary... The regime is trying to place a wedge between Muslims and Marxists. In our view, however, there is only one major enemy – imperialism and its local collaborators. When SAVAK shoots, it kills both Muslims and Marxists. When it tortures, it tortures both Muslims and Marxists. Consequently, in the present situation there is organic unity between Muslim revolutionaries and Marxist revolutionaries. In truth, why do we respect Marxism? Of course, Marxism and Islam are not identical. Nevertheless, Islam is definitely closer to Marxism than to Pahlavism. Islam and Marxism teach the same lessons for they fight against injustice. Islam and Marxism contain the same message, for they inspire martyrdom, struggle, and self-sacrifice. Who is closer to

Islam: the Vietnamese who fight against American imperialism or the Shah who helps Zionism? Since Islam fights oppression it will work together with Marxism which also fights oppression. They have the same enemy: reactionary imperialism.[21]

The *Mojahedin* became even more interested in Marxism in the years after 1972. By the end of 1973, they were reading extensively on the Vietnamese, Cuban, Chinese and Russian revolutions. By mid-1974, they were sending organisers into the factories to agitate among industrial workers. By early 1975 some of their leaders were talking of the need to synthesise Islam with Marxism. And by May 1975, the majority of their leaders still free in Tehran voted to accept Marxism and to declare the organisation as Marxist–Leninist. In a pamphlet entitled *Biyanyeh-i Ela-m-i Movaz'i Iedoluzhek* (*Manifesto on Ideological Issues*), the central leadership declared that after ten years of secret existence, four years of armed struggle, and two years of intense ideological rethinking they had reached the conclusion that Marxism, not Islam, was the true revolutionary philosophy.[22] According to the manifesto, they had reached this conclusion because Islam appealed mainly to the 'middle class' whereas Marxism was the 'salvation of the working class'.

This transformation was vividly described by Mujtabi Taleqani, the son of Ayatollah Taleqani, in a letter to his father:

It is now two full years since I left home, went underground, and lost contact with you. Because of my deep respect for you and because of the many years we spent together fighting imperialism and reaction, I feel the need to explain to you why I and my adopted family decided to make major changes in our organisation . . . From my earliest days at your side, I learnt how to hate this bloodthirsty tyrannic regime. I always expressed my hatred through religion – through the militant teaching of Mohammad Ali, and Hossein. I always respected Islam as the expression of the toiling masses fighting oppression . . . In the past two years, however, I have started to study Marxism. Before I thought that militant intellectuals could destroy the regime. Now I am convinced that we must turn to the working class. But to organise the working class, we must reject Islam, for religion refuses to accept the main dynamic force of history – that of the class struggle. Of course, Islam can play a progressive role, especially in mobilising the intelligentsia against imperialism. But it is only Marxism that provides a scientific analysis of society and looks towards the exploited classes for liberation. Before I used to think that those who believed in historical materialism could not possibly make the supreme sacrifice since they had no faith in the afterlife. Now I know that the highest sacrifice anyone can make is to die for the liberation of the working classes.[23]

The conversion caused a sharp split within the *Mojahedin*. While some members – mostly in Tehran – supported the change, others – mostly in the provinces – remained Islamic, refused to give up the *Mojahedin* name, and accused their rivals of engineering a coup, murdering one of their leaders, and betraying two others to the police. Thus, after May 1975 there were two rival *Mojahedins*, each with its own organisation, its own publications, and its own activities. The activities of the Islamic *Mojahedin* included a bank robbery in Isfahan, a bomb attack on the Israeli Cultural Centre in Tehran, and a strike in Aryamehr University to commemorate the fourth anniversary of the execution of their founders. The activities of the Marxist *Mojahedin* included the bombing of ITT offices and the assassination of two American military advisers. In the course of the next twenty-four months, thirty members of the Marxist *Mojahedin* lost their lives. Among them was a woman from Tehran University – the first woman in Iranian history to be executed by firing squad.

By early 1976, the two *Mojahedins*, like the *Fedayi*, had suffered such heavy losses that they began to reconsider their tactics. The Islamic *Mojahedin* stepped up its campus activities, circulated its own and Shari'ati's publications, and established contact with the Islamic Student Association in North America and Western Europe. Meanwhile, the Marxist *Mojahedin* intensified its labour activities, called for the establishment of a 'new working-class party', started a paper called *Qiyam-i Kargar* (*Worker's Revolt*), and formed links with Maoists heading the Confederation of Iranian Students in Western Europe. It also entered negotiations with the *Fedayi* to merge the two organisations, but soon broke off the talks on the grounds that the latter remained tied to its 'Guevarist ideas', refused to denounce Soviet 'social imperialism', and secretly flirted with such 'dubious entities' as the National Front and the *Tudeh* Party.[24] For its part, the *Fedayi* accused the Marxist *Mojahedin* of 'blindly accepting Maoism',[25] and backed off from merging with an organisation that had shed the blood of the Islamic *Mojahedin* and openly denounced Islam as a 'petty bourgeois ideology'.

Thus when the revolutionary upsurge began in late 1977, there were four separate guerrilla groups – the *Fedayi*, the *Fedayi Monsheb*, the Islamic *Mojahedin*, and the Marxist *Mojahedin* – still functioning in Iran, even though the last three had decided to avoid armed confrontations. All four kept their organisation intact. All four retained their weapons. All four continued to publish journals, recruit members from the universities and send organisers into the factories. And all four had gained not only armed experience but also a mystique of revolutionary heroism. In short, all four were well equipped to move into action and take advantage of the revolutionary situation.

THE REVOLUTION AND BEYOND

The guerrilla organisations were strengthened in late 1977 and early 1978 when the Shah, pressed by mass demonstrations, general strikes and international human rights groups, amnestied 618 political prisoners. Although the amnesty did not cover the guerrilla leaders serving life sentences, it did free over 100 rank-and-file members sentenced to lesser terms. The *Fedayi Monsheb* was further strengthened in January 1979 when the Central Committee of the *Tudeh* elected the leader of the party's left-wing as its First Secretary and declared that since the objective situation was ripe for revolution, and since peaceful protests by themselves could not bring it about, the party needed to distribute weapons and 'prepare for an armed struggle'.[26]

Thus in the last days of the monarchy, when Mehdi Bazargan, on behalf of Ayatollah Khomeini, was secretly negotiating with the US, the SAVAK leaders, and the Chiefs of Staff for an orderly transition of power, the four guerrilla organisations mounted a major assault on the remnants of the army. According to eyewitnesses, the final collapse ccame on 10–13 February as the élite Imperial Guard attacked the main military base in Tehran to put down a mutiny among air force cadets and technicians. As soon as the news of the attack reached the guerrillas, they mobilised their members, distributed guns among their sympathisers, and rushed in full force to help the besieged cadets and technicians. Successfully beating off the Imperial Guards, the guerrillas spent the next three days opening up the prisons, the police stations, the armouries, and the five major military bases in Tehran. Similar events took place in the provinces, especially the Tabriz, Abadan, Hamadan, Kermanshah, Yazd, Isfahan, Mashad, Mahabad and Babol. An Iranian journal, quoting the Iranian Press Agency, reported that in

Tehran alone 654 lost their lives and 2804 suffered serious injuries during these 'final three days that shook the foundations of the 2500-year old monarchy'.[27] The *New York Times* wrote that in forty-eight hours civilians, armed with only light weapons, had been able to rout the élite Imperial Guard.[28] *Le Monde* reported that mere guerrillas had successfully snuffed out the once-formidable army.[29] *Kayhan*, Iran's second-largest newspaper, wrote that in these final days the decisive role had been played by 'the *Mojahedin*, the *Fedayi*, the *Fedayi Monsheb*, and the *Tudeh* Party'.[30] Finally, Bazargan, soon after forming his government, told interviewers from French television that 'the revolution would not forget the role played by the guerrillas and the *Tudeh* Party'.[31]

Since the revolution the *Fedayi Monsheb* has totally merged with the *Tudeh*, and, following the *Tudeh* line, given qualified support both to the central government headed by Premier Bazargan and to the Revolutionary Council formed by Ayatollah Khomeini. It has supported the new administration, especially the Revolutionary Council, on the grounds that Iran is still threatened by a royalist counter-revolution and that the new regime can be encouraged to become more progressive, more democratic, and more anti-imperialist.[32] At the same time, it has criticised the new administration for using force to resolve the Kurdish problem, for failing to create work for the 3 million unemployed, for not ending all military ties with the West, and for hindering the activities of workers', peasants', and soldiers' councils. It has also criticised unnamed 'elements' for creating a goon squad called *Hezb Allah* (God's Party) and hiring thugs to ransack newspaper offices, break up political meetings, burn down bookstores, and even murder leftists.

For their part, the *Fedayi*, the Islamic *Mojahedin*, and the Marxist *Mojahedin*, which is now named *Paykar*, have avoided criticising Khomeini in print since he is the symbol of the revolution, but have openly denounced the regime as 'conservative', 'clerical', 'dictatorial', and even 'fascistic'. They attacked Former Prime Minister Bazargan for refusing to create a new people's army, for trying to collect the weapons distributed during February, and for failing to decree any type of land reform. Moreover, they have accused the Revolutionary Council, which controls the Revolutionary Prosecutors, the Revolutionary Tribunals, and many of the local *Komiteh*s, of censoring the National Iranian Radio and Television Network, closing down twenty-two opposition newspapers including their own, and rearresting anti-Shah activists – one leader of the Islamic *Mojahedin* had been detained for nine months as a 'Russian spy'. They claimed that the Revolutionary Council was inciting religious fanatics to maim and murder revolutionaries who had risked their lives to fight the Shah, and was using armed militia to occupy, ransack, and close down the offices of the guerrilla organisations. Furthermore, they have criticised the Revolutionary Council for refusing to give the electorate a choice between an Islamic Republic and an Islamic Democratic Republic (as promised by Bazargan at the height of the revolution), for rigging the elections to the Assembly of Experts convened to study the draft constitution of the Islamic Republic and for transforming the Islamic Republic into a conservative clerical republic where unelected religious experts will exercise power over elected officials and representatives, where women will be encouraged to restrict themselves to 'family life', and where the goal of creating a 'classless society' will not be incorporated into the whole notion of *Nezam-i Towhid*. In addition, the *Fedayi* and *Paykar* have sided with the ethnic minorities against the central government, have demanded autonomy for the provinces and have sent volunteers to help the Kurdish, Turkoman, Arab and Baluchi rebels.

The momentous developments of 1978 and 1979 transformed the setting in which the guerrilla organisations had operated. Almost overnight the political terrain had been altered. New and immediately pressing political questions were posed for those who had struggled to overthrow the regime, creating new fissures within the political organisations we have been discussing. The rush of events, the complexity and multitude of the questions, and the paucity of reliable accounts and documentation make it impossible to provide more than a preliminary sketch of some important features of this most recent period. A more thorough account and appraisal is a task that lies ahead.

At the time of writing (January 1980) there seems to be two main lines forming on the left. The *Fedayi* and the *Tudeh* now call for the consolidation of the gains won by the 'bourgeois national revolution'. The *Fedayi*, the Islamic *Mojahedin*, and the *Paykar* organisation call for the conversion of the February upheaval into a radical social transformation and for pushing the 'bourgeois national revolution' into a full 'worker–peasant socialist revolution'. Only History, and its companion Hindsight, will be able to judge the relative merits of those two strategies.

NOTES

1. The data on the dead guerrillas has been compiled from interviews, from reports I submitted to the International Commission of Jurists in 1974–5, and from the following newspapers:

Bakhtar-i Emuruz (*Today's West*) the organ of the National Front in the Middle East, August 1970–December 1976. This paper sympathised with the *Fedayi*.

Mojahedin (*Freedom Fighter*) the organ of the Liberation Movement in Exile, June 1972–December 1978. This paper sympathised with the Islamic *Mojahedin*.

Khabarnameh (*Newsletter*) the organ of the National Front in Exile 1969–January 1979. This paper gave extensive coverage to both the *Fedayi* and the Islamic *Mojahedin*.

Mardom (*The People*) the central organ of the *Tudeh* Party, January 1971–February 1979.

Donya (*The World*) the theoretical journal of the *Tudeh* Party, January 1971–February 1979.

Setazeyeh Sorkh (*Red Star*) the organ of the Revolutionary Organisation of the *Tudeh* Party, September 1970–February 1979.

Etelaat (*Information*) the leading newspaper in Tehran, January 1971–December 1979.

Kayhan (*The World*) the second leading newspaper in Tehran, January 1979–September 1979.

Ayandegan (*The Future*) the third leading newspaper in Tehran, January 1979–April 1979.

Kar (*Work*) the organ of the *Fedayi* after the 1979 revolution.

Nabardeh Khalq (*People's Struggle*) the theoretical journal of the *Fedayi* after the 1979 revolution.

Jangal (*Forest*) the organ of the Islamic *Mojahedin*, June 1972–January 1975.

Mojahedin (*Freedom Fighter*) the main organ of the Islamic *Mojahedin* after the 1979 revolution.

Qiyameh Kargar (*Worker's Uprising*) the organ of the Marxist *Mojahedin*, June 1976–October 1978.

Paykar (*The Battle*) the organ of the Marxist *Mojahedin* after the 1979 revolution.

Azadi (*Freedom*) the organ of the Democratic National Front, March 1979–August 1979.

Buletin (*Bulletin*) the organ of the Committee for the Defence of the Rights of Political Prisoners, November 1978–February 1979.

Hambastegi (*Unity*) the joint organ of the Writers Society, the Organisation of University Faculty, and the Committee for the Defence of the Rights of Political Prisoners, December 1978–February 1979.

Jonbesh (*The Movement*) an independent newspaper exposing incidents of violations of human rights, November 1978–March 1979.

Iranshahr (*The Land of Iran*) an independent newspaper published in London, September 1978–July 1979.

2. Amnesty International, *Annual Report, 1974–75* (London, 1975).
3. Anonymous, 'Armed Struggle,' *Mujahid*, I, 4 (November 1974) pp. 5–6.
4. The history of the *Fedayi* has been obtained from the following sources: The *Fedayi* Organisation, *Hasht Sal Mobarezeh-i Maslehaneh (Eight Years of Armed Struggle)* (Tehran, 1979) pp. 1–29; The *Fedayi* Organisation, *Tarikhcheh-i Sazman-i Cherik-ha-yi Fedayi (A Short History of the Fedayi Guerrillas)* (Tehran, 1979) pp. 1–29; The *Fedayi* Organisation, *Tahlil-i Yek Sal-i Mobarez (Study on One Year of Struggle)* (n.p. 1974) pp. 1–28; Anonymous, 'Life of Poyan', *Iranshahr*, No. 11 (5 January 1979) p. 5; H. Ashraf, *Jam'iband-i Seh Saleh (An Evaluation of Three Years)* (Tehran, 1979) pp. 1–107; Y. Zarkar, *Khaterat-i Yek Cherik dar Zendan (The Memoirs of One Guerrilla in Prison* (Tehran, 1973) pp. 1–241; A. Dehqani, *Hameseh-i Moqavemant (Epic of Resistance)* (n.p. 1974) pp. 1–248.
5. The early ties between the *Tudeh* and the *Fedayi* remain ambiguous. Although the *Tudeh* opposed the theory of guerrilla warfare, Reza Radmanesh, the First Secretary and the director of the party's operations in the Middle East, helped Farahani and Ashtiyanri – presumably without authorisation from the Central Committee. When SAVAK published documents proving this link, the Central Committee recalled Radmanesh to Europe and elected a new First Secretary.
6. Ashraf, *Jam'iband-i*, p. 92.
7. P. Poyan, *Zarupat-i Mobarezeh-i Maslehaneh va Rad-i Teor-yi Baqa (The Need for Armed Struggle and the Rejection of the Theory of Survival)* (n.p. 1972) pp. 7–9.
8. M. Ahmadsedeh, *Mobarezeh-i Aslehaneh: Ham Estrategi Ham Taktik (Armed Struggle: Both A Strategy and a Tactic)* pp. 27–30.
9. B. Jazani, *Tarikh-i Siy Saleh-i Iran (Thirty Year History of Iran)* (Tehran, 1979) pp. 69–89.
10. Ahmadsedeh, *Mobarezeh-i Aslehaneh* pp. 11–13; Anonymous, 'The Thoughts of Mao and Our Revolution', *Nabard-i Khalq*, no. 2 (March 1974) pp. 38–48.
11. Jazani *Taukh-i Siy* pp. 8–67, Ahmadzedeh, *Mobarezeh-i Aslehaneh* pp. 12–13, The *Fedayi* Organisation, *I'dam-i Inqelab-i 'Abbas Shahriyar (The Revolutionary Execution of 'Abbas Shahriyar)* (n.p. 1974) pp. 71–142. 'A Nabdel, *Azerbayjan va Masaleh-i Melli (Azerbayjan and the National Question)* (n.p. 1973) pp. 18–32.
12. F. Javan, *Cherik-ha-yi Khalq Cheh Meguyand (What Are the Guerrillas Saying)* (n.p. 1972) pp.1–33; E. Tabari, 'This is Not Marxism–Leninism,' *Donya*, XII, 4 (Autumn 1971) pp. 31–41; N. Kianouri, 'On Methods of Struggle', *Donya*, I, 2 (July 1974) pp. 1–10; Anonymous, 'Message to the Fedayi', *Donya*, I, 5 (November 1974) pp. 1–7; N. Kianouri, 'Again a Message to the Fedayi', *Donya*, II, 3 (June 1975) pp. 7–16; N. Kianouri, 'The *Fedayi* and the *Tudeh* Party', *Donya*, II, 4 (July 1975) pp. 2–10. M. Akhgar, 'Views on the Writings of the *Fedayi*', *Donya*, III, 2 (April 1976) pp. 11–18.
13. For a history of radicalism among the Gilan peasantry, see F. Kazemi and

E. Abrahamian, 'The Non-revolutionary Peasantry of Modern Iran', *Iranian Studies*, XI, 1–3 (1978) pp. 259–304.

14. To Haydari–Begund, *Teor-yi' Tabliq-i Maslehaneh Enheraf Az Marksism-Leninism* (The Theory of 'Armed Propaganda' Deviates from Marxism Leninism) (n.p. 1978) pp. 1–81.

15. The *Fedayi Monsheb, Zindehbad Hezbeh Tudeh (Long Live the Tudeh Party)* (Tehran, 1978) pp. 1–15.

16. The history of the *Mojahedin* has been obtained from the following sources: The *Mojahedin* Organisation, *Sharh-i Tasis va Tarikcheh-i va Vaqa'eh-i Sazman-i Mojahedin* (*An Account of the Formation, Short History, and the Major Events of the* Mojahedin) (Tehran, 1979) pp. 1–87; The *Mojahedin* Organisation, *Az Zindeg-yi Inqelabiyun Dars Begirim (Let Us Learn Lessons from the Lives of Revolutionaries)* (n.p. 1974) pp. 1–32; The *Mojahedin* Organisation, *Ali Mehandoust va Mehdi Reza'i* (Ali Mehandoust and Mehdi Reza'i) (n.p. 1973) pp. 1–135; The *Mojahedin* Organisation *Modaf'at-i Mojahedin* (*The Defence Speeches of the* Mojahedin) (n.p. 1972) pp. 1–101; The *Mojahedin* Organisation, *Akharin Dafa'* (Last Defence) (n.p. 1971) pp. 1–22; The *Mojahedin* Organisation, Matn-i Dafa'at-i Shahid Sa'ed Mohsen (Text of the Defence Speech of Martyr Sa'ed Mohsen) (n.p. 1972) pp. 1–45; The *Mojahedin* Organisation, *Sazmandi va Taktikha* (*Tactics and Organisational Matters*) (n.p. 1974) pp. 1–131; The *Mojahedin* Organisation *Qesmati Az Dafa'at-i Mojahedin* (*Extracts from the* Mojahedin *Defence Speeches*) (n.p. 1972) pp. 1–29.

17. The *Mojahedin* Organisations, *Sharh-i Tasis . . .*, p. 44.

18. A. Shariýati, Eslam Shenasi (Islamology) (n.p. 1972) Lessons 1–2, pp. 88–93.

19. A. Shariýati, *Shiia Yek Hezb-i Tamam (The Shiia A Total Party)* (n.p. 1976) p. 55.

20. The *Mojahedin* Organisation, *Dafa'at-i Naser Sadeq* (The Defence Speech of Naser Sadeq) (n.p. 1972) p. 24.

21. The *Mojahedin* Organisation, *Pasokh Beh Etemat-i Akher-i Rezhim (An Answer to the Regime's Latest Slanders)* (n.p. 1973) pp. 10–13.

22. The *Mojahedin* Organisation, *Biyanyeh-i E'lami-i Movaz'-i Ideoluzhek* (Manifesto on Ideological Issues) (n.p. 1975) pp. 1–246.

23. M. Taleqani, 'Letter to My Father', *Mojahed*, no. 6 (July 1976) pp. 131–44.

24. The *Mojahedin* Organisation, *Masa'il-i Had-i Janbesh-i Ma* (The Critical Problems of Our Movement) (n.p. 1977) pp. 1–392.

25. The *Fedayi* Organisation, *Nashrieh-i Vazheh-i Bahas Darun-i Dow Sazman (Special Documents on the Debate Between the Two Organisations)* (n.p. 1977) pp. 1–76.

26. Central Committee of the Tudeh Party, 'Editorial', *Mardom*, VI, 223 (February 1979) p. 1.

27. Anonymous, 'The Three Days that Shook the Foundations of the 2500 Year Old Monarchy', *Iranshahr*, 17 (16 February 1979) pp. 1–5.

28. P. Lewis, 'Iran's Elite Army Was Routed by Civilians', *The New York Times*, 13 February 1979.

29. P. Balta and D. Pouchin, 'Les Combats de Guerilla Dans Tehran', *Le Monde*, 13 February 1979.
30. Anonymous, 'Armed Civilians Battle Tanks in the Streets of Tehran', *Kayhan*, 11 February 1979.
31. *Ete laat*, 25 February 1979.
32. Tudeh party, *Goftegu.yiba Cherik.ha.yi Fedayi* (*A Discussion with the Fedayi Guerrillas*) (Tehran, 1979) pp. 1–38.

8 The Army*

HALEH AFSHAR

The armed forces have played a central role in maintaining the political order in the past six decades in Iran. A key element in the emergence of Reza Shah as king in 1921, the army remained the basis of support for the subsequent Pahlavi regime. Since the 1979 revolution, the clergy have also used armed men in both regular and irregular forces, to secure their hold over the country. The policy of using armed government forces primarily against internal opponents has continued despite the revolution. Although the current war against Iraq has added a new dimension to the operation of Iranian armed forces, it is the contention of this paper that the primary role of the government's militia is to act as repressive agents of the regime and to eliminate internal, rather than external opposition.

REZA SHAH

Before the Pahlavis, Iranian kings had traditionally depended on tribal forces to defend the borders and on small urban levies drawn from tradesmen, artisans and peasants to act as part-time soldiers defending the government's interest against tribal insurrections. The army was not used to enforce government control, which as a result was not particularly strong, and until the end of the nineteenth century the Qajar kings ruled largely by playing the tribes off against one another and keeping tribal warfare away from the central province.

*I am very grateful to General Fereydoun Djam for his considerable help and for providing much of the information contained in this article.

Thanks are similarly due to Mr Medhi Samyi and Mr Eprim Eshaq. As well, I should like to thank Fred Halliday for his helpful comments on an earlier draft of this paper and for lending me his copy of Dr Salamtian's thesis and the Staff Report on Military Sales to Iran.

However, the responsibility for any misunderstanding or controversial opinion is entirely mine.

The first regular armed force in Iran was set up under Fath Ali Shah Qajar in 1812 by a French general sent by Napoleon Bonaparte. In 1879 (for a second time a regular armed force) the Persian Cossack Brigade was organised by Russian officers to serve as Nasseredin Shah's parade ground cavalry. By the end of the nineteenth century, however, the Qajars were faced with increasing tribal threats which the Cossack Brigade was incapable of meeting and in 1911 the Swedish government was invited to establish a rural gendarmerie. During the First World War the British, who were occupying the southern provinces of Khouzestan set up the South Persian Rifles, mainly with Indian recruits, to protect the oilfields.

Thus under the Qajars the military in Iran was commanded by foreigners, and in the southern regions contained a large proportion of non-Iranian soliders. After the Bolshevik revolution most Russian officers were recalled and, as a result, the Cossack Brigade came under the control of Persian officers. In 1921 one of these officers, Reza Khan took power after a bloodless coup. Initially he acted as commander in chief of the army, but subsequently he became the first Pahlavi shah.

Unlike the Qajars, the Pahlavis were not of tribal origin and came to power with army rather than tribal support; throughout their reign they kept a close relationship with the military.[1] In a radical departure from the previous dynasty, the Phalavis used the military to extend political control of the central government throughout the country. The powerful tribes were defeated and disarmed in a series of military campaigns and once central control was established all opposition was rigorously suppressed. In addition to the armed forces, Reza Shah also revitalised the civil service and created a secular education system which he used to much effect, in curbing the clergy's power, and also to purvey the new notion of modernisation.

Reza Shah embarked on an extensive expansion of the armed forces which was enhanced in 1925 by the introduction of compulsory military service for a two-year period for all adult males over the age of 18. Conscription soon became an effective means of extending the military control throughout the country. At the same time the army became a useful means of social mobility; many conscripts from remote rural areas acquired an elementary education during their military service and chose to remain with the army or work in urban areas after their service. From 1926 onward military schools were set up providing free secondary and tertiary education for those who chose the army as a career. Gradually a new educated and professional élite began to rise from the ranks and at the same time the forces secured a substantial proportion of the government's expenditure, which they have retained to this day. Once the process of suppressing all opposition parties had been completed, the army emerged as the best organised and most privileged group in the country. The tightly-knit higher echelons of the forces commanded by Reza Shah's old Cossack Brigade colleagues, came to exert considerable influence in local as well as national politics.

Under Reza Shah the army grew from five divisions in 1926 to eighteen divisions in 1941 as well as five aviation regiments and three marine units.[2] During this period military personnel increased eightfold from 23 000 to 185 000 men,[3] and the army expenditure accounted for 33 per cent of the government's official income, excluding additional sums from the oil revenue also channelled to the armed forces.[4]

Reza Shah, like Mohammad Reza Shah after him, had a single-minded attitude towards the armed forces. He, like his son, regarded the army as his own personal vehicle of power,[5] as well as a potential enemy. As a result he retained strict and personal control over the army and demanded total loyalty to the person of the king. In return, however, he lavished the forces with material advantages and political prestige. Although military salaries were not the highest in the land, officers did have the opportunity to appropriate large tracts of land in the areas where they were serving;[6] some high ranking officers became among the richest men in Iran.[7] But at the same time the Shah remained suspicious of the young educated élite that were rising from the ranks and retained his old collaborators from the Cossack Regiment in key positions.

This contradictory position of the regime *vis-à-vis* the army has become characteristic of the regime in Iran before as well as since the 1979 revolution. As the best educated and the best organised as well as the best armed group in the country, the army is not only the mainstay of the regime, but also its strongest potential enemy. But there was an uneasy relationship between bright young officers who were not sufficiently experienced to reach the highest ranks and the 'rough and uneducated commanders' under whom they served,[8] and there were sporadic attempts by young officers to initiate army revolts throughout Reza Shah's reign (for example, Major Lahoty's attempted coup in 1922, Colonel Pouladian's in 1926 and Major Janhansouz's in 1938).

THE MOSSADEQ ERA

Reza Shah's 185 000 strong army lost much of its prestige when it was defeated by the much smaller forces of Britain and Russia sent to depose the Shah whose pro-German sympathies were unacceptable to the Western Allies. The Iranian forces lasted only three days against the Allies' 25 000 men and Reza Shah was deposed and his 18-year-old son Mohammed Reza Shah placed on the throne by the Allies who proceeded to occupy the country. The British held the southern oil-rich provinces, the Americans occupied the central provinces and the Russians the northern provinces. Two of the occupied northern provinces, Azarbaijan and Mahabad declared themselves independent democratic soviets, and tribes in the north and the south began a widespread armed insurrection. Like his father, the Shah considered the tribes to be the most serious threat to the country's internal security, and began his reign with a series of campaigns against them. After the withdrawal of the Allies in 1946 the army recaptured the communist provinces and re-established its control over the country.

Once the military was re-established as the major political basis of the regime its support was essential to any group wishing to topple the Shah. There were a series of attempts by pro-*Tudeh* officers, as well as supporters of other opposition parties to gain control of the army but military insubordination remained sporadic and unsuccessful. The most serious political threat to the Shah came from Prime Minister Mohammed Mossadeq who in 1952 sought to assert the constitutional right of the government to control the armed forces. After a number of national demonstrations in support of Mossadeq, he was appointed Minister of War as well as Prime Minister and attempted to reduce the Shah's control over the army. To this end Mossadeq dissolved the Royal Guards, who were by far the most privileged section of the army, and retired 136 senior officers. In addition Mossadeq tried to diminish the importance of the army as an organ of internal oppression by transferring the responsibility for tribal affairs from the forces to the Ministry of Interior, by limiting the jurisprudence of the military to military and not political crime and by appointing two civilian judges to the army's high court.

Although Mossadeq had his supporters in the army, many high-ranking officers saw him as a direct threat to their political and social position and sought to re-establish the old order by a military coup in 1953. The initial coup failed, because of the non-co-operation of junior officers of the Tehran division, and the Shah fled to Rome. Three days later, however, a CIA-backed coup was successful; Mossadeq was arrested, the Shah returned and began the long process of re-establishing and consolidating his power and control of the army.

THE *TUDEH* PARTY

Although the Iranian communist party, the *Tudeh* Party, failed in its bid to gain control of the armed forces, it is of interest to note the extent of the support it enjoyed. In 1945, seventy officers were arrested for 'plotting to deliver the whole of Iran in a space of one night to the *Tudeh* party'.[9] There were a number of other isolated attempts by the pro-*Tudeh* army officers to seize control, but the systematic and widespread penetration of the party within the army followed the uprisings in July 1952 in support of Mossadeq. The *Tudeh* party participated as supporters of the prime minister and *Tudeh* party officials came to the conclusion that had the party been 'armed with a small disciplined military core willing to use violence, it could have exploited the situation' to set up a socialist republic in the wake of a military take over.[10]

As a result the party began a systematic and widespread penetration into almost all branches of the armed forces and *Tudeh* officers set up a tight network operating with maximum security and rigid discipline. Over 600 officers were recruited in a two-year period and the network extended to the police and the gendarmerie; only the navy, which was very small at the time, was not penetrated. The bulk of the *Tudeh* officers were from the lower-ranking groups, mainly lieutenants and captains who, though highly trained, lacked the necessary influence and connections to reach key positions in the forces. Like his father, the Shah selected only his most trusted allies to such positions and for many bright officers the only hope of achieving high ranks was through a military coup.[11]

SAVAK AND THE SECOND BUREAU

The military governorship of Tehran discovered the *Tudeh* network in the army in 1954 and an extensive purge followed; twenty-seven officers were sentenced to death, 134 to life imprisonment and the rest to between two and twenty years of prison with hard labour.[12] The discovery of this extensive dissenting corps within the armed forces highlighted the potential threat presented by the army, which at the same time remained the Shah's main power-base. Therefore, he decided to pre-empt any similar dissent by setting up a tight security system within the forces and by encouraging each branch of the armed forces to control and report on other branches. In addition, the Shah extended his personal control of all army affairs and encouraged all officers to report to him personally on their fellow officers.

The Shah also organised an extensive secret police organisation to operate within and outside the armed forces. With the aid of the CIA, the Shah set up the secret police, *Sazemaneh Etelaat va Amniateh Keshvar* (SAVAK) which was run almost exclusively by 'trusted' and loyal officers – some recalled from retirement – and extended the military jurisdiction to all political acts uncovered by the SAVAK.[13] A separate intelligence organisation, the Second Bureau was set up at the same time to control the armed forces. This organisation had branches in the police, gendarmerie, imperial guards and the military police, each of which was responsible for controlling other branches of the armed forces. Finally in 1959 the Shah appointed the Royal Inspection Organisation, manned exclusively by army officers, to inspect all aspects of political activity in the country and report back directly to him.

Thus the Shah placed the army in a tight self-sustaining surveillance network, and at the same time gave high-ranking army generals considerable political influence by charging them with the task of maintaining national security. On the other hand, top generals were prevented from gaining too much power by a rapid turnover of the top jobs; many were dismissed on the grounds of financial misconduct, disloyalty or incompetence, and on two occasions for treason.

At the same time the Shah accelerated his programme of modernisation and expansion of the armed forces, using substantial American aid and equipment. On the whole, the process of tightening security and increased opportunities for success within the forces effectively secured the allegiance of the army. With the exception of two isolated incidences in the late 1950s and early 1960s the army remained loyal until the 1979 revolution.

US AND THE ARMED FORCES

The interests of the Shah and the Americans in Iran were very close. The Americans desired the Shah's support since they regarded him as the most effective means of securing Western interests in the country and considered the army to be his 'only real source of power'.[14] The Shah for his part, in return for American military assistance, was prepared to give the US exclusive and extensive control over the armed forces. The 1947 agreement to establish a Post-war Military Mission in Iran allowed the Chief of Mission to investigate all matters, including those of security,[15] and the Iranian government agreed not to engage any other foreign personnel 'for duties of any nature connected with the Iranian army'.[16] The Americans set up their first Military Mission to the Iranian Imperial Gendarmeri, GENMISH, in 1943 and their second Mission to the Army, ARMISH, in 1947. The American presence was ostensibly a 'deterrent' to the 'Soviet political encroachment',[17] but in reality the US military assistance was 'aimed at internal security, not national defence'.[18] The American forces were paid by the Iranian government who accorded them highly preferential treatment.

The Chief of the Mission was given formal and wide-ranging authority over the Iranian forces and as a result throughout the Shah's reign the Americans played a central role in shaping and training the Iranian military. In time the American presence in Iran became 'by far the largest US security assistance programme in the world in terms of personnel'.[19] The official numbers of American military Mission personnel in Iran rose from thirty-four GENMISH members in 1943 to 403 ARMISH–MAAG (Military Assistance Advisory Group set up in 1950) in 1956 to 704 in 1960;[20] to an estimated 860 Department of Defence representatives in Iran in 1973, which in turn rose to 1156 in 1974 and 1435 in 1976,[21] the total number of American citizens in Iran however, was estimated at about 24 000, 'a large percentage of whom were involved in military programmes'.[22]

The Americans saw little to worry about in their relationship with their Iranian counterparts. A number of incidents involving single American soldiers and Iranian women and their families resulted in the Americans placing a quota on the numbers of single men sent to Iran and particularly to the provinces. Otherwise the Americans described their Iranian colleagues as 'somewhat formal' and stated that their relationship was excellent.[23] This appears rather uninformed since Iranian officers were all too well aware of the privileged position held by the Americans and the Chief of Missions in particular.

In particular the Iranians were weary of the tendency of the Chiefs of Missions to reorganise the forces almost annually regardless of the country's geo-political and human resources, and to become increasingly involved in arms deals and Iranian politics; in time American advisers became indistinguishable from salesmen and in practice the salesman-role often predominated.[24] Retired Chiefs of Mission often returned to sell arms and by 1976 as many as 1270 retired

US military men were working in Iran as representatives of American firms.[25] Some, such as General Harvey Jablonsky, Major General Harold C. Price and Captain R. S. Haward were arms-sales representatives, while the cleverest one of all, Richard Hallock, succeeded in acting at one and the same time as arms-salesman *and* US Government Adviser to Iran.[26]

ARMS DEALS

The relationship between the Iranian army and its American counterpart was, from the very early stages, personalised as one between the Shah and the representatives of the American government. As a result, the process of defence decision-making in Iran was relatively simple; the Shah decided on all major purchases. 'Once the Shah has decided that a particular system is required by the Iranian forces, it is unlikely that the Iranian defence establishment will challenge it and present serious alternatives. There is virtually no input into defence decisions by the civilian sector of the Iranian government.'[27]

On the question of arms and equipment the Shah was said to have been 'obsessive',[28] and 'obdurately stubborn',[29] and to have been motivated by prestige rather than operational effectiveness.[30] The combination of aggressive American salesmen and the Shah's own capriciousness often resulted in the purchase of totally unsuitable arms with little consideration for the logistics of the transactions or the ability of the forces to accommodate them. At times the arms were far too sophisticated, at other times the Iranian forces lacked the training and infrastructure, to keep them operational and at other times only parts of an equipment was bought and a complementary one ignored. For example, the Shah bought the M107 (175mm sp) artillery with a 32km range, but refused to purchase its target acquisition system. On the other hand the Iranian navy was expected to run the F14 which were so complicated that even the American navy had difficulty running it, as well as the Spruance destroyer which was even more sophisticated than the kind bought by the American navy.[31] Since the Iranians were chronically short of trained personnel to man this equipment, the arrival of each new component resulted in shifting existing trained personnel from other schemes, now comparatively less prestigious than the newest one, to man the new equipment.[32]

The arms deals reached their zenith after 1972 when President Nixon and the National Security Adviser Henry Kissinger agreed for the first time 'to sell Iran virtually any conventional weapon it wanted'.[33] The oil-prices quadrupled in the following year and Iranian arms purchases boomed. But despite employing numerous Americans, the Iranians did not have the necessary back-up to keep the equipment operational; whilst the US deliveries were on schedule the Iranian training and construction programme 'slipped' and fell badly behind.[34] In addition the programme of recruiting Iranian military personnel was not on target, partly because the rapid expansion in the civil sector and the inability of the army to match civilian salaries,[35] and partly because of the high failure rate of officers training to use the new equipment. As a result the Iranian army was unable to use its sophisticated equipment 'without US support on a day-to-day basis'.[36]

Despite the country's inability to absorb the equipment, the Shah continued his vast purchases, proposing barter arrangements when the oil revenue disappeared. 'What we seemed to have ignored was that an army does not consist of equipment alone, it also needs good men and careful direction and planning.'[37] The arms purchases took the country's limited resources away from economic and social development and increased the nation's dependence on the Americans to an unacceptable level; these ill-effects did not seem to trouble the Shah. Possibly the Shah saw the US involvement in Iran as the most effective means of bolstering his regime and securing its survival and therefore welcomed the 'integration' of the Iranian forces into the US logistic and support systems. The resulting 'umbilical relationship' had created an identification of US interest with Iran and the necessary involvement of the US forces in any, but the most rudimentary, of the Iranian military engagements.[38]

THE US POLICY

Although American official policy was favourable to continuing the arms deals there was a substantial minority within the government which regarded with increasing dismay the escalation of the US involvement in Iran.

The American financial involvement in the arms deal, although relatively small, was as impossible to audit as the Iranian-funded transactions. Between 1950 and 1969 the Americans provided an estimated $836m as part of their grant military assistance programme and set up the Military Assistance Advisory Group (MAAG) in 1950 to administer the fund.[39] Nevertheless, as early as 1957 US Congress met serious resistance from both Iranian and American personnel in its attempts to gain access to detailed accounts. Therefore the US House of Representatives' investigation on US aid operations in Iran concluded that the practice of consistently omitting 'the elementary facts needed for an intelligent post-audit' made these funds inauditable and impossible for Congress to control these transactions.[40] Corruption had from the very beginning been a feature of these arms deals and as the scale of the purchases increased, so did the percentages that were received by the intermediaries, often relatives or close friends of the Shah, as well as American Generals, to facilitate the sales.

On the whole the arms deals were very much supported by the US Foreign Office as well as the Department of Defence: 'everyone seemed basically pleased; Iran was getting arms, the State Department enjoyed a good US–Iran relationship; Department of Defence was actively selling and transferring part of the research and development costs to Iran and the contractors were making money'.[41] The American Congress, however, was less easy to please, as one Iranian politician recalls, 'everyone wanted the sales, but Congress always put the brakes on'.[42] Publicly the arms involvement was justified on two grounds, those of political expedience and of economic advantage; the 'broad geo-strategic and political considerations' emphasised the proximity of Iran to Russia,[43] the need to have a friendly policeman for the Gulf where much of American oil imports came from and the importance of Iran as a member of CENTO.

The Americans placed a particular value on their political leverage in the country and in this context they saw the Shah as a 'linchpin' for safeguarding American interests, as well as 'the most effective instrument of maintaining Iran's orientation towards the West'.[44] It was assumed that provided the army did not defect, the Shah could probably remain in power 'indefinitely'.[45] At the time American strategists argued that the relationship of dependence was so extensive and American leverage so powerful that even if the Shah were to be displaced by a revolution and replaced by an anti-US regime, that regime would know that without American help it could not run its army and would therefore 'moderate' its policies towards the West. Furthermore it was assumed that if such a regime failed to comply with American interest, and sought to eliminate the American presence in Iran then the US could retaliate 'by bringing Iran's military machine to a virtual standstill'.[46]

Since ultimately the decision to sell arms rested with the President, the American congressional outcry against the sales of arms in Iran did not prove very effective and Iran was exempted from the provisions of the Carter government's decision to reduce arms sales and not to use these transactions as an 'instrument of foreign policy'.[47] In fact, as late as January 1979, despite the extensive unrest in Iran, Carter was still publicly affirming his government's support for the Shah and the Iranian military.

So extensive was the belief in the power of the Americans in directing Iranian politics that more than one Iranian politician came to blame the revolution on the withdrawal of effective American support. Both the Shah and Bakhtiar (among others)[48] have noted the crucial part played by the United State's government in neutralising the army.[48] In January 1979, at the eleventh hour, the White House sought to unite the military first behind Prime Minister Shahpour Bakhtiar and subsequently in support of the Islamic republic's first Prime Minister Medhi Bazargan. To this end General Robert Hyser was dispatched to Iran. But although he succeeded in winning the general's agreement to the Shah's departure, he failed to set up a new pro-American regime. In part his failure was due to the diminishing influence of the high-ranking officials, who could no longer rely on the men in their command. The bulk of the 180 000 army were conscripts and only 50 000 were professional soldiers. The professionals enjoyed all the privileges of good housing, schooling and medical attention for themselves and their families. By contrast, the conscripts were paid little, and expected to do the most menial tasks. These troops were reluctant to shoot their compatriots and had to be confined to barracks to prevent them from joining the demonstrations.

BUDGET

Since the emergence of the armed forces as a fundamental basis for the Phalavis' survival, the army has always absorbed a substantial percentage of the national budget, on average about 30 per cent of the total from 1921 to 1978. This formal budgetary allocation to the Ministry of War, however, has always been considerably supplemented either directly by oil funds or indirectly by loans and credits negotiated separately and reflected under foreign debts in the national accounts. Nor did the accounts reflect the expenditure of the police and the SAVAK. As a result the actual cost of the army is considerably higher than the apparent one.

There were in fact in Iran three military budgets, one drawn up and calculated by the Ministry of War which was carefully planned and vetted by the *Majlis*. The other two were less visible and not subject to security. The first of these was concerned with the arms deals arranged personally by the Shah 'that was extra; the Shah used to tell Toufanian (Hassan, Vice-Minister of War) to buy the equipment and tell Samyi (Mehdi) to pay'.[49] Only the cash transactions, which were relatively rare, appeared in the official military budget. The bulk of these arms deals were financed by foreign loans or credit; as such they did not involve budgetary allocations from the national budget. The loan credits were ratified by *Majlis*, as general imports funds and repaid as foreign debt and not accounted for as military expenditure. In addition, the Minister of War was able to negotiate loans, guaranteed by the Treasury and ratified by the cabinet, without referring to the central bank nor to the *Majlis*.[50]

The second of these secret budgets was that of the SAVAK and secret police; this was not officially reported anywhere, and was quite separate from the military budget. In addition, expenditure on military infrastructure, such as roads, airports, housing loans to military personnel, etc., were met by other departments, such as the Ministry of Roads and Construction and not counted as military expenditure. Thus, excessive as the *official* military budget was under the Shah, the *actual* amount of military spending was considerably greater.

THE SHAH AND THE ARMED FORCES

The Shah, like his father, was uniquely dependent on the armed forces both for a support base and for the survival of his regime. The Shah himself was well aware of the crucial part played by the forces in Iranian politics: 'the Iranian regime was the advantage that nothing would create an obstacle to it. If a cabinet is ineffective, we sack it; if the *Majlis* is badly organised, we sack it. The most important are the armed forces which were created by my father, with all their traditions.'[51] 'We have seen that king is the king who can effectively command the armed forces, who can play a central role in this country.'[52] Therefore, the Shah regarded army loyalty as pivotal to his success and sought to secure this support by inculcating a strong personal allegiance to the crown and retaining total control of the armed forces. In addition, the Shah offered the army substantial material benefits and a degree of political influence.

Until the late 1960s the army salaries were by far the largest in the country and in addition the forces were entitled to considerable fringe benefits such as cheap housing loans and cost-price consumer goods sold at army co-operatives. These co-operatives were entitled to buy at cost price from State monopolies and were exempt from import duties on foreign products – the co-operatives' imports were considerable and accounted for 40 per cent of the Ministry of War's total imports expenditure in 1958–9.[53] But in the boom years in the 1970s, military salaries failed to keep pace with those in the civilian sector and some of the better-qualified officers resigned to work in the private sector, or took on a second job along with their military one. Others became extensively involved in real-estate speculations. Although military salaries were raised 'the army was no longer attractive as a career'.[54] This aggravated the problems caused by the substantial and sudden increase in purchases of military equipment at the same time.

For the Shah, the armed forces remained 'a tool of personal power',[55] to which he devoted an inordinate amount of time and energy,[56] and maintained a personal control of all its aspects. The army was kept quite separate from all other national institutions;

> there were two independent chains of command; one led to the Prime Minister and his cabinet, including the Minister of War, and the other linked the army and the Chief of Staff who acted as an uneasy link between the Shah and the Minister of War. Hence the armed forces were divorced from government policies which were in any case dictated by the Shah. Therefore, the Shah alone was the co-ordinator of both military and government policies.[57]

As early as the 1940s the Shah had taken his constitutional title of Commander-in-Chief to apply 'not only nominally, but effectively',[58] and to extend to 'every legislative and executive decision within the forces'.[59] The Chief of Staff was required to report to the Shah 'every detail' and 'execute to the letter HM's instructions';[60] even if a private asked for a week's leave to go on pilgrimage, the permission had to be ratified by the Shah personally.

As well, promotions from the level of brigadier onward were 'at the Royal will' and unrelated to length of service; those who did not have the ear of the king were unlikely to be promoted. It was, however, relatively easy for higher ranking officers to gain access; the Shah encouraged officers to regard him as their 'crowned father' and to act as an informal intelligence corps, reporting directly to him about the conduct of their fellow-officers.

This extensive personal control, however, emasculated the army and eliminated its chain of command 'from platoon leader to Chief of Staff, no one had the right to give any orders without the Shah's permission'.[61] 'As a result, although numerous and well-equipped, the army lacked the necessary *esprit de corps*.'[62] In fact, the Shah's practice to play different factions of the army against one another seriously undermined the unity of the forces. Nor was any officer permitted to be too popular or in control of the forces for too long. Popularity, competence and leadership in the Chief of Staff made him a threat to the crown which the Shah could not tolerate.

Since the army was primarily directed against the enemy within, its dependence on the person of the Shah was not thought by him to be inconsistent with its primary function, that of defending his interest. Yet although the main threat was considered to be an internal one, the forces had surprisingly little training in dealing with civil disturbances, the responsibility for containment was placed on SAVAK and spying rather than armed control of the recurring uprisings. After the 1963 riots the armed divisions based in Tehran began anti-riot training, but the programme was short-lived. It was intended that special sections of the army were to support the police and that all the troops in Tehran were to have had sufficient training to be effective against the crowd. The special army units and the police anti-riot control units were placed under a joint command and had begun regular exercises in the capital's potential trouble spots. But the Shah's encouragement of internal rivalries was partly responsible for the demise of the 'civil defence force' when a favoured general asked for and succeeded in obtaining the permission to incorporate the riot control units in the army's first division. In part the riot control was disbanded in the belief that the rising prosperity of the country would in itself undermine the rebellious tendencies and partly on the assumption that SAVAK's control was so extensive that no-one would dare to riot any more. By 1978 the forces appeared to have forgotten the last vestige of their riot-control training and, despite their large numbers, they were totally ineffectual.[63]

The ineffectiveness of the army may also have been the result of its disenchantment with the Shah. The monarch's fear of the army as a potential threat, in the long run, had dominated his desire to placate the forces and the distrust and the network of spies led to widespread demoralisation within the army and made the forces an unhappy and difficult place and an unrewarding career. The Shah resented and distrusted all successful officers and 'treated them like dirt'.[64] 'He expected high ranking officers to dance attendance on him and his family. Generals were expected to bow and scrape, to open doors for him and stand behind him at attention at official functions. One could be in attendance for weeks without a single acknowledgement from either the king or the empress.'[65] Even total life-long loyalty was not proof against the royal whim; General Fereydoun Djam, by far the most able Chief of Staff ever appointed and an old personal friend of the Shah incurred the royal displeasure for confiding to his fellow-generals that he loved the king as his own brother. The Minister of Court, Assadolah Alam was instructed to inform him that 'no-one can be the Shah's brother' and that the General would be well advised to 'take a break for a while'.[66] The General was effectively exiled.

The Shah's total control, as well as the long-established tradition of deferring all orders to the personal decision of the king made the army's effectiveness entirely dependent on the presence of the king, therefore, once he left the country no-one was capable of marshalling the forces in his defence. Once the Shah left, officers followed him in droves; the ones who stayed refused to obey commands not issued by 'our crowned father', so there was little choice left to the generals except to declare their neutrality, which they did as early as 11 February 1979, soon after the Shah's departure.

The air force, the Shah's favourite section of the armed forces was, in fact, the first to declare its support for Khomeini and the pathetic attempt of the land forces to attack the air-force barracks ended in fiasco before reaching their target. The tank commanders who stood up to address the angry crowd were shot one after the other by the people who then attacked and disarmed the whole division.[67]

Thus the edifice of support that the Shah had constructed as the cornerstone of his regime was at one and the same time undermined by his fear of its potential power. On the one hand the army was enlarged, equipped to the hilt and strengthened, and on the other its operational powers were severely restricted and its unity underminded. In the long term it seems that the Shah succeeded in destroying the effectiveness of the only group who were likely to maintain him in power, paradoxically because he feared the power of his creation.

THE POST-REVOLUTIONARY ARMED FORCES

Although the Shah has gone, the habits of mistrust and tight control, as well as the general ambivalence of the regime towards the forces have continued. Initially Khomeini, who also saw the army as a potential threat, decided to disband the forces and replace them with 'the people's army, including all the deprived and impoverished Muslims in Iran and in the world', a kind of international revolutionary *shiia* brotherhood. Surprisingly the army survived both the extensive desertion of conscripts and hundreds of officers, and Khomeini's sacking or execution of over 13 000 of the 25 000-strong officer corps. At the same time the Revolutionary Council set up its own militia: The Guardian Corps of the Islamic Revolution, or the revolutionary guards. The undermining of the army reached its zenith in July 1980, after a series of allegations about the discovery of a plot for an army coup, and might have gone much further had the Iraqis not invaded Khouzestan in September 1980.

The war with Iraq revived the notion of nationalism, which had been declared defunct by Khomeini, and brought a respite from purges for the army. The necessity of marshalling a large army which would remain loyal to the regime led to the inclusion of the clergy as an integral part of the combating forces as well as the rigorous implementation of the conscription and imposition of new and very severe penalties on draft dodgers. Failing to report for service has been declared 'desertion from the fronts' and those committing such a crime are barred from obtaining ration cards, piped water, electricity, gas, telephone, health insurance, any kind of educational certificates or driving licence, or even the registration of wealth or property transferred to them. In addition, all previous servicemen up to the age of 60 are required to be ready for subsequent call-up if necessary.[68] Furthermore, there has been a general call-up of all able-bodied men to form militia units to fight the war. Mosques invite devout Muslim men of all ages to obtain arms and a perfunctory training ranging from thirty-five days for those deemed as untrained to seven days for those who have had some training.[69] Primary school children and teenagers too young for conscription have formed a major intake of the militia.

Since 1983 a new measure has been instituted to encourage all public and private employees to form 'martyrs battalions' for short-term service at the front. Workers, pupils, teachers and civil servants have all sent their battalions for three-monthly periods. In addition, all medical doctors, regardless of their specialities are obliged to serve a similar period each year in the field hospitals. The mainstays of the regime, however, are the revolutionary guards who are specifically responsible for fighting internal opposition and suppressing 'the political currents that may aim to shake the Islamic revolution'.[70] The corps consists almost entirely of devout Muslims who compensate for their lack of 'the superficial discipline in the form that was seen under the Shah' by having plenty of ardour and 'spiritual discipline'.[71] The force, which is under Khomeini's personal command, is almost entirely recruited from the poor and slum-dwellers, for whom being a revolutionary guard is an effective means of gaining both political and economic benefits. In practice the revolutionary corps is now acting as the most effective vehicle of upward mobility for those who have no education and no skills. The corps does not even demand literacy of its members, but it does exact fanatical devotion to the revolution in general and to the person of Khomeini in particular, and all members must be willing to give their lives for their cause. According to the corps commander, Morteza Rezai, in the first two years of its formation 11 000 guards 'achieved' martyrdom, which he described as 'a means of reaching God and the exalted state'.[72] Besides being heavenly-rewarded, however, the corps also offers substantial material benefits to its members. In addition to a regular salary (which although not large, compares favourably with the wages paid to other unskilled workers) the guards are entitled to land and housing as well as cheap loans and they are guaranteed medical care. The guards are expected to fight both at the front and against tribal uprising in the provinces, as well as acting as the law enforcement arm of the urban Islamic revolutionary committees. The guards' ubiquity and unchecked authority has given them considerable power, which is often abused. Even the Commander of the Corps has shown public concern over the excesses of his men and their tendency to 'interfere in some affairs that they should not'. Nevertheless, despite public pronouncement to the contrary, the corps members continue to take effective control both of political and at time economic organisation of localities. In 1983 the Ministry of Revolutionary Guards was set up to represent their interests at cabinet level. At the same time military service was redefined to include conscription to the guards. Conscripts could enlist for four years urban duties or two years service at the front. In terms of internal politics it is the total devotion of the corps members to Khomeini and their presence in ever-increasing numbers in all spheres of life that has buttressed the regime and given it a degree of security.

SAVAMA

The revolutionary guards work closely with the new secret police Sazemaneh Etelaat va Amniateh Mihan SAVAMA, which has taken over and expanded the external functions of the SAVAK. The internal

control and repression has been taken over by the revolutionary guards
and local committees who are still using the files and the previous secret
police. Already the regime has gained considerable notoriety for its
extensive infringements of human rights, for using SAVAK's torture
chambers as well as its methods of interrogation and for having the
highest rate of political execution in the world.[73] There is also great
emphasis placed by the current regime on sending SAVAMA members
and revolutionary guards abroad in pursuit of its opponents. The secret
police, often engaged under various guises by the Embassies abroad,
have had a degree of success. One of the Shah's nephews, Shahryar, as
well as a leading general, Qolam Ali Oveissi, were assassinated in Paris
and there were a number of attempts to kill Shahpour Bahktiar and
other personalities abroad. In addition, the regime has extended its
network of spies to most universities abroad and there are numerous
attacks on individuals, much of which pass unrecorded.

IDEOLOGY IN COMMAND

The entire propaganda machine in Iran is currently working to
generate loyalty to the regime. But not all the work is done through the
media; the revolutionary guards, for example, have a specifically
ideological role to play in their capacity as the 'powerful arm of the
revolutionary religious institution, *Rohaniat*'. The single most powerful
organ devoted to raising the nation's Islamic zeal, however, is the
Ideological and Political Section, which is Khomeini's clerical
information and security network set up within all national
organisations and particularly active within the armed forces and the
revolutionary corps. The ideological and political section was set up in
September 1979 to purge the army of 'counter-revolutionary and
imperial agents' and to take 'speedy measures' in making the army an
'Islamic' force.[74] Through their membership of this section, the clergy
have now successfully permeated the forces at all levels and have in the
process 'demolished' what they have labelled the 'destructive image' of
the army to replace it by a truly populist one.[75] The new image is said to
convey the new character of the army which is no longer Westernised
but *maktabi*, orthodox. This is exactly the kind of army that the Head
of the Ideological sector, Hojatoleslam Safayi, thinks the country
should have: 'any genuine Islamic government requires a very powerful
and active armed force in order to safeguard orthodox and divine
values, cleanse decadence and illuminate the way'.[76] Safayi argues that

the regime cannot survive without relying on a powerful army base, and the power of the army, he adds, must be rooted in its faith. Faith in this context is described in terms of merciless vengeance and martyrdom. Vengeance in turn is seen as a worthy attribute, one that has reportedly been praised by the leader of all Shiias, Ali, Mohamad's son-in-law. Ali is said to have revenged himself in the most bloody manner against the *Khavarej*, Muslims who turned against him and chose to leave him unaided in the battlefield.

> The day *Hazrateh* Ali *Aleyha Salam* (may peace be upon him) realised the danger posed by them (*Khavarej*) he announced in a fierce and deadly voice 'only I have the strength to cut through the protection of faith, enhanced by daily prayers and cut open their heads with my sword and shatter their frail bodies which are protected by years of fasting and devotion', and proceeded to kill them.[77]

The untrained militia were exhorted by the General Secretary of the Combating Clerics, Ayatollah Mahdavi Kani, to remember that 'martyrs are the building blocks of our society',[78] and the Commander-in-Chief of the Armed Forces, Colonel Sayad Shirazi, emphasised that 'faith' is the forces' 'strongest weapon enabling them to rush and give their lives on the battlefields'.[79] Much of this faith centres on the 'bright, glorious and heavenly prospect' of the 'blessed state of martyrdom',[80] and the belief that martyrdom is able to 'revitalise death and give it the essence of life'.[81] Thus death is made glorious and the enemies are made impotent since either way the Shiia soldiers would achieve glory, whether in this world or the next. In fact, so exalted is the state of martyrdom that the state has instituted the practice of congratulating widows and orphans for the death of their nearest and dearest, as well as offering them condolences.

However, despite repeated public statements about the 'great unity of the militia, the guards and the army',[82] the regular armed forces have not found it easy to accept the messages of faith and martyrdom. They have continued to regard the clergy with deep suspicion and have placed them at the head of the militia, who have become the standard-bearers of the battlefields. The militia and the guards, exhorted by the clergy have, in practice, been used as cannon fodder while the regular forces have tended to choose less suicidal war tactics.

The leading role of the clergy at the fronts and the high risk to their lives has resulted in a marked reluctance on their part to join the forces, and a tendency to 'spend their time making public speeches at home'.[83] This reached such critical dimensions that, although exempt from conscription on religious grounds, the clergy were publicly invited by the establishment 'to go to the front and provide the necessary guidance and leadership'.[84] The Iranian army has, nevertheless, held up surprisingly well. After two years of stalemate, the forces regained the areas lost to Iraq in 1982 and mounted major offensives into Iraq in 1983 and 1984.

Despite repeated purges the army remains resilient and the training and skills gained in the past fifty years have enabled it to survive. After the hasty flight of the country's first President, Abolhassan Bani Sadre, to Paris in 1982, many high-ranking officers were sacked or imprisoned. In 1983, a major drive against the *Tudeh* party led to the discovery of numerous *Tudeh* cells among the junior officers, and a further purge. As a result, the army is now entirely commanded by junior officers; the Chief of Staff is a brigadier general, the army is headed by a colonel, and the navy by a captain. It is in death and martyrdom that the elusive unity of the regular and irregular forces is achieved. The Martyrs Organisation orchestrates the death of martyrs using one of the old gambits of the resistance movement in Iran, which was to publicise the last testament of the heroes tortured and killed by the regime. The practice has now gained mass application; every day Islamic papers carry photographs and last testaments of devoted soldiers stating their loyalty to the regime in general and Khomeini in particular and their willingness to die for the cause. The heavy, ideological onslaught, directed against all internal opposition to the regime, against the 'pagan' Sunni Iraqis, who represent the great devil America, and against the great enemy of Ali and Shiism the Sunni Yazid, must however be occasionally tempered with a soothing message for the Sunni brothers of the regime in Iran. In particular the propaganda machine seeks to identify the Sunni Arabs in Khouzestan and some Sunni Kurdish tribesmen as its supporters, a task not made easy by the long-standing tribal revolt against Khomeini both in Kordestan and in Turkomanestan in the north of the country.

In its containment strategies, however, the Khomeini regime is more effective than the Shah in that it has appointed a particular force, the revolutionary corps, for the specific task of fighting against the internal enemy. As a result there is an unprecedented delineation of responsibility within the forces. The army is, by and large, concentrated at the front line to fight against the external enemy, while the revolutionary guards are sent to tribal areas, provinces, as well as to the trouble spots in the capital. The guards' regular skirmishes with the resistance movement in turn, over the past three years, have provided it with invaluable training in urban battles, a training that the Shah's forces did not have.

CONCLUSION

The importance of the armed forces in Iranian politics has if anything increased over time. The current regime is heavily dependent on the revolutionary guards and the secret police for its survival internally, and on the army for the protection of its borders. The war with Iraq has resulted in the channelling of even larger funds to the armed forces. Although the American speculations about grounding the Iranian forces have not been realised, largely thanks to the army's pre-revolutionary training as well as the thriving black market in arms, the Iranian economy has been burdened by the prohibitive cost of making its army operational. The problem has been aggravated by the destruction of large parts of the oil industry in the war zone and the oil glut since 1982. However, despite predictions of national bankruptcy and dark hints at empty coffers by many exiled ex-heads of the national bank, the government has so far succeeded in staving-off disaster by its austerity policies and severe cuts in public expenditure.[85]

As to the forces themselves, although Khomeini's control is not as all-pervasive as that of the Shah, the clergy have reinstituted the climate of distrust and competition that existed under the Shah. Once more the army and the new revolutionary corps have become instruments of power, used to great effect by the regime which, like the Shah, has established the practice of regular purges in order to prevent the emergence of the forces as a potential source of threat.

Sadly, it appears that the revolution has contributed little to the cause of liberty in Iran. Once more a dictatorship has emerged, buttressed by its own militia and the secret police, and using the forces primarily as an instrument of internal repression.

NOTES

1. F. Kazemi 'The Military and Politics in Iran, An Uneasy Symbiosis' in E. Kedouri and S. Hain.
2. A. Salamatian, 'Historique du Rôle Politique de l'Armée en Iran', thesis

for the Faculty of Law & Economics at Paris University, February 1970, p. 106.

3. Ibid, p. 115.
4. Ibid, p. 109.
5. Ibid, p. 111.
6. A. K. S. Lambton *Landlord and Peasant in Iran*, p. 463.
7. Salamatian, p. 110.
8. General H. Arfa *Under Five Shahs* (London: John Murray, 1964) p. 283.
9. Ibid, p. 342.
10. S. Zabih *The Communist Movement in Iran* (University of California Press, 1966) p. 178.
11. For a detailed analysis of the *Tudeh* penetration within the armed forces and the aspiration of junior officers, see Kazemi, *Military and Politics*.
12. Salamatian p. 162.
13. M. R. Pahlavi, *Answer to History* (New York: Stein & Day, 1980) p. 157.
14. Draft report to the National Security Council by NSC Board 21 December 1953. Quoted by Y. Alexander and A. Nanes (eds) *The US and Iran: A Documentary History* (University Publication of America, 1980) p. 268.
15. Article 12.
16. Article 24.
17. General Arfa, *Under Five Shahs*, p. 325.
18. Note from Acting Secretary of State, Lovett, to the Embassy in Iran 3 March 1948. Alexander and Nanes, *The US and Iran*, p. 189.
19. US Military Sales to Iran Staff Report (Washington: US Government Printing Office, 1976) p. 37.
20. Ibid, p. 34.
21. Ibid, p. 37.
22. Ibid, p. vii. William H. Sullivan, US Ambassador, notes that many of the American instructors 'proved to be a partially disruptive element in US–Iranian relations', W. H. Sullivan, *Mission to Iran* (W. W. Norton & Co, New York and London 1981) p.80.
23. Ibid, p. ix.
24. Ibid, p. 49.
25. Ibid, p. 36.
26. B. Rubin *Paved with Good Intentions* (Oxford University Press, 1980) pp. 164–5.
27. Staff Report, 1976 p. 7
28. Wiley, US Ambassador to Iran on 18 November 1948, quoted by Alexander and Nanes, *The US and Iran*, p. 198, and ARMISH Chief Evans, ibid, p. 197.
29. Wiley, letter to the Secretary of State 11 September 1948, in Alexander and Nanes, *The US and Iran*, p. 197.
30. Staff Report, 1976 p. xi.
31. Rubin, *Paved with Good Intentions*, p. 166.
32. Staff Report, p. 32.
33. Ibid, p. vii.
34. Ibid, p. 54.
35. Ibid, p. viii.
36. Ibid, p. ix.

37. General Fereydoun Djam, interviewed by the author in November 1981.
38. Staff Report, 1976, p. 52.
39. Ibid, p. 4.
40. Alexander and Nanes, *The US and Iran*, pp. 298 and 302.
41. Staff Report, 1976, p. 46.
42. Mehdi Samyi, previously Governor of the Central Bank in Iran, interviewed by the author.
43. National Security Council on US Strategy for Iran, 1963, quoted by Alexander and Nanes, *The US and Iran*, p. 353.
44. Draft report to the National Security Council by NSC Planning Board, 21 December 1953 in Alexander and Nanes, *The US and Iran*, p. 268.
45. Ibid, p. 317.
46. Staff Report, 1976, p. 52.
47. Alexander and Nanes, *The US and Iran*, p. 447.
48. See Pahlavi, *Answer to History*, p. 172, Rubin, *Paved with Good Intentions*, p. 246, and Bakhtiar interviewed by Fred Halliday, MERIP No. 104, March–April, 1982 and Sullivan *Mission to Iran*, pp. 227–34.
49. General Djam, interviewed by the author.
50. Mehdi Samyi, interviewed by the author.
51. Etelaat 8 June 1960, quoted by Salamatian pp. 188–9.
52. Ibid, 27 June 1967; ibid, p. 189.
53. Ibid, p. 171.
54. Djam, interviewed by author.
55. Staff Report, 1976, p. 37.
56. Ibid.
57. Djam, interviewed by the author.
58. Arfa, *Under Five Shahs*, p. 331.
59. Djam, interviewed by the author.
60. Arfa, *Under Five Shahs*, p. 331.
61. Recruitment of Armed Forces Act, 1957, articles 18 and 32.
62. Djam, interviewed by the author.
63. Anthony Parsons British Ambassador notes that the Iranian army were quite unable to disperse even small crowds by baton charges and anti-riot techniques; 'the Iranian army was behaving as though it was fighting a war against a national enemy'. Anthony Parson *The Pride and the Fall*, Jonathan Cape, London 1984, p. 104.
64. Djam, interviewed by the author. Also see Sullivan, *Mission to Iran*, p. 83.
65. Ibid.
66. Ibid.
67. General Kazemi interviewed in Paris, Summer 1982.
68. Hassan Rohani, Head of the *Majlis'* Defence Commission, interviewed by *Kayhan*, 19 August 1982.
69. Qalomhosein Naderi, MP for Najafabad, speaking in the *Majlis*, reported by *Kayhan*, 6 January 1982.
70. Morteza Rezayi, Head of the Corps, interviewed by *Kayhan International*, 24 June 1981.
71. Ibid.
72. Ibid.
73. Amnesty International, January 1982.

74. *Kayhan International*, 19 April 1981.
75. Ibid, 17 November 1981.
76. Ibid, 15 March 1981.
77. Naderi reported by *Kayhan*, 19 August 1982.
78. *Kayhan*, 6 November 1983.
79. *Kayhan*, 1 September 1983.
80. *Kayhan*, 9 November 1981.
81. Ayatollah Ali Khameneyi addressing the forces, reported by *Kayhan*, 20 January 1982.
82. *Kayhan*, 24 September 1983.
83. Ayatollah Montazeri's address to the Clergy, *Kayhan*, 2 February 1984.
84. *Kayhan*, 4 February 1984.
85. For a more detailed discussion of these measures, see chapter 10 on theocracy in this volume.

Part III
The Islamic Revolution

9 The Nature of the Islamic Revolution*

MORTEZA MOTAHARI

What is 'revolution'? 'Revolution' is an expression for the rebellion or uprising of the people of one region or one land against the existing ruling order for the purpose of installing some desired form of rule. According to another explanation, 'revolution' is a kind of rebellion or uprising against the governmental *status quo* with the aim of establishing another *status quo*. It will be understood, therefore, that two features lie at the root of every revolution: one is discontent and exasperation directed towards the existing situation, and the other is the aim of establishing another, different situation. Understanding a revolution means knowing the causes of discontent, and knowing the aim which the people have.

In connection with revolutions in general, there are two (prevailing) theories. One theory is that all the world's social revolutions have a single basic spirit or nature, even though they may appear to assume different and varied forms. The supporters of this theory say that all the world's revolutions, the revolution at the birth of Islam, the great French Revolution, the October Revolution, the Chinese Cultural Revolution, and so on, are actually one kind of revolution, although their expressions are diverse. It may appear that one revolution, for example, is scientific (in character), another political; another may be a religious revolution, and so forth; however, the spirit and nature of all

---

*This chapter has been composed from extracts from a selection of speeches and interviews which Ayatollah Morteza Motahari gave after the Revolution, and which were gathered together in a volume called *Piramouneh Enqelabeh Eslami*, published by the Entesharateh Sadra in Qum in 1980. The common strand to this volume is an analysis of the Revolution, and it marks the first steps towards an understanding of what the Iranian people had been through, the tremendous upheaval which had occurred and the direction in which they were to go.

of them is no more than one. The spirit and nature of all revolutions are economic and material.

From this point of view, revolutions resemble a disease which manifests different effects and symptoms in different circumstances; but a doctor can understand that all these various symptoms and all the indications which appear to vary, have no more than one origin. Those who believe this also say that in every revolution the discontents in fact ultimately reduce to one discontent, the frustrations boil down to one frustration, and the aims to one aim. All the world's revolutions are in fact revolutions by those who have not, against those who have. The foundation of all revolutions is ultimately deprivation. (Of course, the point that deprivation is itself the effect of advances in the means of production which increase the gaps within society is something that needs to be investigated in its proper place.)

In our own times, this idea – the class origin of revolutions – has gained much currency, so that even those who talk in terms of the ideas of Islam 'and hold forth about Islamic culture' lay a great deal of emphasis on the question of 'the deprived', 'deprivation' and 'being deprived', with the result that these people have become involved in a kind of distortion of the facts.

The second theory holds that revolutions do not have a purely material foundation. Of course, some revolutions may spring from a polarisation of society with respect to economic factors and material gains . . . but (this is) not a necessary condition; it is quite possible for a revolution to have a purely human character. Rebellion because of hunger is not unique to man: animals, too, when starved, often turn against man, or other animals, or even against their own sort. But, in many cases, revolutions can have an entirely human character. A revolution can sometimes be human when it has a freedom-oriented or political nature, not an economic one. Thus it is quite possible that stomachs may be full and hunger minimised or abolished, in a society, but the people have not been given the right of freedom; that is, the right to self-determination and the right to express one's own beliefs have been denied. We know that none of these matters has anything to do with economic causes. In such a society, it has been observed, the people rise up to claim these rights that they have been denied, and set a revolution in motion. In this way it is not a revolution with an economic nature which comes into existence, but one with a democratic and liberal nature.

In addition to the two kinds of essential nature that we have mentioned, revolution can have a belief-oriented or ideological nature, in the sense that people who have faith in a religion or ideology and firmly adhere to its spiritual values will rise up when they see their religion or ideology exposed to harm and when they see it made the target of radical attacks against its ideas, because they are angry and grieved on account of the injuries which the body of their religion or ideology has sustained, and because they wish to establish it in a complete form without any imperfection. The revolution of such people is not related to the fullness or emptiness of their stomachs, nor to their having or not having political freedom, since it may well be that their stomachs are full and they have political freedom; but they rebel and rise up because they observe that the religion in which they believe and have their aspirations has not been adhered to.

If we try to gather together the causes which bring about a revolution, we shall reach the conclusion that they can either be of an economic and material kind, that is, that their cause lies in the polarisation of society and its division into two extremes – the well-off and the deprived, the prosperous and those who have no share. Naturally, the aim of such an uprising will be to arrive at a kind of society in which there is no kind of class division, that is to say, a classless society, or else the governing factor of the revolution may be man's freedom-loving qualities. One of man's lofty principles is his love of freedom, which means that to be free, to have no master over one, is more valuable to a man than any amount of material welath ... A human being prefers freedom to anything else, so it is perfectly natural that a people's movement should be a political one and not an economic or material one. As an example, the French Revolution was a revolution like this; when the philosophers and *savants* like Rousseau had propagated all their ideas about freedom and love of freedom, about man's self-respect, his liberty and value (as a human being) they had prepared the ground for an uprising, and the people, who had been awakened, made the revolution to achieve freedom.

The third cause of the appearance of revolution is the desire for an ideal, the pursuit of beliefs; these are the so-called ideological revolutions. These revolutions are struggles for beliefs, and not economic struggles in the guise of struggles for beliefs. Religious wars are a good example of conflicts which are rooted in creeds and ideals. The Koran also emphasises this point. A subtle observation is inserted at the thirteenth verse of the surah 'Al Imran' (III). This verse has to do with an engagement between the Muslims and the unbelievers at the battle of Badr. Where the verse names the believers, it calls their struggle an ideological or belief-based struggle, but it does not call the unbelievers' struggle a belief-based one. The verse says 'There has already been a sign for you in the two companies that confronted each other, one company fighting in the way of God (that is, fighting for their faith and beliefs) and the other unbelieving.' The verse does not say that the second group was fighting for its beliefs too, because its struggle was not really tempered by any doctrinal quality. The protection of the idols by the likes of Abu Sufyan (the principal Meccan opponent of the Prophet) was not on account of any faith in them, for Abu Sufyan knew that if the new order took over, nothing would remain of his power and glory: in fact, he was defending his own interests, not his beliefs.

*   *   *   *   *

Our movement must now answer the question, 'what is the basic nature of the Iranian revolution?' Is it based on class (struggle)? Is it motivated by liberalism? Does it have an ideological, belief-based, Islamic nature? Those who believe that all revolutions have a material, class-oriented nature say that in effect the Iranian revolution was a rising-up of the deprived against the rich; that is to say, two classes stood up against each other, the wealthy and the poor, and, if the revolution is to continue, it must follow this way. This group, who believe themselves to be Muslims but who think like materialists, try to paint the picture in Islamic colours. They take the verse 'Yet we desired to be gracious to those who were abased in the land, and to make them leaders, and to make them the inheritors, and to establish them in the land, and to show Pharaoh and Haman, and their hosts, what they were dreading from them' (XXVIII: 4 and 5) and on the basis of this, claim that Islam too interprets history in terms of the polarisation of societies, the struggle of the oppressors with the oppressed, and the victory of the latter over the former; and they say that the revolution (in Iran) is an example of this. But there is a significant point in the Koran which these people have not noticed, which is that although Islam recognises that spiritual resurgence is on the side of the oppressed, it does not recognise the oppressed alone as the source of every resurgence or revolution. Contrary to materialism, which asserts that resurgence is basically the responsibility of the deprived alone, and is directed by them against the wealthy classes, Islam recognises that the uprising of the prophets was to the advantage of the deprived, but does not recognise that it was exclusively their responsibility. The failure to perceive this difference, between the alliances within, and the source of, a revolution, is the origin of many errors.

Those who believe that it is the material factor that is intrinsic to, and causes, revolutions, see them as essentially social. That is to say, they believe that revolution does not have its roots in the nature of man, but in social transformations, whereas Islam on the contrary, stresses (the role of) man's nature and humanity. It is for this very reason that Islam does not see itself as addressing only the deprived. Islam addresses itself to all social groups and classes, even the well-to-do and oppressing classes. For the Islamic world-view finds a human being in yokes and chains inside every oppressor, every Pharaoh. According to the reasoning of Islam, Pharaoh did not put only the Israelites into chains, he put a human being inside himself into chains – a man who has a divine nature and who is capable of perceiving divine values – and he became imprisoned within this external Pharaoh. So we can see that when the prophets begin their calls to mankind and start their struggle against false gods, the beginning of their quest is this man who has been dragged into chains: they go right inside the Pharaohs, with the intention of inciting this man against the Pharaoh ruling over him, so that they can in this way bring about the revolution from within. Of course, the success here (with the Pharaoh type of person is not as great as that with an individual whose inner self is freed from chains. Concerning especially this kind of internal revolution are the words 'Then said a certain man, a believer of Pharaoh's folk that kept his belief hidden ...' (XL:28). This states that in the court of Pharaoh, among those who, as far as their standard of living was concerned, passed their days in complete ease, and who, as members of the wealthy and oppressing class, worked and co-operated, and thought the same as the ruler, Pharaoh, there was a man who believed in Moses and came to his aid.

Pharaoh's wife is an example of someone who found herself in the ruling class but who became aware of the reality when she heard the words of truth, and put herself at her Lord's command. When she had accepted Moses' call, she rose up against Pharaoh; right at the beginning she ripped off the shackles from the feet of that human being who was chained up inside her. Then, when she had freed her own humanity, she rebelled against Pharaoh, who was both her husband and a symbol of the power of oppression and cruelty. This uprising was that of one of the Egyptians for the sake of the Israelites.

The Israelites were a people who were in chains in the land of another people, the Egyptians, but their own interior selves were not in chains, or at least were not so captive. Naturally, Moses' call attracted more support among them, who could in fact be counted as the deprived in that country, just as the call of the Prophet (Mohammed) was accepted more by the deprived, than in the wealthy classes where there were fewer who surrendered themselves. In our own time also, the deprived welcomed the Islamic Revolution much more wholeheartedly because this revolution is in support of the oppressed and for their good; that is to say, it follows the direction of justice, and naturally, since it is for the establishment of justice, it is necessary for the wealth that has been accumulated by one group to be taken from them and put at the disposal of the deprived. It is quite natural that it should be a piece of good fortune and a joy for the one who is to take: it is both a response to his own natural feelings and a vindication. But as for the one who must give up his wealth, of course it is an answer to his nature too, but he must see all his aspirations come to an end; so, from this aspect, it is very difficult for such a person as this to accept the new order, and, for this very reason, the degree of agreement (with the aims of the revolution) met with in this stratum of society has been slight.

The speaker now focuses on the Iranian revolution and, by examining the way in which the leader was chosen and the special qualities which he possesses, proceeds to demonstrate that this was a truly Islamic revolution in the sense he had previously outlined. The division between religion and politics is traced back to colonialist origins, and nationalism is criticised for perpetuating this idea. A truly Islamic leader, a *marjaeh taqlid*, it is claimed, is the only person who can dispel the confusions of the non-Islamic way of thinking, and thus restore to the people confidence in their own abilities to govern themselves. Finally, Motahari points to certain features of Islam which make it a suitable 'ideology' for a revolution, and draws the distinction between an Islamic revolution and revolutionary Islam: Islam as an end, and Islam as a means to some other end. Strongly condemning the latter, he issues a cautionary word about the examplary nature of Islamic justice and the need to be scrupulous in administering it, and this leads on to an advocation of freedom of thought and expression within the Islamic society. (This part is to be found on pages 48 to 67 of Piramounch Enqelabeh Eslami.)

Concerning our own revolution, if it is true that it has an Islamic nature, that is, that it is a revolution which in all respects – material and spiritual, political and ideological – has an Islamic spirit and identity, then its continuation and growth will only be possible on the very same basis. Therefore the duty of each one of us is to strive to preserve the true identity of the revolution. I mean that our revolution must hereafter also be Islamic, not just liberalistic; it must ultimately be Islamic and not just spiritual, or only political.

However, let us now look at how it can be established that our revolution has been an Islamic revolution, with no other kind of essential nature. One way to understand the revolution is to investigate the nature of its leadership.

Looking now at its leadership, it was not the case that on the first day someone put himself forward as a candidate and then people voted for him, and chose him as a leader; and that this leader subsequently marked out a policy. In fact, many groups – those who felt some responsibility – tried to take over the leadership of the movement; but gradually each was dropped and the leader was chosen quite spontaneously. Bear in mind what a great number of different layers made up this revolution; the *ruhaniyun* (the *ulama*, whether *marja* or not) and others, laymen (whether Islamic groups or not). Educated people, uneducated people, students, workers in factories and on the land, and merchants: together they took part in this revolution. But among all these diverse people, only one individual was chosen quite naturally as a leader, a leader whom every group accepted as such. Why? Was it because of the leader's honesty? Undoubtedly he was entirely honest, but was honesty the monopoly of Imam Khomeini, possessed by no-one else? Of course, we know that this is not so, and that honesty did not belong exclusively to him. Was it because of his courage, and because he was the only courageous individual, because there was no other truthful, honest and courageous person other than him? Of course there were other brave people. Was it because of his decisiveness, which no-one else possessed? We know that it was not only he who was decisive. It is quite true that all these strengths were combined in him, but it is not true that they could not be found in others. So why did the whole society choose him quite spontaneously for leadership? The answer to this question takes us back to a fundamental question which comes up for consideration in the philosophy of history: do movements produce leaders, or leaders movements? Briefly, we know that the truth of the matter is that there is a reciprocal influence between these two, that is between the movement and the leader. On the one hand, the leader must possess an array of strengths and distinctions; but on the other hand, there must be certain characteristics in the movement as well. The sum of these preconditions is that the particular individual arrives at the position of being leader.

Imam Khomeini became the unopposed and unchallenged leader because, over and above the fact that the preconditions for, and strengths of, leadership were to be found together in him, he was completely in harmony with the thinking and feelings of the people of Iran and their needs, while others who had tried to occupy the position of leader of the movement did not have the same degree of harmony as he did. What this means is that, with all the personal strengths and excellences that he has, if the levers on which he placed his hand and applied pressure, and with which he got the people moving, had been of the kind which others could have used, and if the logic which he employed had been like the logic of others, it would not have been possible for him to have succeeded in moving the society. For example, if the question of the influence of class confrontation on the consciousness of the people, or the concepts of liberalism and the search for justice according to the standards of the ideologies of East and West had been put forward by him, they would have caused no reaction within society; whereas when he presented the same ideas to people according to Islamic criteria, and by using the fertile culture of Islam, society received them favourably.

If Imam Khomeini had not had the makings of a religious and Islamic leader, if the people of Iran had not had some kind of acquaintance and familiarity with, and sympathy for, Islam deep within their spirits, if the love which our people have for the Family of the Prophet had not existed, and if they had not felt that it was the call of the Prophet, the call of Ali and the call of Hosein coming from the mouth of this man, then it would have been impossible for a resurgence and a revolution of this amplitude to have taken place within our nation.

The secret of the success of the leader lay in the fact that he advanced the struggle within the mould of Islamic concepts. He fought against oppression, but he expounded the fight against oppression using Islamic criteria. Imam Khomeini fought against oppression, injustice, colonialism and exploitation by means of the belief that a Muslim should not crouch beneath the burden of oppression, that a Muslim should not submit to strangulation, that a Muslim should not allow himself to become servile, that a believer should not be under the heel of the unbeliever (see Koran IV, 141: 'And God will never grant the unbelievers any way over the believers'). It was a fight under the banner of Islam, and according to Islamic criteria and standards.

One of the fundamental measures taken by this leader was to take a firm stand against the separation of religion and politics. Perhaps the merit of having been the first in this should belong to Sayyed Jamal al-din. Perhaps he was the first person to realise that if he wanted to start an uprising among the Muslims he had to make them understand that politics was not something separate from religion. It was he who brought this matter clearly before the attention of the Muslims. Later, the colonialists tried hard to sever the link between religion and politics in Muslim countries. One of their efforts has been the programme of secularisation, which means the disjunction of religion and politics. After Sayyid Jamal al-din, many people came on to the scene in Arab countries, especially in Egypt, who proceeded to propagate the idea of the separate nature of religion and politics, getting their support from feelings of ethnic identity and by assuming the stands of nationalism, Arabism, or pan-Arabism. Lately, you have seen how Anwar Sadat has re-kindled the same sentiments. In his later speeches, he has emphasised that religion belongs to the mosques and should get on with its own business there: religion should have absolutely nothing to do with politics.

In our country as well the same point has frequently been brought up, so that people have almost come to accept it; but when it is explained quite clearly from the lips of a *marjaeh taqlid*, from the lips of one to whose directives people scrupulously try to make their smallest religious observances conform, that religion is not separate from politics, and when people are told that if they have distanced themselves from the politics of their country then they have in fact distanced themselves from religion, then we have all seen how they are stimulated and how they proceed to a sort of general mobilisation. Or observe that although the question of freedom and liberalisation has frequently been discussed in the community, it has not had much of an effect on people; but when the same question is raised by the leader, that is, someone who is a religious leader, people understand for the first time that freedom is not just a political matter but, more importantly, an Islamic matter, and it becomes clear (to them) that a Muslim should live in freedom and seek after liberty.

In the last few years, problems have cropped up in Iran which may not have been so very important from an economic or political aspect, but which were important from a religious aspect, particularly from the point of view of religious observances. For example, one of the great mistakes of the agents of the (previous) regime was their decision in the latter part of 1355 shamsi (1977) prompted by their extraordinary self-glorification to change the (Islamic) *Hejri* calendar to the so-called *Shahanshahi* calendar. (The Shah decided to abandon the Iranian Islamic calendar *shamsi* and adopted the historical one dating back to 2500 years of royal rule in Iran (ed.).) From the point of view of economics or politics, it was of very little importance among the people whether the date was *Hejri* or *Shahanshahi*, but it was this very matter which wounded the religious sensibilities of the people and put a useful weapon into the hands of the leader with which he could attack the regime. By proposing the slogan that such an action was an act of hostility against the Prophet and against Islam and was tantamount to the massacre of thousands of this people's loved ones, the leader succeeded in instigating disobedience among the people and in exploiting in the best possible way the awakening of their Islamic conscience in order to advance the movement.

Therefore, by studying the question of leadership and its nature, by fixing our attention on which leader the people chose out of the many who had the competence to be leaders (it should particularly be observed that this leader had no power with which to impose himself on the people – no-one proposed him, nor did he propose himself, as a candidate – his 'election' was entirely natural and spontaneous) and by analysing the path the leader took, the levers which he used on the people and the logic which he employed, we come to the clear and unambiguous conclusion that our movement is a truly Islamic one. The movement was for justice, and, in another respect, to seek freedom and independence, but it sought justice under the banner of Islam, and freedom and independence in the light of Islam. To express it more succinctly, our movement was looking for everything it wanted in Islamic form, and this was the same form in which the nation wanted it.

Let me give an example. I have a friend who all his life has been constantly in a state of conflict with the regime, and has spared absolutely nothing for this, either of himself or his property. Because of his particular outlook, he became quite astonishingly attached to the *Mojahedin*, who were also a centre of struggle against the regime. When what they call an 'opportunist' current swept through the *Mojahedin* organisation, I became very worried for this friend of mine. I said to myself 'Let us hope that when he finds out about this tendency he does not say that it is no matter that they have come and made this a Marxist organisation since we must concentrate at the present time on the struggle which is the imporant thing.' However, later, at a meeting where I met him and asked him what he thought about the *Mojahedin*'s becoming Marxist, he said something in reply which I shall never forget 'The fact is that we want justice under the banner of God. If we get justice, but it is not a result of invoking God's name and His help, we should feel a revulsion against that kind of justice'. It was because of such a state of mind as this that our people succeeded in rising up in such strength.

At the beginning of my talk, I made a point which I must now fill out. I said that every revolution is the result of a chain of discontents and frustrations. What I meant was that when people became discontented with, and indignant at, the ruling system, and aspire to some desired system, the groundwork for a revolution has been laid. Now I want to explain this point more fully, and say that discontent is not enough. It may be that a nation is discontented with the existing system and aspires to another, yet does not revolt. Why? Because it is in an acquiescent and submissive state; a state of acceptance of oppression is prevalent among these people. Such a people are discontented but at the same time they submit to oppression. If a nation is discontented but, more than that, is in a condition to protest and to reject, then it will revolt; and it is here that the programme of each ideology or religion becomes clear. One of the characteristics of Islam is that it imbues its followers with a feeling of protest, of struggle and of the rejection of any undesired situation. What is the meaning of *jehad* or bidding to good and forbidding evil (*al-amreh beh maruf-va nahy al-monker*) if not this? I mean, if the ruling system is undesirable and inhuman, one must not submit and acquiesce to it – one should, at the most, exert oneself to reject and refuse to put up with the system and to establish the ideal system one wants.

Christianity, which is based on submission and acquiescence, has for centuries criticised Islam. 'What kind of religion is this?', they have said. The sword and war have no place in religion; religion speaks the word of peace and serenity; religion says that if your left cheek is struck you should offer your right cheek.

Now Islam has no such logic. Islam says that 'the most excellent *jehad* is to speak of justice before a despotic ruler'. That is to say that the most exemplary and supreme form of struggle is that a man should stand before an oppressive leader and speak the word of justice. I have said elsewhere that this short sentence has been the inspiration for so many epics written in the history of Islam.

If there is an element of pugnacity and combativeness in relation to

oppression, tyranny and suppression within an ideology or religion, it
will then be able to plant the seeds of revolution among its followers.
Happily, these seeds have today been sufficiently sown among us. I can
remember at the first meetings of the Islamic Association of Engineers
(*Anjomaneh Eslamyeh Mohandesin*) that I held a discussion about
'bidding to good and forbidding evil'. In connection with this topic, I
made some study of its history, during which I came across a suprising
point which caused me much amazement. I noticed that in the past
twenty years the section on *al amreh beh maruf va nahy al-monker* has
been removed from our manuals on religious obligations (*resaleyeh
amaliyeh*), whereas previously it had taken its place alongside the
sections on prayer, fasting, the religious fiscal duties (*khoms* and *zakat*)
etc, in both Arabic and Persian manuals. But it seems that later on, for
no apparent reason, the discussion of this topic came to be seen as quite
superfluous, and just as other sections are now left out, like those on the
prescribed punishments and the such like, and it is said that such topics
are no longer worth discussing, so also the topics of *jehad* and *al-amreh
beh maruf va nahy al-monker* are (thought to be) irrelevant to the times.
(But now) after years ... during which (these matters) have been
forgotten among us, and the memory of the path of fighting erased,
(they) have ... been raised again and have started to gain in importance
within the community.

Now we come to a point at which our path forks. I said that Islam
has a connection with revolution, that the seeds of revolution are to be
found in the teachings of Islam, and now as a result of this the
following question faces revolutionary Muslims: should the future path
be Islamic revolution or revolutionary Islam?

Islamic revolution means the way whose aim is Islam and Islamic
values, and which rises up and fights uniquely to establish Islamic
values. In other words, in this path the struggle is not the end, but the
means. However, there are some who confuse Islamic revolution with
revolutionary Islam; that is to say, for them the revolution and the fight
is the aim – Islam is a means for the struggle. They say that they accept
whatever there is in Islam which points them in the direction of the
struggle, but they reject whatever there is in Islam which leads them
away from the struggle. It is altogether natural that with this difference
in approach between Islamic revolution and revolutionary Islam, there
will be conflicts and contradictions in the two interpretations of Islam,
man, divine unity (*tohid*), history, society and the verses of the Koran.

There is a difference between someone who recognises Islam as an
aim and sees fighting and *jahad* as a means to establishing Islamic

values, and one who recognises the fight as the objective and says that he must always be struggling, that Islam really came to advance the struggle. In reply to such people, it must be pointed out that contrary to what they think, although the element of struggle exists within Islam, this does not mean that Islam only came to further struggle and that it has no other objective than to fight: there are countless precepts in Islam, and one of them is to fight.

The idea that the struggle is what counts comes from a manner of thinking which materialists apply to society and history. According to what they believe, history and nature follow a so-called 'dialectic' course: they both advance through contraries. The war of contraries is forever present in the world, and the war of contraries proceeds in a dialectic form: every single thing in nature and history necessarily nurtures its own negating factor within itself, and as it grows, there arises a struggle between the first thing – the thesis – which is seen as the old element, and its negator – the antithesis – which is counted as the new element. This struggle ends with a new victory, or, in another sense, with a new order – the appearance of the synthesis. Then the process starts all over again and the synthesis which resulted from the struggle itself starts to operate as a thesis, and so on and so forth. On the basis of this way of looking at things, nature, life, society and anything you care to put your finger on are combats and just that. Correct behaviour means always being in the form of the antithesis, rejecting everything there is, rejecting the present situation. Everything that struggles against the present situation, irrespective of the result, is progression and perfection. With the arrival of any new situation, another state immediately comes into existence inside it which is the denial of the actual situation. From then on, this progressing man becomes one of the old elements which must disappear. The struggle never ceases even for a moment, nor will it cease. At every moment, whatever is engaged in the struggle is legitimate. It is on the basis of this mode of thinking that these people try, in their own words, to make Islam revolutionary, not to make the revolution Islamic; they introduce combat as everywhere the criterion of Islam. (More could be said here, but) the differences between this interpretation of Islam, that is, revolutionary Islam, and the thinking that conceives revolution to be Islamic are so great that it is impossible to mention all of them (in the time at our disposal).

According to the explanations which have just been given, if we accept that our revolution is a revolution with an Islamic nature – of course, Islamic in the same sense as I have expounded, that is to say, the sum of all ideas, values and objectives within the mould of Islam – then this revolution will remain secure on one condition, that the course of the desire for justice should continue for ever. I mean that future governments should genuinely walk the path of Islamic justice, work to mend class rifts, really do away with all kinds of discrimination, and strive to establish a unitary (*tohidi*) society in the Islamic sense of the word, not in the sense that others have used it, because the difference between these two is the difference of the heavens from the earth.

In an Islamic government, there should be no oppression or unjust dealing; even if a guilty person deserves the death penalty. Here I must reproach some of our young friends, for, although their fine sentiments are commendable, they sometimes pass judgements according to a logic which has more to do with the logic of the emotions than the logic of Islam. A few days ago, I had a meeting, for some reason, with Mehdi Bazargan, and heard that the Revolutionary Guards who were there had been complaining about the revolutionary executions and saying that these people were not worthy to be shot and should be thrown alive into the sea.

These young friends should be reminded that according to the logic of Islam, even if someone has killed a thousand people and it would be an insufficient punishment to have him executed a hundred times, he still has his rights which must be observed. In such circumstances, the best patterns for us to follow come from the teachings of Imam Ali. Observe the way he behaved with murderers – there is a whole world of humanity, affection and love there. When Ali was on his deathbed (having been fatally attacked) he called his family, the Banu Abd al-Mutallib, around him, and told them

O Banu Abd al-Mutallib, let it never happen that after me you seek revenge for my blood among the Muslims, and say that because Ali has been killed, the culprit, the instigator, the one who helped him, each and every one must be put to death. I was one person; Ibn Muljam (the attacker) did not strike me more than once either, so do not strike him more than once.

We read in history that during the time that Ibu Muljam was kept prisoner in Ali's house, there was not a single instance of bad behaviour towards him. Ali even sent his own food to him and gave instructions that the prisoner should never be allowed to go hungry. This kind of justice must be a model for us all; there can be no doubt that it is the existence of values such as this which has protected our religion for one thousand four hundred years and kept it healthy and vigorous.

I repeat here that if our revolution does not continue in the direction of establishing social justice, it will surely never reach its objective, and there is a danger that it will be replaced by another revolution with another nature. However, an important point which must be considered is that in this revolution the foundations must be laid on an Islamic sense of brotherhood. That is to say, that which others obtain by harshness and the use of force must be accomplished in this revolution by moderation, because of a willingness and consent to act, and through a feeling of brotherhood. One of the pillars of our revolution, if it is truly Islamic in nature, is spirituality. This means that people should move forward to mend class rifts and economic differences with spiritual maturity, humane sentiments and Islamic brotherliness. This is the way; as our leader, Ali, said:

Let it never happen that my feelings get the better of me and my greed lead me to pick and choose my food, as long as in the Hijaz and Yamamah there are people who do not have a round of bread to eat nor hope to leave off eating satisfied; or that I should fill my stomach as long as there are hungry bellies and parched livers around me. (*Nahj al-Balagha* – letter 45)

Such an attitude must be an example to us all. A spirit of devotion towards others must find a place in the hearts of all of us. You have all noticed that Imam Khomeini recently called for a general mobilisation for housing. The reason for this is that the Imam wanted this revolution to remain Islamic, and all its objectives to be achieved through Islamic methods. He did not just want to establish a new regime and then force things to move forward, and impose the establishment of social justice. When our people employ their resources for the welfare of the deprived because they want to, and because of Islamic brotherliness, our revolution will have found a sure path.

Our revolution will not be a true revolution until families refuse to give their children new clothes on the days of religious festivities unless they are quite certain that the families of the poor have new clothes. The words of the Prophet must be realised among us: 'The love of (true) believers, one for the other, is like a body in which, if one of the members is suffering, the other members do not remain calm, but show a reaction by becoming inflamed and painful'. Our society will become an Islamic society when the suffering of each individual is not just his own suffering, but the suffering of all Muslims. Ali was the exempler of such a Muslim; he said:

> Should I feel content that they say: 'This is the Commander of the Faithful (*Amir al-Mu-minin*)', as long as I do not share with them the hardships of the times? (*Nahj al-Balagha* – letter 45)

Of what value are names and titles, the Imam says; the revolutionary is not encumbered with names and titles. How insignificant he must be if he is happy with these titles but does not share in the people's suffering. Imam Hasan said:

> When I was a child, I remained awake one night, and lay watching my mother, Zahra, who was busy with the night prayers. I noticed that in her prayers she was naming the Muslims one by one and praying for them. I wanted to see how she would pray for herself, but I was amazed to see that she made no supplication on her own behalf. The next day I asked her why she had prayed for everyone but not for herself. She replied: 'O my dear son, first your neighbour, then yourself'.

Elsewhere we find Zahra (the Prophet's daughter) on her wedding-night giving a poor woman who had asked her for help her only chemise which she had brought to her husband's house as a wedding-dress. This is what the spirit of true revolution and the ethics of Islam are like, and our revolution will have begun to bear fruit when we are ready to make such sacrifices and give eagerly.

Since the nature of the revolution is one of a search after justice, it is the duty of all of us to be very respectful towards freedoms in their true sense; because, if it should happen that the government of the Islamic Republic starts to maintain a stranglehold on things, it will surely be defeated. Of course, freedom is something other than social chaos and we mean by it what sane reason understands by it.

Islam is a religion of freedom, a religion which promotes freedom for everyone in society. In the Koran we find: 'Surely we guided him in the way, whether he be thankful or unthankful' (LXXVI:29) and: 'Let whosoever will, believe, and whosoever will, disbelieve' (XVIII:29). Islam says no religion can be forced on anyone. People can be forced not to say or do certain things, but they cannot be forced to think or not to think in some particular way. Beliefs must come from reason. Of course, matters related to 'bidding to good and forbidding evil' are safeguarded by certain conditions which pertain to them. In such matters, the fundamental point is guidance and not force.

Everyone must have freedom of thought and expression, both in speech and writing and only in this form will our Islamic Revolution continue on the road to victory. Incidentally, previous experiments have shown that whenever society has any kind of freedom of thought, even though this may be through bad intention, it never results in any detriment to Islam, but in the end is to its advantage. If in our society an environment of freedom is created, opinions and beliefs will exist in such a form that proponents of opposing ideas will be able to express them while we express our own ideas. Only on such a healthy ground will Islam be able to send down more roots. It is not altogether irrelevant at this point for me to tell you something which has just come into my mind. A few years ago at the Theological Faculty (of Tehran University) one of the professors, who was a materialist, regularly went into his lectures and disseminated materialist and anti-Islamic propaganda. The students complained about this, and the faculty gradually fell into a kind of pandemonium. I wrote an official letter which I still have with me, in which it was explained that in my opinion there was a need in the Theology Faculty for the establishment of a course in dialectic materialism and that a professor who was an expert in this subject, and who believed in dialetic materialism, should be responsible for this course. I said that this was what was needed in this case and that I would give all my support to such a project, but that someone should surreptitiously try to delude simple students who were not very well-informed was something I could not accept. Later, I proposed to this same man several times that instead of talking to a few uninformed students, he should discuss with me, and that if he wanted we should hold our discussions in front of the students, and even, if necessary, invite a bigger audience, from professors and students from the universities, so that we could set forth our arguments in front of a general audience of a few thousand persons, and have a kind of debate. I even told him that, although I was not normally prepared to speak on the radio or appear on the television at any price (of course, this was in the time of the previous regime), would be willing to debate with him on the radio or television in this one instance.

In my opinion, this is the only way to confront opposing ideas; otherwise, if we want to control thought, we shall have defeated Islam and the Islamic Republic. But of course, as we have explained, meeting with other beliefs does not mean being deluded or taken in, by which I mean uniting with what is false, joining hands with spurious propaganda.

For example, suppose that someone omits a part of a sentence, or a verse of the Koran, and adds his own part to it, and then brings the altered expression forward as evidence. Or suppose that someone relates something from history and omits something else and then draws the conclusion he wants by employing this incomplete information, or, for example, claims that his conclusion is scholarly. Deception cannot and must not, be freely permitted. It is because of this social harm that Islam forbids commerce in books which mislead and does not even allow their purchase.

But let me finish what I was saying and draw my conclusion. I said that the future of our revolution will only be secure if we preserve justice and freedom, if we keep political, economic, cultural, intellectual and religious independence. I shall not discuss the question of political and economic independence here, because you yourselves understand these things better than I do, but I intend to say a little more about intellectual and cultural independence – what I called ideological independence.

Our revolution will succeed when we let the world know of our own ideology and religion, which is pure Islam without any addition. That is to say, if we have an independent ideology and can tell the people of the world about our beliefs without any embarrassment and as they really are, we can hope for victory. But if it is decided to set up a concocted ideology with the name of Islam and if our way is to collect something from everywhere, to take one idea from Marxism, one from existentialism, something else from socialism and something from Islam as well, and then to make a hotch-potch from this collection and say that it is Islam, perhaps people will accept it in the beginning, because the truth can be concealed for a short time; but such a thing cannot remain hidden for ever. Someone will come along, a person who can think clearly and investigate matters, who will understand the truth, and will start to object that whatver Mr So-and-so is saying in the name of Islam is not really Islam at all. The sources of Islam are well-known: the Koran, the Sunnah of the Prophet, Islamic law and the authentic principles of Islam are all quite explicit, while, on the other hand, whatever Mr So-and-so says in the name of Islam is also quite explicit. By comparing the two it can easily be seen that such-and-such an idea, for example, has been taken from Marxism and has had an Islamic veneer put on it. The result will be that when the very people who had eagerly resorted to Islam, and had accepted these concocted ideas, thinking them Islamic, come to know what the truth is, they will violently and abruptly turn away from Islam. The fact is that, in my opinion, if the damage that such concocted ideologies can do to islam is not greater than that which completely anti-Islamic ideologies can do, it is at any rate not less. If our revolution is to continue on its victorious way, it must purify itself from all these embellishments and move along the road of the revival of the true values of Islam, the Islam of the Koran and the *Ahl al-Bayt* (the Household of the Prophet).

10 The Iranian Theocracy

HALEH AFSHAR

The 1977 revolution in Iran was based on a widespread opposition to the Shah rather than in a chiliastic attempt to reach an Islamic Utopia. The loose alliance formed by reformists, Muslim radicals and Marxists used the Islamic medium to advocate their cause. The contradictory Islamic slogans bandied about during the revolution reflected the diversity of this uneasy alliance and its support amongst the merchants, the slum-dwellers and the urban middle and working classes. The revolution guaranteed to respect the sanctity of private property and provide a welfare state. In the event the Islamic government has failed to do either and as a result has lost much of its popular support. The absence of a coherent socio-economic policy, the continual power struggle and the substantial flight of capital have all contributed to the deterioration of the national economy and rapid underdevelopment in Iran.

THE ULAMA

To understand the current national disarray it is important to analyse the character of the *ulama* (eminent members of the religious establishment) and their relationship with the state. The *ulama*, which literally translated means 'learned men', had in the nineteenth century held an important position in Iranian society; they not only preached and taught but also administered justice and charitable religius endowments.[1] Traditionally, the *ulama* have been independent of the state and have theoretically held the Shah to be a usurper, since according to the Shiia belief legitimate succession has passed through Ali, the first Imam, through to his descendants and remains with the twelfth hidden Imam; there could be no legitimate rule until he reappeared. Meanwhile the *ulama* have acted as 'the guardian of those who are without protection' and controlled 'the enforcement of divine ordinances concerning what had been permitted and prohibited'.[2]

The *ulama* form an affluent semi-closed élite with tightly-knit matrimonial patterns linking families together. Although *ulama* status can be reached by individuals from the most humble origins once high status has been achieved clergy solidarity is usually cemented by creating family ties through marriage.[3] The high ranking *ulama* are amongst the wealthiest classes in Iran. For example in the Isfahan area in 1946, 47 per cent of the landowners in the area were *ulama*, by far the largest single group; merchants and aristocrats were each only 15 per cent of the total.[4] Because the prophet Mohammed was himself a trader, Muslims have always held merchants in great respect and many of the *ulama* are wholesale merchants. Traditionally there has therefore been a close alliance between the merchants and the *ulama*; the latter have played a significant part in the moral intellectual and political lives of the *bazaar* merchants, artisans and workers. 'Merchants had no legitimate political power but depended on strikes and uprisings to express their opposition and on the intervention of the clergy to sanctify their conduct and protect them against the state.'[5]

The *bazaar* in turn was the main channel for the payment of religious taxes which formed the most important source of income for the *ulama* and enabled the religious establishment to be financially independent of the state. There are a number of Islamic taxes which the Shiia pay to the *mojtahed*, the religious leader of their choice. These are *khoms*, an annual tax paid by those who earn their income from trade, commerce or industry; after paying for their own expenses and that of their dependants and family, one fifth of any surplus must be paid to a *mojtahed*. *Zakat* is a similar religious tax on wheat, oats, dates, raisins, silver, gold, camels, cows and sheep. Once more those who had owned them for an entire year must, if there is a surplus after paying their own expenses, make a contribution to a *mojtahed*. In addition there is a small tax on land which landlords should pay. Religious minorities which are exempt from these taxes are expected to pay *jezyeh*, which is a small per capita tax paid by employed males. The *mojtahed* is in turn expected to draw his personal livelihood from these taxes and to divide the surplus between the poor and needy and the Islamic teaching institutions, *madaress*.[6]

THE PAHLAVIS

The most fundamental blow to the power and authority of *ulama* was dealt by Reza Shah's modernisation policies. In the span of one decade

Reza Shah secularised education to such an extent that even *madaress* were required to teach a curriculum approved by the lay Minister of Education. At the same time *ulama* were deprived of their judicial functions by the secularisation of the *Sharia*, Islamic, laws. These were reformulated into the 1928 Civil Code and all judges were required to hold a law degree. Finally in 1937 the secular Endowment Office was given full power of supervision over all public endowments thereby extending bureaucratic control over one of the important sources of income for the *ulama*.

The success of the modernisation policies, which contributed to both economic growth and social development, and were to some extent supported by the intelligentsia, helped to contain opposition. In part this containment was doubtlessly due to Reza Shah's ruthless elimination of all political opposition, but the general rise in the standard of living also helped. Apparently unable to resist the regime, the *ulama* who had played a decisive role in the 1906 revolution again withdrew from the political sphere. Although constitutionally the *ulama* had secured their control over the legislature and were entitled to veto all *Majlis* bills which contravened Islamic laws,[7] in practice they were never able to exercise this right and eventually stopped trying.[8]

THE POLITICISATION OF THE ULAMA

The religious establishment remained essentially separate from the political sphere in the late 1940s and 1950s. In fact in 1949 Ayatollah Mohamad Hassan Boroujerdi, the *marjaeh taqlid* (the most learned religious leader selected as the wisest and the ultimate authority for interpreting the Koranic laws) prohibited the *ulama* from joining parties and participating in politics.[9] There was concern for the future of Islam in the face of the Pahlavi regime's modernisation programmes, which threatened to give the state 'total control to regulate life from birth to death',[10] but with few notable exceptions, the religious establishment accepted this separatist position. Even Ayatollah Khomeini favoured this position: 'bad government is better than no government ... the *ulama* always co-operate with the government if that is needed'.[11]

After Boroujerdi's death in 1961, however, a sector of the clergy began a fundamental revision of *ulama*'s role within the state, and a move to assert both the importance of Islam as a way of life and the need for the religious establishment to engage in active political opposition. It was argued that 'unless there is a change of pattern, politics will annihilate religion'.[12]

The ensuing debate about the involvement of clergy in politics is of particular importance. Some religious leaders believed that Islam should guide all aspects of life and not be seen as a mere ideology. Therefore, they argued that the high clergy, *mojtahedin*, must not be concerned only or even primarily with religious rituals and practices, but rather with political and socio-economic activities; a concept which though fundamental to Islam had not been a reality in the recent past in Iran.

Fundamental changes were advocated, both in administrative and financial organisation of the religious establishment and its hierarchical structure; *khoms*, which had always been regarded as the major sources of *ulama*'s financial independence was seen as something of a constraint since it enabled 'the masses to control the *ulama*'s income', so that 'attempts at reforming the structure of the religious institution needed their approval. Unfortunately for the reformers, the masses have proved to be conservative with regard to social change'.[13] This led to attempts to organise an alternative and effective financial establishment to fund the *ulama*.

There was also a move to liberalise the religious hierarchy by some influential *foqaha* (leading religious figures) including Morteza Motahari, Morteza Jazaeri and Rouhola Khomeini. They disputed the correctness of choosing a single *marjaeh taqlid* and argued for a degree of scholarly specialisation and a *shorayeh fatwa*, a committee of *foqaha* issuing joint interpretations of the Koranic laws. Since he was not among the most learned of the *ulama*, Khomeini supported the idea of a committee in order to retain his own claim to participation at such a high level of decision-making.

Khomeini himself, however, did not play a significant part in the politicisation of the *ulama* until the 1970s. It was a layman, Ali Shariati, who was instrumental in popularising the idea of Islam as a way of life and attracting mass support among the youth and the intelligentsia for the establishment of an Islamic government. Shariati used Shiism and the teaching of the first Imam, Ali, as the basis for his powerful arguments for changing society and discarding the burdens of dependence and false western values. Shariati denounced Marxism as tyrannical and capitalism as exploitative and called for the return to what he saw as a spirit of equality and compassion taught by Ali. Shariati extended his criticisms to the hidebound *ulama* whom he said had been obsessed by esoteric theological arguments with the result that an uneducated believer was better able to understand and live within the bounds of Islam than many a sophisticated *faqih*. What mattered, according to Shariati, was devotion, commitment and engagement.

In fact, Shariati and his intellectual predecessor Mehdi Bazargan were both wary of theocratic control. Although they sought to radicalise the religious establishment they did not envisage it as holding political authority. Bazargan in particular argued specifically against the establishment of a theocracy. He noted that although there were 'linkages and contradictions between religion and politics', moderation was needed in 'treading the fine line between religion and politics and creatively interweaving them together without fully integrating them into a monolithic whole'.[14]

VALAYATEH FAQIH

When eventually in 1971 Khomeini published his version of Islamic government, *Valayateh Faqih*, the fine line between religion and politics was absent, as was the spirit of equality and compassion. *Valayateh Faqih* sets out the parameters for the rule of theocracy. Khomeini dismisses the very concept of democracy as unacceptable. People, he states, are in no position to ratify laws since 'Islamic governments is the rule of divine law over people'.[15] 'Herein lies the difference between the Islamic government and the constitutional monarchy or republican government. In these regimes people's representatives or the king take charge of legislation, whereas in Islam this power is the prerogative of God.'[16]

The Islamic government was to be 'neither authoritarian, allowing a ruler to play with people's money and punish and execute at will, nor constitutional in the modern sense, but constituted by the Koran and *sunnat*. Since all Muslims wish to follow God's law, Islamic government does not depend on force, but merely serves to map out programmes.'[17]

Thus the art of government is simplified to the extreme and bureaucracy and the judiciary became unnecessary: 'superfluous administrative organisations and the administration method accompanied by fabrication of files and bureaucracy which are alien to Islam, have imposed expenses on the state budget, which are ... inadmissible ... This administrative system is remote from Islam.'[18]

The entire secular legal process was similarly dismissed as cumbersome and unnecessary:

the procedure prescribed by Islam for adjudication, settlement of disputes imposition of punishment and penal code are simple, practical and fast. When the Islamic legal procedure was practiced, a religious judge in a city with two or three officials, a pen and an inkpot, would settle the disputes and would send the people away to conduct their daily life. But now God knows how vast the administrative apparatus of justice and its formalities are, yet without achieving any results.[19]

Khomeini is equally simplistic in his economic analysis. In a convenient exaggeration he stated that the Shah spent 50 per cent of the national income on himself. Consequently Khomeini deduced that 'if there were no extravagant royal ceremonies, no squandering or embezzlements, then there would be no deficit in the state budget and no need to humiliate ourselves in front of the United States or England and ask for a loan or aid'.[20] Nor did Khomeini expect his Islamic government to need to levy any taxes other than the religious ones. He states that *khoms* and *zakat* are more than enough to meet the needs of the poor and 'the provision of necessary expenditure of a large government'. *Khoms*, he says, provides 'a large revenue destined for the administration of the Islamic state and meeting its financial requirements'.[21]

It is perhaps the extraordinarily simplistic approach of Khomeini that helped to make his ideas so attractive. All that was needed, he stated, was 'conviction and ethical solutions'; it is only then that the country could achieve 'prosperity and mental exaltation and solve its social problems'.[22] In practice, however, not only have Khomeini's statements proved hollow, but also he has abandoned many of the more acceptable of his principles of government. The wholesale dismissal of the judiciary and piecemeal introduction of Islamic justice, the political repression and mass executions are well-known.[23] Khomeini states that 'Islam ... kills several corrupt and malicious persons in order to make men submit to the laws that are beneficial for human beings'.[24]

Khomeini's meteoric rise to power is also against his own stated aims and the traditions of the religious establishment, which had enjoyed a plurality of leadership. Although there had been one single *marjaeh taqlid* in Iran until 1961, he did not have the kind of authority enjoyed by the Christian Pope. The religious establishment though influenced by the *marjaeh taqlid* was not controlled by him. Khomeini himself had envisaged a pluralistic theocracy in *Valayateh Faqih*: 'since no *faqih* can dismiss the opinions of another *faqih* the guidance of the just government will be collegial'.[25] The religious establishment was for the most part insistent that the Islamic republic should retain this 'collegial' characteristic and the leading *foqaha* were opposed to the emergence of Khomeini as the sole ruling power in Iran. Of these, by far the most learned and among the most senior is Ayatollah Kazem Shariatmadari, of thé holy city of Qum and one of the early protectors of Khomeini. Others were the Ayatollahs Mahmoud Taleqani and Morteza Motahari, both of whom had played a central part in radicalising the religious establishment and popularising Shiia ideology. Both Motahari and Taleqani have been assassinated; Motahari by the rightist religious guerrillas Forqan, and Taleqani – it is suspected on the orders of Khomeini – for publicly warning the Muslims against 'despotism masquerading as religion'.[26] Shariatmadari, who is the *marja* for Iran's largest minority group the Azarbaijanis, has been considerably less outspoken. Nevertheless he invoked his right as a *faqih* and demanded to be consulted about the constitution, he warned Khomeini against flaunting his own teaching in *Valayateh Faqih*. As a result Khomeini placed Shariatmadari under house arrest and more recently decided to eliminate this last of his influential religious opponents by an unprecedented act of 'dismissing' him as a *faqih*. Shariatmadari has been imprisoned and branded as a traitor for not opposing the Pahlavi regime at a time when Khomeini himself is on record for supporting it.[27] The Azarbaijani and all other followers of Shariatmadari have been instructed to find another *marja*.

ECONOMIC PROBLEMS: TAXATION

It is however the economic policy of the Islamic government which is the particular concern of this chapter. The deep divisions between the few trained economists remaining in the administration and the *ulama* has resulted in the payment of lip-service to Khomeini's aims while the previous regime's fiscal arrangements are still implemented. The impracticability of Khomeini's economic policies and the total absence of any effective government mechanism for collecting Islamic revenues makes this inevitable. So far the *mojtahedin* have not shown any tendency to pay over their main means of subsistence and that of their supporters to the state. Nor has their partial redistribution of *khoms* helped to eliminate poverty, or achieve any other of the stated aims of the revolution. Part of the problem in this context is Khomeini's assumption that the *ulama* would not be corrupt and would necessarily seek to help the Islamic government. It is difficult to reconcile the egalitarian slogans of the revolution with the *ulama*'s relative affluence and their present exalted position in Iranian society. It is unlikely that such a group would encourage policies conducive to either land reforms, which have since 1960s been strongly opposed by the religious establishment, or any real redistribution of wealth. Khomeini, however, does not appear to be aware of the practical and ideological problem in appointing the *ulama* as channels for transmission of *khoms* to the government purses. Such collaboration would in fact undermine the *ulama*'s own support, secured by the redistribution of *khoms*.

In addition there is increasingly a problem of accommodating the rising expectation of the poor and needy who have supported the regime. Khomeini in *Valayateh Faqih* does not envisage the emergence of an egalitarian society. In fact he argues that the needy ought at the end of the year to return the surplus from the alms they have received; 'We know that the *Sadat* (the descendants of the prophet) and the needy are entitled to the amount necessary for their subsistence', but he adds 'It has been said in the *Hadith*, that *Sadat* should return what is left after the expenses to the Islamic government at the end of the year'.[28]

Khomeini's incorrect forecasts have opened a widening rift between the state and its most important financial backers, the merchants. 'The income from *khoms* of Baghdad *bazaar* let alone Tehran *bazaar* would be sufficient for the *Sadat*, all theological schools and all Muslims – should such a large budget be thrown into the sea?'[29] In the event this income has proved smaller than expected. Of course there are no figures available as to the exact amount of *khoms* paid, but that it is not meeting the Treasury's needs can be surmised by the continuation of the pre-revolutionary system of taxation and repeated calls by the government's spokesmen to make people pay these secular taxes. 'The question is are we going to win this war? To win we must finance it, yet as soon as we suggest taxation everyone is up in arms.'[30] The Governor of Central Bank has repeatedly said 'taxation is the right of the Islamic governments' and the government should 'change our culture and way of thinking in this respect and make the payment of taxes an Islamic duty for the people'.[31] Such calls, however, fall on deaf ears when addressed to the merchants or artisans who are already paying their *khoms*, and who are urged to continue doing so. The *Majlis* speaker, Hashemi Rafsanjani, addressed the faithful at a Friday prayer meeting to repeat yet again that *khoms* was 'of the essence of Islam' and 'only the infidels and insurgents denied the Islamic government this rightful income'.[32] Under the Pahlavis the payment of taxes was compulsory and were not precluded by payment of religious taxes. Under the Islamic government, however, Muslims are most unwilling to continue this double burden of taxation and in this many enjoy the support of some *ulama* who would also be affected.

INTEREST

Khomeini's projected economic plans included the abolition of interest payment. Usury is condemned by Islam as it has been by Christianity but merchants had always found ways of evading its prohibition by measures such as calling the interest a gift or a true equivalent of the money lent, etc.[33] As a result the *bazaar* was able to operate as the financial heart of the traditional economy, where not only commerce but also investments, credit transactions and other financial transactions were conducted. Many merchants had in the past three decades invested substantially in the modern sector of the Iranian economy and some had even funded Western-style banks.

The strict imposition of the ban on usury, however, directly threatened one of the most important sources of income for merchant capital in Iran. The Islamic government nationalised the banks and imposed a 4 per cent service charge on all loans, at a time when the official estimate of the rate of inflation ranged from 25 to 50 per cent. Borrowers clearly preferred to apply to the nationalised banks rather than to the merchants for loans. The wealthy in turn withdrew their money from the banks and either offered it for transactions on the black market or more often began transferring their capital abroad. Merchants who had longstanding trading ties with the West were particularly well-situated for transferring their capital abroad and many did so.

There followed a serious crisis of confidence in the nationalised banks and repeated calls from successive Governors of the Central Bank for support. 'Our compatriots must have full confidence in the banking system, they must deposit their money there.'[34] A year later the new Governor found it necessary to state 'of course we have no intention of appropriating people's private savings. There are plenty of legal provisions to prevent such an action.'[35] Potential savers, however, were not reassured and the problem remains acute.

TRADE

A basic problem of Khomeini's economic theory is its reliance on morality as a vehicle for economic prosperity. He argued that the appointment of *ulama* as tax-collectors would eliminate financial corruption and assumed that merchants would act according to the Islamic moral codes and would cease to be motivated by profit. Accordingly the Islamic party drew up its theoretical framework on the basis of morality; economy is said to 'draw and contribute to morality and morality must at no time be neglected'.[36] Since it is assumed that 'inflation is based on the pursuit of the profit motive', the Manifesto of the Islamic party concluded, 'When the fight against profits is successful then internal inflation is likely to be eliminated, although external inflation in the West will always continue'.[37]

The failure of the Islamic government to check inflation or impose Islamic morality on the merchant led to serious deficits in the budget and sharp price rises. These led to a sustained attack on the merchant classes. 'The Islamic market can only operate successfully if people and the merchants acquire an Islamic consciousness. People have gone a long way to meet this end, but merchants have not changed.'[38] Furthermore it was stated that 'The Koran does not permit the ungodly to rule over Muslims, and following the dictum of our high and respected leader of the revolution (Khomeini) we must realise that any trade relations that facilitate the control of foreigners over our country are against our religion and *haram* (Islamically impure) and unacceptable. Yet these wealthy merchants have grasped the control of 71 per cent of all our national imports and conduct 90 per cent of that trade with their seven major imperialist masters.'[39] The situation was said to be worsening and *Majlis* deputies were warned against the merchants' stranglehold on the economy: the private sector's share of foreign exchange bought for imports was said to have increased from $5.5bn of the total of $11.8bn (46 per cent of total) in 1977 to $4.7bn of total $7.2bn (63.3 per cent of total) in 1979, to $8bn of total $11.3 (70 per cent) in 1980.[40] These increases of 18.7 per cent in the first instance and 4.3 per cent in the second were announced in an equally true but far more spectacular way:

that is to say that in the first nine months of 1980 private sector imports increased by 45 per cent over their 1977 levels and 69 per cent over their 1979 level, so we can see that large merchants who control over 70 per cent of our imports are major contributors to our critical economic situation. This group is continuing to play a central part in the current inflation and rapid price rises.[41]

Furthermore merchants were denounced for using trade as a means of transfering national assets abroad. The dramatic rise in the value of exported carpets, from \$62.5m for 4467 tonnes of carpet in 1978 to \$320m for 7608 tonnes was attributed to the merchants exporting the very finest quality carpets abroad and thereby 'smuggling' the assets of 'the rich expatriates' out of the country.[42]

To curtail the ungodly control of the merchants, the *Majlis* voted to implement the provisions of the Islamic constitution for nationalisation of trade and it was suggested that 'all who have expertise in the field of foreign trade should place themselves at the service of the government in the spirit of brotherhood and realise that even though they won't make spectacular profits they will earn spiritual benefits',[43] – hardly an incentive for merchant capital. Although theoretically the law of nationalisation of trade has been ratified and for good measure a few merchants have been executed for un-Islamic activities, the government has not succeeded in gaining control of trade. What has happened instead, is a far more serious shortage of all consumer goods and many necessities such as cooking oil, soap, meat, onions, potatoes, iron, aluminium, cement, etc.

NATIONALISATION OF COMMERCE

The failure to solve the economic crisis by curbing the largest merchant interest led to further attempts by the government to control the market by taking over internal commerce and the distribution process. This time the 'exploitative middle man' was singled out as the guilty party. A new term 'economic terrorists' was coined by the establishment to denounce these 'anti-Islamic hoarders'.

A national Headquarters was set up with the intention of 'distributing everything with ration books'.[44] To begin with the Headquarters issued rations for fuel, sugar, vegetable oil, meat and chicken. Once more the system was plagued by the diversity of the sources of power and authority within the country. The clergy were given ration books to distribute through local mosques, but at the same time the local revolutionary committees, *Komiteh*, which are operating as the organs of government in each locality and the civil service were also given ration books to distribute. As a result many people succeeded in obtaining more than one ration book, while others got none.

The nationalisation of commerce failed to meet the consumer demands and also failed – far more dramatically than the nationalisation of trade – to retain adequate support from the influential religious establishment. The consumers could not find any goods in exchange for their ration coupons. 'We have a ration book for a supermarket, but in the past three months there has not been a trace of meat, and in the last month there has not been any butter, cheese, rice or eggs.'[45] 'We have had our ration books for forty days and in this period the five of us have only had chicken twice.'[46] 'Sometimes we have to queue for three hours to get eggs.'[47] 'I waited since 6a.m. in a queue to get a chicken, but they ran out before it got to me. Some people had started queueing at 4 a.m.'[48] The government's answer was to advise the consumers to be more austere and refrain from wasteful consumption. As soon as the implications of the nationalisation of commerce were understood, an influential group in the religious establishment withdrew its support.

As part of the process of nationalisation of commerce the Headquarters had decided to take over all transactions in the rice trade. Rice is one of the main staples with an annual consumption of 840 000 tonnes which cannot be met by the national production of 600 000 tonnes. To meet the estimated 240 000 tonnes shortfall the government imported 450 000 tonnes in 1981.[49] These large imports and the direct purchases from all rice-producers was intended not only to stabilise the price of rice, but also to eliminate the 'few hundred wholesalers who raise the rice price and make profits of billions of rials every month'.[50] The programme met with grave resistance by rice-producers who preferred selling to the wholesalers offering a price higher than that of the government. The peasants were reprimanded for 'acting against national interest' and transmitting the higher prices to the lowest income groups including the peasants themselves',[51] but they continued to withhold the produce. The Headquarters then set up road-blocks and began confiscating rice smuggled out of the northern rice-growing regions. Owners of private cars, however, were permitted to bring back 50kg of rice each.[52] These measures failed to relieve the shortages; rice queues grew longer than ever, prices soared and the Headquarters was obliged to admit defeat. The failure of the rice-distribution programme was said to have been caused by 'the influential supporters of the revolution who call these measures un-Islamic and are able to prevent their implementation'.[53] These influential opponents included the Majlis' deputy speaker, Sheikh Mohamad Yazdi, who denounced the Headquarters for being 'socialistic' and called the rice-distribution programme irreligious, immoral and

> against the directives of Ayatollah Khomeini who has specified that the government has no right to make cultivators sell their produce to them rather than the merchants. So these officials have asked can we set up road-blocks? and Ayatollah Khomeini has answered that roads, electricity and water belong to the government and this has enabled them to take the letter and not the spirit of the law and bar the way to honest traders.[54]

Yazdi denounced these measures as contravening the Islamic right of an owner to choose to whom he sells his produce and whether or not to sell it.

ECONOMIC POLICIES: NATIONALISED INDUSTRIES

Khomeini had predicted a government which would serve the people and 'merely map out programmes',[55] and would not 'overrule people's lives and properties and wilfully interfere in them'.[56] But such separation of government from the economy was hard to achieve in Iran where the state had been for more than two decades, in close co-operation with foreign capital, the largest investor in productive processes. Nationalised industries in partnership with foreign concerns ranged from tobacco and textiles to coal, steel, iron, oil and wood and paper mills, as well as a number of agri-business concerns. After the fall of the Shah the foreign expertise and capital withdrew leaving the country with half-completed projects and without the technical know-how to complete them. Even where the work was almost completed, as was the case with the Sarcheshmeh copper complex in Kerman, projects remained incomplete two years after the revolution in 1981, despite the further expenditure of some 12bn rials towards their construction.[57] By 1982 these concerns were making an estimated loss of 76bn rials.[58] The only successful state-owned concerns other than oil, were the tobacco industry, which made 12bn profits 'largely through the sale of foreign cigarettes', the Shiraz petrochemical company, Mazandaran Textiles and four other smaller industrial units.[59] But large concerns such as the Khouzestan steel complex, which has been partly operational before the revolution, were not working at full capacity even though the steel plant was paying out 730m rials to its 12 000 workers and producing half a million tonnes of steel annually. Similarly the coal complex hear Isfahan although completed in 1978 was well below its full potential production, with 550 000 tonnes of coal each year.[60] This failure, which could not be attributed to lack of credit were generally blamed on the absence of expertise and the inability of the government to run these industries.[61] 'We have so little control over these nationalised industries that many are not even paying their taxes.'[62] The government attempted to deal with the problem by removing the plan organisation's administrative control of these concerns and running them directly, without any intermediaries. The results were marginally worse.[63]

CO-OPERATIVES

The failure of the government to run industrial concerns was to be rectified by returning these concerns to the people themselves and setting up co-operatives. In fact the very nexus of the post-revolutionary economic policies was to be the development of co-operatives across the board for all activities. The revolutionary constitution had stipulated that co-operatives would be set up 'to provide the able-bodied toilers with the necessary means of production and create the opportunity for full employment for all those seeking work'.[64] Co-operatives were to provide the new revolutionary solution which was neither capitalist nor socialist; co-operatives were to 'prevent the concentration of wealth in the hands of the few in the private sector and prevent unnecessary bureaucracy and prevent the government from becoming a major employer'.[65] In fact the co-operatives were to realise Khomeini's dream of a simplified economy run by small independent groups free of bureaucracy. To this end the government allocated a vast budget of 55bn rials for co-operative ventures, with a further 30bn earmarked for their future use.[66]

Co-operatives had been a central part of the land-reform programme in Iran and were to have replaced the landlord by providing cheap credit and improved seeds to the peasants. By 1968 the co-operatives' registered membership was 1.2m consisting mainly of the new peasant proprietors.[67] After the revolution the movement virtually collapsed although its headquarters the Central Organisation of Rural Co-operative (CORC) survived despite falling membership. The current co-operative of only 36 000 includes man urban members such as the 12 000 steel workers in Khouzestan who have been presented with a productivity deal disguised as co-operatism; the steel complex was split into numerous small co-operative units consisting of technical staff, scientific staff, administrative staff, production workers, etc, who were paid according to the work they did.[68] Given the current low production levels, the negotiations have resulted in a pay-cut for the steel workers.

The co-operatives have not been successful despite many similar measures and repeated government encouragement and massive investment amounting to an average available credit of 150 000m rials per member as against the 20 000 rials offered to peasants under the previous regime. The failure has been attributed by the government to lack of equipment, raw materials and, surprisingly, inadequate funds and the absence of a proper mechanism for transferring these funds as well as a marked absence of expertise. Even though CORC had been running courses in co-operative management for the past two decades, the government claimed in 1982 that there were only 500 members with any co-operative training at all;[69] it is possible that all other trained personnel have been dismissed for collaborating with the Pahlavi regime.

PLANNING

Thus various attempts at the realisation of Khomeini's *laissez-faire* and simplistic economic policies failed to solve the increasingly critical economic problems of Iran. At the same time, the clergy's political control was severely tested by critical opposition led by Bani Sadre. There were also public anti-government demonstrations by women, by the unemployed and by university students, and a series of assassinations of prominent political figures. Finally, in the summer of 1981, the secular elements lost the power struggle; Bani Sadre took refuge in France and the regime set about its ruthless elimination of all opposition. The economic situation was also deteriorating.

The Iraq–Iran war and American trade embargo necessitated the purchase of military equipment at exorbitant black-market rates.

Finally the government decided to formulate a nationa plan 'based on the Islamic revolutinary principles of the Imam's (Khomeini) line'.[70] The Minister of Islamic Guidance announced 'I am the bearer of good tidings, the central plan organisation has begun planning'.[71] By this time the attempts to make the *ulama* finance the national budget by handing over part of the *khoms* had long been abandoned; the government's debt to the Central Bank had increased by 100 per cent over a one-year period, rising from 1000bn rials in March 1980 to 2000 in March 1981 and the Prime Minister was obliged to admit that 'the amount of the government's debt to the Central Bank indicated the bitter fact that the government has accomplished little in the sphere of the economy'.[72] Over the same period government receipts had fallen by 50 per cent from 177bn rials in 1980 to 89bn rials in 1981, and the national industries had registered a loss of 160bn rials.[73] War expenses were estimated at about 82.5bn rials (25 per cent of the total national budget)[74] while at the same time the GNP had been falling by an estimated annual rate of 11 per cent since the revolution.[75]

As a result the government was faced with a deficit of 878bn rials and a cash flow deficit of 285bn rials.[76] The only solution offered by the cabinet had been to increase oil sales. As one of the government's critics pointed out at the time 'suddenly meeting budgetary shortfalls becomes elementary and no longer requires complicated planning, calculation and expertise'.[77]

THE RISE OF MONETARISM

The plan to meet the budget deficit by raising oil sales had to be abandoned in the face of the oil glut and falling oil prices as well as the Iraqi attack on Iran's oil installations and the Saudi's decision to increase their oil sales. Despite earlier public statements to the contrary the government was obliged to admit that the war has caused 'falling production . . . rising demand and hoarding and has led to inflation and economic stagnation'.[78]

Eventually a new, planned economic policy was introduced by the Prime Minister, Mir Hosein Mousavi. There was an unexpected monetarist principle behind the policy; 'to counteract inflation the government will seek to control the quantity of money in circulation',[79] and it was announced that 'to save our economy from total collapse it is necessary to save on current expenditure on development expenditure and cut down on all unnecessary appointments'.[80] Khomeini was quoted as saying that 'superfluous administrative organisations, and the administrative methods accompanied by the creation of files and bureaucracy, which are alien to Islam, have imposed expenses on the state budget and are inadmissable ... These redundant ceremonies which bear nothing for people except expenses, toil and retardation, are not from Islam.'[81] Civil servants were, therefore, required to become 'productive' and new appointments were to be reduced to a replacement rate of 1 per cent.[82] In addition all government-sponsored training and education for civil servants were cut as were subsidies for canteens, nurseries and other facilities; the only exceptions were to apply to schools and hospitals.[83]

The demand for productivity led to an attack on the small traders who were branded as 'unproductive' and who were required to become 'healthy and productive'.[84] A government spokesman announced that 'a large section of our labour force is active in the distribution section instead of concentrating on the processes of production. This country is in dire need of productive activities in order to reach its revolutionary goal of self-sufficiency. Hence the government has decided to redirect labour and capital away from distribution and service sectors into production.'[85] To this end the 1982 budget has allocated 3bn rials to 'encourage' small businesses.[86] But instead of meeting this sector's demand for cheap loans, access to raw materials and to technology, the government decided to spend the money on 'relocation' of small industries to twenty-two industrial zones and to insist on the use of indigenous techniques and production of 'useful' objects. The process included the banning of the production of fifty 'unsuitable, unnecessary or luxury items'.[87] Canning and bottling and the manufacture of stockings were prohibited.

The most disturbing aspect of the new economic policies, however, was the decision to dispense with the limited number of welfare programmes that existed. 'We will no longer emphasise welfare projects, times are hard and we must concentrate on growth and development.'[88]

It was decided to stop welfare payments, such as unemployment benefits and family allowances, which in any case had only been introduced on a limited scale since they were 'not practical nor a basic solution to our economic problems'.[89] This directly affected the mass of the poor and slum-dwellers who had provided the bulk of support for the government and were still providing the soldiers and 'martyrs' for the cause both in the country and against the Iraqis.

The poor were praised by Khomeini: 'our parents, our protectors and our patrons are those bare-feet slum-dwellers. Without them we would still be in exile or in prison. It is these people who came out and brought us where we are to serve them till the end of our lives.' Service in this context is, however, not equated with redistribution of wealth or provision of welfare facilities. Khomeini excuses this by stating that 'there are such rich and powerful people in this world that if one of them distributed his wealth amongst our 36m people, all this 36m people would become affluent and rise from their so-called social class ... But people should recognise that there is no-one in government whose wealth if distributed among 36m people would make them rich. So we have a country that has only one social class and we are weary of those who want to create false divisions among them.'[90] The poor were also promised that in due course the government would 'expand the middle classes as far as possible so that there would no longer be any rich or poor ... and no-one would be allowed to benefit from another person's work without the latter's consent'.[91] But far from meeting these objectives, in practice the minimum wage requirements were relaxed and new employees were exempted.[92] Workers' control over wage negotiations was revoked and the government decided that 'wage increases must be linked to productivity' and local agreements between workers and management were to be 'subject to ratification by the General Council of the Ministry of Labour'.[93] In the climate of terror and state of unemployment that prevails, the government has not found it difficult to implement these measures. Early demonstrations by the unemployed, which appeared threatening in April and October 1979 when the demonstrators began shouting anti-government slogans, have been effectively defused first by the attack on the American embassy and subsequently by the nationalist fervour whipped up by the Iraq–Iran war. Furthermore the war fronts have provided a source of employment for hundreds of thousands of young men, many of whom will never return. The uncompromising implementation of monetarist policies has shored up the budget deficits and for the first time in decades Iran's national and international debts have ebbed. But the drastic cuts in public expenditure have seriously eroded the government's popularity.

CONCLUSION

After four years of Islamic government in Iran the deep contradictions of Shiia ideology have remained unresolved. The revolution was to help the poor and yet remain within a theoretical framework that does not favour egalitarian measures nor provide any means for their implementation. Shiism is frequently seen as the religion of the oppressed, yet it does not oppose inequalities and does not provide for radical distribution of wealth. In fact the very influence and authority of the *ulama* is in part based in their ability to extract *khoms* and *zakat* payment from the rich and give part of these to the poor. This process permits the religious establishment to maintain its patronage of the poor and retain their allegiance. Any radical measures which would result in the elimination of this process, either by eradicating poverty or by the state taking over taxation and welfare provisions, would in fact erode the most vital links between the religious establishment and its support base.

The Islamic government has been unable to reconcile the traditionalists in the religious establishment to its theocratic rule. Despite the elimination of many influential ayatollahs the power struggle continues between those who identify closely with the state and those who feel threatened and seek to retain their independence and their financial and spiritual control over their followers. There still remain a few religious leaders who continue to argue for a more extensive process of democratisation. It is this group which is regarded as one of the immediate threats by the state. The recent arrest of Ayatollah Shariatmadari has deprived them of their most eminent spokesman.

It is, however, by the alienation of one of the most important elements in its support, namely the merchants, that the theocratic government is most threatened. Without co-operation from the merchant classes the activities of the remainder of the private sector within the economy is gradually coming to a halt, and the goverment appears to have neither the ability nor the means to counteract the acute economic stagnation that the country is experiencing. The only solution offered, other than severe budgetary cuts and elimination of the few government-funded welfare services that existed, appears to be an attempt to secure socio-economic change through ideological propaganda. Iranians are asked to abandon their 'cultural habits of dependence' and realise that 'consumerism' is a Western value which has bound the nation firmly to its previous imperialist masters. Iranians are asked to break these bonds by acquiring the habit of 'Islamic austerity' and by accepting that 'saving is an Islamic revolutionary duty which mitigates against the Shah and the Western values of consumerism'.[94] The new austerity includes the abandonment of 'false needs' such as washing machines, hoovers and rice-cookers which are classified as 'foreign products'. It is interesting to note in passing that all these items are those traditionally used by women in the home; electric shavers, cars and televisions, though similarly foreign-based, are not included in the list of false needs. As well, the exclusion of these products, which are assembled in Iran under licences, would increase unemployment. The relation of dependence may appear easy to break, but as the Iranian theocracy has come to realise, the long-term results of expulsion of foreign capital has been a greater dependence on importing expensive foreign goods. In practice economic independence and political freedom require far greater experience and sophistication than that of the current regime.

It seems that the revolutionary slogans of liberty, equality, independence and freedom from exploitation, have been abandoned as unproductive and have been replaced by what appear to be rather severe monetarist policies which are unlikely to gain widespread popular support. It is arguable that the nationalist fervour whipped up by the war with Iraq is becoming the mainstay of the Islamic republic's survival and may explain the ardour of the government to continue the war despite Iraq's unilateral withdrawal in July 1982. The war not only legitimises the demands for austerity and self-denial, but also becomes a useful means of explaining away all economic failures. The war also provides employment of a kind for thousands of young men and keeps the potentially dangerous victorious army at a distance.

Attempts to purge all opposition, autocratic closure of the universities and many of the leading newspapers, total reorganisation of television and the radio and death sentences on 'un-Islamic' media personalities failed to forge the unity that the government sought of its people. Finally on 16 December 1982 Ayatollah Khomeini announced what appeared to be an end to police persecutions: the Eight Points Decree. Accordingly the entire judicial and law enforcement system was to be reformed to ensure that people felt 'protected' rather than 'threatened' by the Islamic government.

The decree stipulated that 'Judges, the army police, militia and the committees must behave Islamically so that people feel safe under the protection of the law of Islam and realise that Islamic justice does not dishonour and disappropriate them and protects their life honour and property'.[95]

Summary arrests, execution and confiscation of assets were banned and the leader of the nation magnanimously granted Iranians the right to their own privacy, as well as the right to commit their own 'sins'.

'No-one has the right to repeat other people's secrets.' Law-enforcement officers who inadvertently find 'instruments of debauchery or gambling or prostitutes or other things such as narcotics, must keep the knowledge to themselves'. 'They do not have the right to divulge this information' since doing so would 'violate the dignity of Muslims'.[96]

The decree has been rapidly implemented and a number of high-ranking officials ranging from regional chiefs of the revolutionary guards *Spaheh Pasdaran* to Public Prosecutors were sacked. Many of the civil servants dismissed during the purges were allowed to appeal against their dismissals and, to speed up the process, theological students from Qum were incorporated into the judiciary. The Tehran Public Prosecutor explained to reporters that 'in the absence of a Faculty of Law, we have no choice other than employing religious scholars to achieve 'judicial efficiency'.[97] Nevertheless the government is yet to succeed in forging a new alliance with the mass of the urban poor, or in regaining the support of some of the capitalist classes to revitalise the productive sector, and it seems unlikely that the present regime would survive the war. The government is still relying on its powerful secret police and revolutionary guards, and the reign of terror seems considerably worse than that of the Pahlavis, without offering the small salve of consumerism that made many people more tolerant of the Shah than they would have otherwise been. It is difficult to believe that the Iranian people will continue accepting the total collapse of law and order and the current economic and socio-political disarray after the conclusion of the war with Iraq. However, one hopes that if there is another revolution it will be more than a rejection of a dictatorship and will have realistic and humane objectives and clearly formulated means of achieving them.

NOTES

1. N. Keddie *Religion and Irreligion in the Early Iranian Nationalism, Comparative Studies in Society and History*, vol. IV, 1961–2, p. 289.
2. H. Algar *Religion and State in Iran* (University of California Press, 1969) p. 11.
3. S. Akhavi *Religion and Politics in Contemporary Iran* (Albany: State University of New York Press, 1980) p. 66.
4. M. M. J. Fischer *Iran from Religious Dispute to Revolution* (Harvard University Press, 1980) p. 96.
5. N. Jacobs *La Religion et le Développement Economique le Cas de l'Iran Archives de Sociologie du Religion 1963*, vol. 15, p. 45.

6. R. M. Khomeini *Valayateh Faqih, Kayhan International*, 15 March 1981.
7. 1906 Constitution, article 2.
8. In 1926, 40 per cent of the 6th *Majlis* were from the religious establishment; by 1930 this percentage was reduced to 30 per cent and in the 7th *Majlis*, and by the 11th *Majlis* in 1937 there was not a single well-known cleric among the deputies (Akhavi, *Religion and Politics*, p. 59).
9. Ibid, p. 63.
10. Mehdi Bazargan, '*Marz Mianeh Mazhab va Omoureh Ejtemaii'* in *Mazhab Dar Orupa* (Tehran, 1965) p. 119.
11. R. M. Khomeini *Kashf-al-Assrar*, 1943, p. 189.
12. Bazargan *Mazhab Dar Orupa* p. 119.
13. M. Motahari, '*Moshkeleh Assassi Dar Sazemaneh Rohaniat'* in *Bahsi Darbar-eyeh Marjayiat Va Rohaniat* (Tehran, 1962) p. 118.
14. M. Bazargan *Marz Mianeh* in *Mazhab Dar Orupa* p. 110 and 112.
15. *Valayateh Faqih* explained by Khomeini in *Kayhan International*, 15 March 1981.
16. Ibid.
17. Ibid.
18. *Valayateh Faqih* explained by Khomeini in *Kayhan International*, 12 April 1981.
19. Ibid.
20. Ibid.
21. *Valayateh Faqih* explained by Khomeini in *Kayhan International*, 15 March 1981.
22. *Valayateh Faqih* explained by Khomeini in *Kayhan International*, 8 March 1981.
23. Amnesty International Reports and *At War With Humanity*, People's Mojahedin Organisation of Iran, May 1982.
24. *Valayateh Faqih* explained by Khomeini in *Kayhan International*, 1 March 1981.
25. *Valayateh Faqih* quoted by Fischer, in *Iran from Religious Dispute to Revolution*, p. 153.
26. Fischer, *Iran from Religious Dispute to Revolution*, p. 222.
27. See p. 222 of this article.
28. *Valayateh Faqih* explained by Khomeini in *Kayhan International*, 15 March 1981.
29. Ibid.
30. Prime Minister, Mir Hosein Mousavi, interviewed by *Kayhan*, 30 October 1983.
31. M. Nourbakhsh, Governor of the Central Bank, *Kayhan*, 3 February 1982.
32. Hashemi Rafsanjani, *Majlis* speaker, during the Friday prayer, 17 February 1982.
33. See Fischer *Iran from Religious Dispute to Revolution*, p. 278n.
34. A. R. Nobari Governor of Central Bank, *Kayhan International*, 2 December 1980.
35. M. Nourbakh *Kayhan*, 26 November 1981.
36. Manifesto of the Islamic Party, *Kayhan*, 29 February 1982.
37. Ibid.
38. M. R. Vali, spokesman for the Centre for the Production and Distribution of Food, *Kayhan*, 1 December 1981.

39. K. Massouri, *Majlis* Deputy speaking in *Majlis, Kayhan*, 3 December 1981.
40. Ibid.
41. Ibid.
42. *Kayhan International*, 25 February 1981.
43. *Kayhan* 1 March 1983.
44. *Kayhan* 1 March 1983.
45. A woman interviewed by *Kayhan* 1 March 1981.
46. Ibid.
47. Ibid.
48. Ibid.
49. *Kayhan*, 23 September 1981.
50. Ibid.
51. Ibid.
52. Ibid.
53. *Kayhan*, 1 February 1982.
54. Ibid.
55. See p. 224.
56. *Valayateh Faqih* explained by Khomeini in *Kayhan International*, 12 April 1981.
57. *Enqelabeh Eslami*, 9 May 1981.
58. A. Atari *Vasleh beh Vasleh, Kayhan*, 22 February 1982.
59. Ibid.
60. *Kayhan*, 24 February 1981.
61. A. H. Bani Sadre *Enqelabeh Eslami*, 9 May 1981.
62. Ibid.
63. Ibid.
64. Article 43.
65. *Kayhan*, 12 January 1982.
66. *Kayhan*, 26 April 1982.
67. H. Afshar *Co-operatives in Iran* mimeo (Bradford University, 1980).
68. *Kayhan*, 12 January 1982.
69. *Kayhan*, 16 November 1981.
70. *Kayhan*, 8 November 1981.
71. Ibid.
72. M. A. Raja'i *Kayhan International*, 22 April 1981.
73. Ibid.
74. M. Dizchi, Under-Secretary of Ministry of Finance and Economy, *Kayhan*, 16 March 1982.
75. A. H. Bani Sadre, Commenting on the Budget, *Enqelabeh Eslami*, 13 May 1981.
76. *Kayhan International*, 22 April 1981.
77. Derakhshandeh, *Enqelabeh Eslami*, 24 May 1981.
78. M. Nourbakhsh, Governor of Central Bank, *Kayhan*, 2 March 1982.
79. M. H. Mousavi *Kayhan*, 16 November 1981.
80. M. T. Banki, Head of Plan Organisation and the Budget Office.
81. *Valayateh Faqih* explained by Khomeini in *Kayhan International*, 12 April 1981.
82. 1982 Budget, *Kayhan*, 1 May 1982.
83. Ibid.

84. *Kayhan*, 26 September 1981.
85. S. Samyi *Kayhan*, 29 September 1981.
86. *Kayhan*, 24 April 1982.
87. Ibid, and 29 June 1982.
88. M. T. Banki, Director of Plan Organisation and Budget Office, *Kayhan*, 2 November 1981.
89. *Kayhan*, 22 November 1981 and 1 May 1982.
90. *Kayhan*, 9 February 1982.
91. Hashemi Rafsanjani, *Emam Jomeah* of Tehran *Kayhan*, 23 January 1982.
92. *Kayhan*, 27 October 1982.
93. Ibid.
94. M. T. Banki, Minister without Portfolio, *Kayhan*, 3 November 1981.
95. Article 3 of the Eight Point Decree.
96. Article 8.
97. The Public Prosecutor, Ayatollah Yousef Saneyi, *Kayhan*, 20 January 1983.

Epilogue

Despite many predictions to the contrary, the Islamic revolution has survived for half a decade and appears set to continue. As the earlier chapters in this book have indicated, this success is partly due to the continuation of the war which has created a nationalistic unity and has enabled the government to impose strict economic, social and political controls which would have otherwise been quite unacceptable. At the same time, the regime has successfully repressed all criticism by imposing a tight control on the media and closing down all papers and publications which had at any time been critical of the regime. The only papers allowed to appear are either the official organs of the regime or those willing to endorse its politics and perpetuate the current religious hysteria. The universities which were the only other forum of open discussion, have also been closed for the past four years.

There are distressing similarities between the government's centralist and propagandist approach and some aspects of Fascist governments in Italy and Germany. The same fanatical devotion to the regime is demanded and the same intolerance of opposition is shown. The government's attitudes towards women are also similar. Like Hitler in 1935, Khomeini in 1979 sacked all women judges and barred women from enrolling at the Faculty of Law. Like Mussolini, Khomeini has barred women from entering many if not all engineering and technical training schools and faculties. Above all the Islamic government holds a similar view of the position of women and regards them primarily as the guardians of the home fires and sees their main function as one of procreation and care of children, a role which is similar to that envisaged for women in Fascist countries. Motherhood, however, is seen strictly as existing within the context of marital relations – one of the earliest measures introduced by the Islamic government was to revoke the legal rights of custody in divorce, gained by mothers in the late 1970s.

Educational establishments have also been subjected to a wholesale control. All curricula have been totally revised to include a strong and central element of Islamic teaching and schools have been segregated to prevent un-Islamic contact between male and female children. It is, however, the universities who have suffered a much more serious fate. All have been closed for at least four years and only some have finally been allowed to reopen.

To close this book we will briefly consider the plight of those groups or institutions which have fallen foul of the regime, in particular women, the educational institutions and the media.

WOMEN

One of the first demonstrations of the regime's Islamic character was in terms of the official edict demanding that women should appear in Islamic veil at all times in public. There followed a series of official instructions indicating how women civil servants should behave and what Islamic demeanor consisted of. Anyone found not conforming to these requirements was summarily sacked.

Increasingly women have become marginalised in the labour market and, with the exception of the traditionally female jobs such as nursing and teaching, they have been gradually forced out of paid employment. Despite the current war and the heavy demands it has made on able-bodied young men, male unemployment remains relatively high. Rapid de-industrialisation and the flight of capital that preceded and followed the revolution made industrial jobs scarce. The situation was exacerbated by the government's policies of cutting public expenditure, and the decision not to replace the hundreds of civil servants that had been sacked in the cleaning-up process (*paksazi*) that followed the arrival of the Islamic government. Thus the war has been useful in absorbing some of the unemployed and in preventing others from entering the labour market. Military service at the moment is an essential prerequisite for gaining access to jobs, education or even facilities such as electricity, running water and telephone. Women have not found many employment opportunities in this process. Instead they have been exhorted to return to motherhood and give birth to future martyrs; it is mothers who are rocking both cradle and coffin. Devotion to the cause is not merely imposed from above; like Mussolini, Khomeini has substantial support amongst fanatically devout women who, wrapped in their black veils like the black-clad women in Fascist Italy, take to the streets in massive numbers to demonstrate their support for the Islamic government and fuel the nationalistic hysteria. Many mothers visiting the graves of their dead sons are accompanied by younger sons wearing a red armband to indicate that they too will be going to the front as soon as they are able.

By and large it is the poorer women who have given Khomeini their wholehearted support. For those women who were paid the lowest of wages for the most arduous work and who on such a wage often supported an idle husband as well as their children, the withdrawal to the sphere of domesticity was a welcome prospect. But poverty has prevented many of these women from actually withdrawing from the labour market and many remain the main wage-earners of the family. Nevertheless, it is these women who have been 'politicised' by Khomeini to take to the streets in support of the clergy and who are hailed by the establishment as virtuous examples to all Muslim women.

It is middle-class women and those who had joined the professions in the past fifty years who have suffered the greatest loss of social and economic status. Many of these women are among the most articulate members of groups opposing the regime and actively seeking its downfall. A major concern of these women is the loss of access to equal educational opportunities. Iranian women now have their own form of *bantu* education. Girls are being educated in single-sex schools where they are expected to wear their Islamic clothing at all times. They are taught a curriculum which has been devised to meet the social needs of women as perceived by the religious establishment. Given that women are barred from gaining any further education in industrial, technical and agricultural areas, the establishment clearly does not perceive a great need for including scientific subjects in the pre-university educational curriculum. But there is an even more serious problem in that even before the revolution only 34 per cent of girls at school age attended school; of those who did go to school 75 per cent did not proceed to secondary levels and only 7 per cent had any tertiary education. Hence the segregation of schools has inevitably resulted in an inferior education for women and has disbarred them from access to technological knowledge at almost all levels.

EDUCATION

The process of Islamification of the educational system was one of the first priorities of the post-revolutionary government and initially all schools and educational establishments were closed. The curriculum was radically revised to include a central element of Islamic teaching and there was a conscious attempt at returning to the less complex *maktabi* approach which was rooted in the traditional religious teaching methods used by the clergy before the secularisation of the educational system in the twentieth century. Although segregated schools which taught a new curriculum were reopened relatively rapidly, the universities, closed after the departure of the first Iranian president Abolhassan Bani Sadre, remained so for over four years and even in 1984 only some have been reopened. The closure of the universities was hailed by Khomeini and his supporters as the Iranian Cultural Revolution. It was intended to clean up the foreign-orientated, dependent, imperialist and biased nature of academia and replace it by a new revolutionary and specifically Islamic context and content. The Iranian Cultural Revolution, however, was not merely a matter of curriculum improvement. In fact the most Western-orientated faculties, such as medical schools, were soon reopened and by 1984 a number of technical and scientific faculties were also allowed to reopen. The closure of the universities was both a political decision – made to control the discontented youth – and a cultural one, aimed at simplifying education to make it more similar to the unquestioning style of rote learning practised in the old clergy-controlled school, *maktab*.

A committee of cultural revolution in universities *jahadeh daneshgahi*, was set up to revise the curriculum and cleanse it of the foreign ideology which, it was argued, had permeated the Iranian culture through the educated youth and their received wisdom. After three years of preparations, the *jahad* sanctioned the setting up of a new Islamic training college to train university teachers. The college which was opened in 1983 accepted university graduates who had achieved grades of 60 per cent or more and prepared them for the serious task of un-westernised instructions. After a year in the college's preparatory classes these students were allowed to sit an entrance examination; successful candidates could then embark on a three-year training course.

At the same time the government introduced the simple *maktabi* approach by launching the Independent Islamic University, although no funds were allocated to support the scheme. The university is intended to ease the demand for university places and to provide appropriate education for fee-paying students whose ages range from 12 to 50 years. Both specialist courses and a general education are offered and students can obtain twelve year school certificates (equivalent to 'A' levels) or the equivalent of a university degree. The Free Islamic University holds all its sessions in public buildings such as mosques, mystery play theatres *takieha* or other religious centres such as *Hosseinieha*. Inevitably all the teaching is based on books and teachers' notes and there are no facilities for experimental or laboratory work. It is hard to see how this university as constituted at present, can ever provide adequate training in scientific and technical areas. It is not surprising that as yet it has not been able to fill all the available places and is still advertising in the Iranian daily press to find new students.

The closure of universities had in the short run a damaging effect. With the departure of many of the technocrats and inability of the educational system to deliver new ones many institutions have suffered seriously. But to some extent the government has responded quite effectively to the problems that it had created. In the legal system, government decided on two consecutive measures, the first of which was a return to Islamic law. Before the twentieth century the Sharia courts implemented Islamic laws, but the law was not codified. The Islamic government decided to draw up a new Islamic legal framework, and provided a detailed set of Islamic laws, *Qassas*. The second was to recruit young theologian students with two years' studies behind them in large numbers to administer the new laws while law students were still awaiting the opening of the universities to continue their training. The Ministry of Foreign Affairs meanwhile launched its own Faculty of Politics to train future diplomats.

To meet the serious shortage of medical personnel and doctors the government has not only allowed medical schools to reopen but has also provided doctors with numerous incentives; these include the decision to waive all doctors' taxes, except the basic tax on salaries, and allow them to run their own clinics to earn an extra income. In return, they must spend a specified time in hospitals and must serve at least four weeks each year at the war front.

The closure of universities, however, was not merely to initiate Islamification, it was also a conscious attempt by the government to prevent the young and educated from gathering in an open forum for discussions. This decision followed a period of unrest and recurring demonstrations in the universities protesting against the Draconian measures of the new Islamic government. There was a long-established history of organised resistence to dictatorial oppression in universities and they had been the hotbed of revolutionary ideas which preceded the arrival of the Islamic revolution. The universities nurtured many of the radical authors and thinkers who had for long opposed the Pahlavi regime. It was also in the universities that the guerrilla movement was formed in the early 1960s and it was university students who in 1962 took to the streets and were murdered in large numbers when demonstrating for the demands formulated by the clergy. But once in power, Khomeini was only too aware of the central political role that the universities could play and was therefore more than willing to close them down.

After four years the departments of Humanities, identified as 'the den of Westernised ideologies' remain closed and there is little likelihood of their reopening. The 4000 students who had enrolled in this section of the universities had traditionally been most radical and it is not surprising that the government remains unwilling to readmit them to their faculties. However, the government is also grappling with the problem of inventing an Islamic curriculum. Ironically technical subjects which depend largely on Western research and educational materials have now been declared sufficiently Islamic to be acceptable by the government, but Humanities which are rooted in the Iranian culture remain unacceptable. Part of the problem is, of course, the 2500 years of Iranian history which has been rejected by the religious establishment, partly because it pre-dates Islam, but ostensibly because it is a long history of oppressive royal rule and unacceptable to the revolutionary spirit of Iran today. Similarly the entire literary base of Iran has been denounced for its open and at times assertive irreligiosity and it celebrations of wine, women and song. Iranian epic poetry is also dismissed for praising the virtues of kings and kingdom. Even the poets writing in the Sufi tradition are frowned upon for verging on the heretical. Iranian history is, of course, totally unacceptable since it too is concerned with the rule and battles of kings, many of whom had fought long and hard against the Islamic invasion. Thus it is not Westernisation but the Iranian culture and its un-Islamic traditions which have proved unacceptable to the current regime. It is unlikely that the government will solve this particular dilemma in the near future.

THE MEDIA

A free press flourished briefly after the revolution. Political parties across the spectrum, ranging from the communist *Tudeh* party and the Marxist *Fedayan* to the Islamic Party and the National Front, which supported a pro-Islamic but secular policy, all issued daily or weekly papers. The radio and television also enjoyed a brief spell of relative freedom. But the post-revolutionary euphoria was short-lived and radio and television were the first to lose their newly gained autonomy.

By 1978 Iran had already had an extensive broadcasting network, including eighty-five relay stations, twelve regional televisions, and over fifty local radios. They were all under the direct control of the Ministry of Information. To reach the general public before the revolution, Khomeini by-passed the officially controlled media by sending in cassette recordings of his speeches as well as using the international news broadcasts. The BBC in particular had been meticulous in 1978 in broadcasting many of Khomeini's speeches and announcing dates, times and starting-points of public demonstrations. Many Iranians still believe that the BBC both stage-managed and orchestrated the revolution and was to some extent instrumental in its success. To prevent the opposition from using similar means, Khomeini, on coming to power, banned all cassettes as an illicit Western medium which corrupted the mind of the Iranian youths and at the same time he decided to impose strict controls on radio and television. The first four directors of the networks were sacked in rapid succession for failing to exercise sufficient control. Finally, Mohamad Hashemi, the brother of the *Majlis* speaker Ali Akbar Hashemi Rafanjani, was appointed as the Controller of the network and succeeded in eradicating all liberal elements from this sector. By 1984 most women announcers had been dismissed and those who remain appear on the screen wearing the Islamic veil, *hejab*. Many of the light variety programmes, music and poetry series and comedy serials have been replaced by sermons broadcast direct from various mosques, Koran reading sessions as well as religious mystery plays and religious chants.

The great importance of the network is recognised by both the government and the opposition. Khomeini is all too aware of the network's extensive influence and refers to them as the Open University of Iran. In a country where more than half the population is still illiterate, radio and television are the universal medium of communication and have become a useful tool in the hands of Khomeini, himself a past master in media-manipulation. The opposition groups have tried numerous times to gain access to the media; during the uprisings in Tabriz many of the battles were centred on the local broadcasting station. Now all these stations are under heavy armed protection by the revolutionary guards.

The subjugation and control of the press took somewhat longer. In the initial struggle for power between the secularists and the clergy, each group relied heavily on their respective papers to defend and explain their case. The President's own daily paper, *Enqelabeh Eslami*, published regular editorials by Bani Sadre listing the shortcomings of the government. In the last year of his presidency the media battles intensified; Bani Sadre took to attacking the Prime Minister, who was appointed by and enjoyed the confidence of Khomeini, and the Prime Minister, in turn, sent in the revolutionary guards to raid many of the offices of the *Enqelabeh Eslami* and arrest its writers and junior editors. They responded with hunger strikes which were only reported by the remaining *Enqelabeh Eslami* journalists. By contrast, all the government-controlled papers contained daily reports about Bobby Sands and the IRA prisoners' hunger strikes, but failed to mention those in Iran. Finally in 1982 *Enqelabeh Eslami* was closed down and Bani Sadre fled to France. The Pro-Islamic but secular newspaper, *Mizan*, which advocated the National Front's policies, was also closed soon after, despite a passionate plea for the freedom of the press made by Iran's first Prime Minister, Medhi Bazargan, in the *Majlis*. Bazargan was pilloried by the government-controlled press for being an ally of the then-discredited Bani Sadre, and the brief renaissance of Iranian journalism came to a sudden halt. The government decided to end the problem once and for all by banning all publications and asking publishers to reapply to the government to obtain the right to publish. The Ideological Islamic Guidance Council, *Shorayeh Ershadeh Eslami* was empowered to recognise those publishers who were deemed sufficiently Islamic and to allow them to re-open. Thus since April 1982 the only legitimate publications in Iran are those which wholeheartedly support the government's Islamic line.

CONCLUSION

Despite a tumultuous beginning and initial chaos and instability and despite repeated assassinations, the theocracy in Iran has for the moment established and maintained full control. The process has been extremely bloody and many of the erstwhile supporters of Khomeini have met their death either at the hands of the regime or of its opponents, while others have been driven to exile abroad. After changing one President and eight Prime Ministers in three years, Khomeini has finally found a reliable and compatible President in

Ayatollah Seyed Ali Mousavi and a Prime Minister in his brother Mir Hosein Mousavi who, since November 1981, have maintained power and implemented their fundamentalist policies.

The survival of the regime is in part the result of the nationalistic fervour that was aroused by the Iraqi invasion in 1980 and in part the result of the ruthless suppression of all opposition both outside and in the government and even among the clergy. But this stability, although extremely costly in terms of human life, is very fragile. The regime is still fighting on three major fronts. The first is the war with Iraq which seems to serve no other purpose than that of securing the survival of the current theocracy. Men and even 11-year old boys are being sacrificed in this inconclusive war of attrition, but it seems unlikely that the Iranian government would agree to end this useless bloodshed in the near future. Khomeini insists that before there can be peace, the Iraqi President Sadam Hossein must resign (or be assassinated); an unlikely event and one which is not surprisingly unacceptable to the Iraqi government.

The second is the war against tribal insurgents which has been going on since 1980. When the Islamic constitution was ratified, Iranian tribes were left without the autonomy they had wanted and at the same time lost the very few concessions that they had managed to extract from the Pahlavi regime. As a result, there have ever since been constant tribal uprisings in Iran. The war against the Kurdish tribes, fought by the revolutionary guards against the Kurdish *pishmargan* assisted by the Fadayan and the Mojahedin, is still continuing and seems as inconclusive as the war against Iraq.

The third continuing battle is against the urban guerrillas who have continued their resistance to the regime despite enormous loss of life and continual persecution, arrests and death sentences. According to the figures published by the Mojahedin over 8000 freedom fighters have been killed in the past five years; these include women and children and the ages of the victims range from 11 to 75 years. Khomeini who had ascribed the sobriquet of bloodsucker, *khoun asham*, to the Shah, has proved even more insatiable than his predecessor. Government by terror has resulted in a rapid loss of support for the regime and the general disillusionment has been such that even Khomeini has been obliged to admit to some of the excesses of his regime. In 1983 Khomeini criticised the revolutionary guards for exceeding their authority and invading people's privacy. Khomeini issued an eight-point declaration intended to reassure Iranians that they were safe under the protection of the Islamic regime and that they need not live in fear. In addition, a number of committees were set up to hear complaints and to restrain the revolutionary guards.

There has been a degree of relaxation of the reign of terror following Khomeini's declaration and the setting-up of the committees. There has also been some attempt at liberalisation; in particular people are now allowed to behave as they please in the privacy of their homes without the constant likelihood of an intrusion by the revolutionary guards. The government has also been conciliatory towards technocrats, industrialists and doctors. All such people currently living in exile have been publicly invited to return and have been given guarantees that their lives and their property will be protected provided they return and begin to help the economy. Whether these measures are more than temporary or cosmetic it is too early to say, but there is little doubt that on the whole they have not had much effect on the lives of the poorest sections of the society. Once the enthusiasm for the war has waned (and there is increasing evidence that this is happening) then the regime will have to justify its Draconian political and monetarist economic policies. The rural population has now taken to hiding their able-bodied men and producing ever-smaller surpluses. Not only has the rural labour force been seriously reduced by the war, but also the policy of maintaining relatively low urban food prices, has made agriculture an unprofitable occupation and many cultivators are no longer willing to sell their surplus. The situation is particularly serious in the rich rice-growing northern regions where the government has been obliged to send the revolutionary guards to the rice paddies to prevent illegal sale of rice to merchants and enforce obligatory sales at low prices to the government agencies.

Rural improverishment has, in turn, intensified the rural–urban migration. Slum-dwelling migrants swell the poor quarters of the cities, intensify demands on the already inadequate facilities and are more and more dissatisfied with the government policies of withdrawal of welfare provisions and food subsidies. It is the poor who are experiencing the worst shortages, of water, electricity, food and fuel, and yet they can see the relative opulence of the wealthy living in the rich quarters of the cities. It was this close juxtaposition of opulence and dire poverty that prepared the grounds for the 1978 revolution. The failure of the government to make any lasting impact on these tensions may in the end prove decisive in its own downfall.

Index